DAY TRIPS
TO THE
DESERT
A sort of travel book

DAY TRIPS TO THE DESERT

A sort of travel book

GEOFF NICHOLSON

Hodder & Stoughton

LONDON SYDNEY AUCKLAND

British Library Cataloguing in Publication Data

Nicholson, Geoff
  Day trips to the desert: A sort of travel book.
  I. Title
  910.91
  ISBN 0-340-55371-5

First published in Great Britain 1992

Published by Hodder and Stoughton,
a division of Hodder and Stoughton Ltd,
Mill Road, Dunton Green, Sevenoaks, Kent TN13 2YA.
Editorial Office: 47 Bedford Square, London WC1B 3DP.

Photoset by Rowland Phototypesetting Ltd,
Bury St Edmunds, Suffolk.

Printed in Great Britain by
St Edmundsbury Press Ltd,
Bury St Edmunds, Suffolk

Contents

1

A Paddle in the Sahara (Morocco)

It was a Sunday evening in May 1991 and I was sitting in Room 206 of the Desert Villa Motel in Barstow, on the edge of the Mojave Desert, drinking tequila and Minute Maid orange soda; the nearest I could get to a tequila sunrise. We had just arrived in town after one of the most exhilarating drives I've ever made; not an especially difficult or dangerous drive but a couple of hundred miles from Vidal Junction, through Twentynine Palms and Joshua Tree, then up Highway 247, through Johnson Valley (a kind of suburb in the desert with the houses half a mile away from each other) and across harsh, mountainous desert country until we came to Barstow.

Looking out of the room's window I could see a 1956 blue and silver Chevy, and a white early-seventies Corvette parked in front of the motel. Neither of these was mine, alas. Mine was the characterless rented Buick Century with all the dead bugs and butterflies splattered on the windscreen, the paintwork coated in all kinds of different-coloured desert sand and dust. Beyond the parked cars and beyond the main road were strips of irrigated greenery, then some rising, sandy ground and then the blue mountains of the Mojave.

In the motel room Sue, my girlfriend, was ordering club sandwiches from room service. We were in the Mojave Desert because I was gathering material for a book, this book. In fact, our flight home to England was booked from Las Vegas for the day after tomorrow. I wasn't all that sure I had enough material for the book, or that the material was of the required quality (whatever *that* meant), but sitting there in Room 206, sharing a club sandwich and a bed with someone I loved beyond good sense, I couldn't remember a time when I had ever felt happier.

About three years earlier I had sat in a very similar room to this one, in the Vagabond Inn, just a couple of miles up the main strip in Barstow, with my then wife. Our marriage was unhappy but at the time I didn't know just *how* unhappy. My wife, Tessa, and I were on holiday in California and I was determined to see some desert. We had driven out from Los Angeles, stayed in Barstow a couple of days, and gone out from there to explore the desert. We only had a Ford Escort and I wasn't feeling at all brave, but we did a little driving on dirt roads through some fairly forbidding spots. We encountered nothing that required four-wheel drive, and yet we were in places where a little idiocy would have got us into all sorts of trouble. I kept looking at the landscape, all dirty yellow sand, Joshua trees, a wide horizon, a massive sky, not another soul in sight, and I kept thinking: this is where the spaceship first lands in the science fiction B-movie.

We parked, and walked away from the road. I was feeling great. Here was I, an Englishman, an out and out urbanite, standing in all this space and heat and light, and it was perfect. I felt I could have stayed there for ever. Then my wife slipped and fell and twisted her ankle, just like in the science fiction B-movie.

Of course, in the movies the couple who first see the spaceship are always deeply in love and he always saves her from the aliens. I felt like dumping Tessa there in the desert.

Later we were back at the Vagabond Inn. We'd had some routine bickering arguments, our standard repertoire. Tessa went to bed and I stayed up drinking weak American beer and watching the final pose-down of a female body-building contest on TV, and I wished I was alone in the desert, or at least that I was in the desert with somebody I loved beyond good sense, and I wondered if there was a moral dimension to landscape, and it must have been about then I got the idea that one day I might write a book about deserts.

This is not the book I thought I would write. I thought I would probably write solely about the American deserts. I thought I would write a wry, oblique, possibly comic account of travelling through the desert south-west with a certain timidity and a rented car. I think I have not completely abandoned wryness or obliqueness, and I would have been quite prepared to be comic about the end of my marriage, which I had certainly not anticipated when I conceived the book. However, I had barely started work when my father, totally unexpectedly, was diagnosed as having terminal renal cancer. He died quickly and in great pain when I was barely halfway through my travels. His death was so much a part of my thoughts and feelings while travelling and writing that to have omitted it from this account would have been dishonest, not to say impossible.

When my wife told me she didn't want to be married to me any more I did three things, none of them too bright. I immediately moved to

London, placed an ad in the Lonely Hearts column of *Time Out*, and decided to spend some time in the desert.

Why London? Well, I didn't really know where else to go. Tessa and I had moved out of London a couple of years earlier and gone to live in Yorkshire. Our motives were almost entirely materialistic. Yorkshire was a cheaper place to live. It was possible to buy a big detached house there with a double garage, and my paltry earnings from writing stretched considerably further. But it was certainly essential that Tessa should be living with me. Living alone in Yorkshire held no attractions.

Tessa's desire not to be married to me seemed not unreasonable. She found me bad-tempered, anti-social, self-absorbed, isolated: just like a writer. She claimed I wasn't enough fun. She said I wanted sex too often, and she said I didn't respect her or the job she was doing: writing the staff newspaper for a building society.

I pleaded guilty on all charges and said I'd try hard to change. There was no doubt that I still wanted to be married and living with my wife. When she stopped considering this as an option I didn't feel I had any choice but to get out, and London was the only other place I knew. London was where most of my friends still were, as well as my few contacts in publishing and journalism who helped me make a living.

I had lived alone in London for a good few years before I got married and I had often been lonely and unhappy there. The chances of being lonely and unhappy again looked high but I hoped I could change the pattern.

Putting the ad in *Time Out* was a dim-witted attempt to do this. It was meant to be an act of independence and resilience, a way of saying, though I'm not sure to whom, 'All right, so my wife doesn't want me, but there are plenty of other women who do. I have all my hair, my own teeth. I'm literate, I'm not physically repellent, why wouldn't somebody want me? Why should I grieve over being kicked out?' Of course, today I see the placing of the ad as a symptom of that grief, and an act not of independence and resilience but of eccentric desperation. Needless to say, it only made me feel more desperate.

No doubt the urge to travel to the desert was a similar paradoxical gesture of independence and desperation. If my wife didn't want me then I could manage on my own, in fact utterly on my own, devastatingly alone in the centre of the pitiless and unredeemable desert.

I was not entirely blind to, nor entirely averse to, the fact that I was adopting a dramatic pose here, and at least I thought I wasn't being as bad as some, not as bad for instance as Geoffrey Moorhouse. Early in his book *The Fearful Void* he confesses to his wife – whom he bafflingly refers to as 'J', I mean why not just say 'my wife' or use her real name? – that he's been unfaithful, and the next thing you know he's crossing Africa on foot and camel from west to east, from the Atlantic coast of Mauritania to the Nile. I thought he was over-reacting. I wasn't planning to go that far.

But why, as people often asked me, the desert? I didn't know why. I liked the few areas of desert that I'd seen, but even then I wasn't entirely sure what it was I liked. Was it perhaps that I was looking for a geographical equivalent of my own emotional state? Was I looking for some deserted city of the heart? Did I want the desert to be a metaphor? Was the desert to be part stage set and part emotional correlative? Was it to be part aid to meditation and part spiritual theme park?

Don't be absurd. No, of course it wasn't.

I had always been more or less immune to the joys of the English landscape. I had grown up in Sheffield, not far from the Peak District, and there had been frequent days out to Hope or Castleton, featuring a steep climb up some dramatic but not too difficult hillside. It was okay but I was never moved by the scenery. Then there were all those years of studying English Lit, studying Wordsworth, Clare, even Pope and Blake, all those divine relationships with landscape. I never knew what they were talking about.

A bit of foreign travel taught me that there were certain landscapes that had a bit more poke to them. You'd have to be a lump of rock to see the Niagara Falls or the Grand Canyon or even the Alps and not be moved. I saw and was duly moved, but there still didn't seem to be anything personal about it. The Niagara Falls seemed a bit *obvious* somehow.

Then I spent a summer hitch-hiking round the States. It was the mid-seventies, I was twenty-one and I was pretending to be Jack Kerouac, and I saw, if only through the windscreen of someone else's car, the deserts of New Mexico, Arizona and California, and suddenly it felt personal. I'd found my landscape, though I wasn't sure quite what I'd found.

Certainly I liked the *idea* of the desert, and the kind of ideas that attach themselves to the desert; ideas about solitude, silence, space, harsh beauty, danger, revelation, self-knowledge. I was in favour of all these things, yet it would be dishonest to pretend that I discovered profound spiritual solace in the desert. I just liked being there. I felt good in the desert. I felt different there from the way I felt anywhere else. The desert seemed to put me in touch with something that I wasn't generally in touch with. That was as much as I could say about it.

On that Jack Kerouac trip I was hitching somewhere near Lancaster, somewhere near the Edwards Air Force Base. I'd been waiting at the roadside, close to a gas station, for half an hour or so, and I had no idea what the temperature was, but it felt hotter than anything I had ever experienced. Then it struck me that I wasn't sweating. It was too hot to sweat. The moment moisture reached the surface of the skin it evaporated, leaving a dry, salted coating. I drank some water, took a salt tablet and went into the washroom of the gas station. I was wearing a sweatshirt, soft, quite thick, quite absorbent. I took it off, put it in the sink and ran cold water over it until it was soaked and heavy. I put it on again and left the gas station. By the time I'd walked the hundred yards to the spot where I'd been hitching the shirt was completely dry. I was very impressed by that.

A few years later, in 1978, when I still had no idea I was ever going to want to write about the desert, I was taking a bus out of Salt Lake City, across the Great Basin, heading ultimately for San Francisco.

The desert formed a white crust all the way to the horizon where receding silhouettes of mountains marked the desert's end. But the crust was apparently quite thin, and joyriders who'd taken their cars out across it had broken through the surface, as if through ice on a lake, and their wheels were stuck in the soft sand underneath. The cars had been abandoned, it being too difficult or expensive to get them out.

As the sun went down there was a storm. Picture-book forks of lightning spiked down out of the low, heavy clouds, shooting down at the mountains, illuminating the white desert like a giant flashgun.

There was a girl on the bus. She had corkscrew blonde hair and a big bust, and was young but hard-bitten. She was wearing a tee-shirt with a high round neck. After a while she went to the on-board toilet and when she came back to her seat she had on a very low-cut top that showed a huge cleavage, and dead centre between her breasts there was a tattoo of a butterfly. And it did occur to me even then that if I was a certain sort of travel writer I'd fall into conversation with this girl and ask her about her tattoo. But I wasn't, so I didn't.

I had been surprised by how much of the American desert was fenced off. Barbed wire asserted private ownership and told people to keep out, although there never appeared to be any difference between the land inside the fence and the land outside, and it was hard to imagine what harm trespassers might do; there didn't appear to be anything for them to damage.

When there is ownership there is commerce, buying and selling; and I had been amazed to see hoardings from realtors offering parcels of desert for sale at reasonable prices. Owning a patch of desert seemed absurd (see *Paris, Texas* passim) but it had its appeal. Certainly it was hard to see what anybody would do with such a parcel of land, until I saw what they *had* done. Purchasers had laid fat rolls of barbed wire around a three- or four-acre plot, set a trailer at the centre of it. There would be a portable generator, a chicken hutch, a few motor vehicles, some working, most not. And where the plot bordered the road there would be big hand-painted signs that said things like, 'Stan's place. Keep out. Strictly no callers. You have been warned.'

I imagined Stan, prematurely aged and frazzled by the sun or the wrong combination of drugs or by some personal Vietnam; sitting out in the desert all alone, his brain grilling in the heat, some sixties rock on the big speakers, and a variety of weaponry close at hand: bowie knives, crossbows, a sawn-off shotgun, a magnum, guns that needed to be fired from time to time to make sure they were still in perfect condition, fired at passing trucks, at ghosts, at nothing in particular, at nosy English travel writers. I felt I'd had worse neighbours than Stan.

There is no absolute and universally accepted definition of a desert. One simple definition, and it's the one I've tended to accept for the sake of this book, says that a desert is a place that receives less than 10 inches or 250 millimetres of rain per year. This isn't entirely unproblematic. By this definition, for instance, the Antarctic is a desert. Las Vegas receives only 4 inches of rain per year, but you can stand on the Strip watching the fountains gush extravagantly outside one of the casinos and your ideas about what constitutes a desert will be severely challenged. By contrast, Menzies, in Australia, has a mean annual rainfall of 250 millimetres, and is therefore barely a desert town at all, yet if you were there in midsummer with the temperature hitting a hundred degrees every day and no rain in sight, you might beg to differ.

But a definition that depends solely on precipitation doesn't seem to tell the whole story. Temperature, evaporation rates, soil types and the presence or absence of vegetation would all seem to be determining factors. There are certainly those who would wish to make a distinction between arid zones and true deserts. These people would say, for example, that the Kalahari Desert is not a desert, and that Australia has no true deserts at all. They would say that both these areas are arid, but that aridity does not in itself define a desert. The true deserts, by this account, would only be the Sahara, Sinai, Arabian, Central Asian and Atacama Deserts. These places have less than 10 millimetres of annual rainfall and are characterised by rocky and sandy plains and an absence of vegetation. But it seems to me this is an argument about degree rather than about essence. Yes, the Sahara is hotter, rockier and less fertile than the Gibson but that doesn't stop the Gibson being a desert.

Another definition says that a desert is a place where vegetation covers less than thirty-five per cent of the land surface. I think this is moderately persuasive, although it does mean that the summit of Mount Everest might be called a desert, to say nothing of the average supermarket car park.

Definitions apart, we all know what we mean by deserts. We mean sand dunes, camels, cacti, Bedouin, cattle skulls, water holes, Ayers Rock, the Pyramids. We share a vision that derives partly from the Bible and mostly from the movies; a cinematic amalgam of *Stagecoach*, *Walkabout* and *Lawrence of Arabia*. This is largely incorrect. Sand dunes, for example, make up only a tiny fraction of the world's deserts. Not all deserts are hot. Camels, surprisingly, are not at home in all deserts. Nevertheless, we still know what we mean.

The advertising men know this too. An ad for Du Pont Stainmaster Carpets shows a stretch of blue carpet fitted around the buttes of Monument Valley as evidence of its 'Styling, texture and durability'.

A newspaper ad for Martini shows an obviously faked desert landscape, montaged from three or four photographs, showing dunes, rocks and footprints and assures the reader that 'the dry you're looking for is Extra Dry'.

An ad for Michel Herbelin wrist-watches shows a man sitting on a high sand dune, with a superimposed photograph of a watch, and the selling line is: 'In an age of conformity some things are still made for the individual.'

The first two of these obviously contain some irony, but they, and many like them, play on the fact that we conceive of the desert as exotic, rugged, beautiful and potentially dangerous. In my experience this is more or less the case.

There is much talk of deserts expanding, a belief that deserts are getting bigger and bigger and swallowing up the earth's fertile land. In his book *The Threatening Desert* Alan Grainger makes a convincing case that desertification only occurs because of human mismanagement, through overcultivation, overgrazing, deforestation, and inefficient irrigation. This is inevitably all tied to population growth, economic development and government policies. It is worst in the Third World because everything is worst in the Third World, but desertification is happening to some degree in the United States, in Canada, in Australia, even in Spain. It is not very hard to create a desert, as America's Dust Bowl proved.

I have thought from time to time that perhaps I should have visited the deserts of, say, Ethiopia or Sudan and seen that far from being places of beauty and solace, deserts are also places where people starve to death. And perhaps I should. But that would be a very different book and I would need to be a different person in order to write it.

People always ask me what I find to do in the desert. Surely, they say, there's nothing to do. It's true that compared with Disneyland, deserts are lacking in leisure facilities. That is the attraction. I don't do much in the desert but it's enough for me.

I walk in the desert when I can. I drive through it. I look at the scenery, at the flora and fauna, and at how human beings have succeeded or failed to come to terms with the desert. I take a few photographs, though it's very easy to take some profoundly uninteresting photographs of deserts. I pick up interesting rocks. Sometimes I sit and think. Sometimes I just sit. From the very early days I liked the idea of making love to a woman in the desert, but that took a certain amount of organisation. My wife would certainly not entertain the idea.

I am an enthusiast for the desert but I make no pretence at being an expert. I am someone who enjoys deserts and reports what he does and sees. I am, at best, a man in a rented car, a man on a day trip.

As I have said, the American desert, specifically the Mojave, was my desert of first reference, and I knew I wanted to go back there, but as I sat in London nursing my broken marriage it occurred to me that if I was going to profess an interest in deserts in general I ought to look at another desert or two, so that at the very least I would have a standard of comparison. And if you're going to write about deserts you have to be perverse not to take a look at the Sahara.

I started to investigate the possibility of seeing the Sahara Desert. I started reading books and looking at maps, and I sent off for details of 'adventure holidays'. I was envisaging a four or six week group trek on the back of a truck through Morocco, into Algeria, down to Tamanrasset, 'the crossroads of the Sahara', then back home by way of Tunisia. It sounded good to me.

I was having dinner in a Thai restaurant in Crouch End with a woman who taught art in a prep school in Hampstead; Salman Rushdie's son was one of her pupils. She had answered my *Time Out* ad. In her letter she had called herself stylish and well travelled. I told her I was planning a trip through the Sahara.

'I don't see why you'd want to go to the middle of the desert,' she said. 'I think it would be a very rough trip unless you were a seasoned traveller, and you don't look like a seasoned traveller to me. You don't look like a seasoned traveller at all.'

I tried to say that maybe that was the point.

'But *why?*' she insisted. 'Why would you really want to go to the desert?'

'I suppose the real reason,' I said, 'is because I think there might be a book in it.'

My parents' reactions to my splitting up from Tessa were mixed. My mother reacted with anger, my father with sorrow. My mother's opinion was that Tessa should have 'tried harder'. My father was sympathetic for both of us. He even phoned Tessa a couple of times to make sure she was 'all right'. He insisted he had no argument with her. They were both relieved that Tessa hadn't left me for someone else. It felt to me that she'd left me for *anyone* else.

When I told my parents I was hoping to visit the Sahara they were horrified. We had never been a family that liked to go places. We had spent the regulation week-long holidays in Blackpool and Yarmouth, the days out in Skegness or Bridlington when I was a kid, but never with much enthusiasm. I was an only child and never enjoyed these holidays much, and my parents, who might have said they were only doing it for my benefit, didn't seem to enjoy themselves much either.

After I left home, my parents had a spell of taking holidays in Somerset farmhouses and had got as far as going on package weekends to Amsterdam or Paris. But that had been some time ago, and they hadn't been away on holiday for some years. My father claimed he had done all the travelling he ever wanted to do in the war when he served in the Navy. He had been forced to go to places he didn't want to go, in discomfort, with the threat of being killed when he got there. From time to time I suggested that if he travelled these days he'd be going because he wanted to, could travel in comfort, with very little likelihood of being killed when he got there. This didn't cut much ice with my father.

He had always said very little about his experiences in the war but he did have one story about going into a bar in Gibraltar with two sailors he'd just met. They talked and had a few beers. At one point the other two sailors went to the toilet, came back and continued drinking and talking. Five minutes later the Military Police arrived, arrested all three of them and carted them off to jail. It appeared that while the two sailors had been in the toilet they'd gone berserk and completely wrecked the place, smashing doors and windows and porcelain, ripping plumbing out of the walls, the lot. My father seemed to think that was the least of what might happen to you when you travelled.

He wished me well on my Sahara trip, but long days spent sitting in a truck and nights spent camping in the desert amounted to one of his versions of Hell.

At this time my father was sixty-four. He was about to take early retirement from his job as a 'multi-trade supervisor' with the council (he was a carpenter by trade). He seemed fit, healthy, young for his age. There was not the slightest hint, not the faintest reason to suspect, that he would be dead from cancer in considerably less than a year.

Emile Gautier, author of the classic *Le Sahara*, says there is no great mystery about exploring the desert. 'Oh, it is very simple,' he says, 'you just get some camels and some food and go.' This was not quite what I had in mind. I didn't want to be an Emile Gautier, not even a Bruce Chatwin, not even an Alan Whicker. All I wanted to be then was a tourist on the back of a big four-wheel-drive truck, seeing the desert with a dozen or so fellow travellers, one of whom might surely be female, desirable, and not averse to romping in the desert with an English writer.

Several companies did the sort of trip I was looking for. They all had hairy-chested names like Exodus, Dragoman, Guerba. Their brochures were as glossy as holiday brochures always are, but they all stressed that they ran tours for 'travellers' rather than oiks and they all contained paragraphs like this: 'For nearly 2000 miles (3,300 kms) the Sahara stretches before us, haunting, evocative, its faces, colours and moods in constant flux.'

My picture of the Sahara was as ill-informed as most people's: undulating, corrugated sand dunes, camels, the merciless sun; the stuff of girly calendars and Foreign Legion movies. The brochures didn't do much to challenge this picture. I read about sulphur springs, volcanic rock pinnacles, Berber villages. I read about Tamanrasset, the very centre of the Sahara, the place where caravan trails meet. I read about the Tuareg, the blue men of the desert, their skins coloured by the dye from their blue robes. I read about the Trans-Sahara Highway, a route carved through the desert but which the desert fights relentlessly to reclaim. I read about night in the desert, absolute stillness and silence and a sky smeared thick with stars. I was seduced.

I rang up my chosen company to make a reservation.

'Hello,' I said. 'I'd like to book one of your holidays.'

'Oh yes?' said the girl on the other end.

'Yes, the Trans Sahara Plus.'

'Fine,' she said. 'Are you English?'

'Oh yes,' I said with a certain pride.

'British passport holder?'

'Yes,' I said, starting to wonder whether pride in being English might be misplaced in these post-colonial days.

'Ah well,' she said. 'This is a problem. I'm afraid Algeria isn't letting in British nationals at the moment.'

She didn't seem very clear about why, although she thought it might have something to do with the Salman Rushdie business. But whatever the reason, a couple of phone calls to other companies confirmed that Algeria wasn't going to be on my itinerary. Since the largest part of the Sahara is in Algeria and quite a lot of the rest is in Libya, and since I didn't have the bottle to go willy nilly to Mauritania, Mali, Niger et al., my plans were in serious disarray.

Having got all keen and excited, and just as important, having told people that I was going to the Sahara, I needed to do something quickly. The Sahara just about creeps into Morocco, so I did the easiest thing, I rapidly booked a cheap and cheerful Desert Truck Adventure that claimed to give 'a taste of the desert'. I already had a taste *for* the desert, but this was going to have to do.

Having envisaged this wholehearted plunge into the romantic

wastes of the deepest Sahara, I found myself reduced to having a paddle in the outer fringes. Perhaps this was the story of my life. Anyway, at least it claimed to be an adventure.

I was well aware of the contradictions that attach to setting out deliberately to have an adventure (I had read some literary criticism of the *chanson d'aventure*). An adventure is what happens unexpectedly, thus once you have declared that you are looking for adventure, you are expecting the unexpected, therefore it is impossible to *have* an adventure. And so on.

The Desert Truck Adventure was, I suppose, a package tour masquerading as an expedition. A converted ex-army Bedford truck, kitted out with lockers, roof seats, gerry cans, sand ladders, etc, was to plunge south through the Atlas Mountains, hit the Merzouga Sand Sea, 'one of the most famous of all Saharan sand seas', wander through desert rock and gravel plains for a while, then back into the mountains and home via Marrakesh and Tangier.

Even from the trip dossier it was obvious that there was going to be quite a lot of truck and probably not enough desert in this scenario, but I was a beggar, not a chooser and it did at least provide a glimpse of the Sahara. It contained exactly the amount of risk and danger I was looking for: none.

The travel company I booked with publishes a pamphlet of general travel information about passports and visas, what to pack, how to dress and so on. It has a lot to say about health. AIDS is, of course, much on everybody's mind and the pamphlet says, 'Avoid having sex with local people or strangers while abroad.' This seemed to me to limit the possibilities for 'adventure' to a crippling extent. Who was I likely to meet if not locals or strangers? Who else was I going to get the chance to sleep with? The only hope seemed to be that I might run into some long-lost girlfriend in the Merzouga Sand Sea.

The Department of Health and Social Security publishes two leaflets that make up 'The Traveller's Guide to Health'. One is called 'Before You Go' and the other is 'While You're Away'. They take a more pragmatic view than my travel company. They advise that you should take as many condoms with you as you think you are likely to need, 'as they may not be easily available or of good quality in the country you are visiting'.

This too seemed to create difficulty. How many condoms could I see myself using on this trip? Would a pack of three be enough? How about a gross? Imagine the ignominy of returning through British customs with the same number as you went out with. I decided to go for a pack of twelve. This seemed to strike the right balance between modesty and optimism.

Now, nobody in their right mind would imagine that being locked up in the back of a truck with a group of complete strangers was likely to be an unalloyed delight, and it wasn't, but it could all have been a lot worse. We assembled in Malaga, lager lout capital of the world. There were nineteen of us, more than I'd imagined. There were twelve women and seven men. There were eight English, five Australians, two Dutch and one each from Ireland, Belgium, Canada and Japan.

We varied in age from twenty-two to fifty-nine. The oldest was a retired lady schoolteacher whom I began by thinking was wonderfully brave, tough and independent, but who turned out to be none of these things, and spent the whole trip complaining about the state of her bowels and tut-tutting about the Moroccan treatment of donkeys. The youngest sold spare parts for Vauxhall cars and frittered away his weekends with the Territorial Army. There was Dawn, a production secretary for the BBC. There was Chikako, she was a Japanese ex-ballet dancer who had damaged her knee competing in motocross, was now a shoe designer, and had an English vocabulary of at most a hundred words. There was Ursula, a doctor from Nottingham. There was Steve who had been kicked out of South Africa and now repaired washing machines in Cambridge. There was Andy who sold office furniture in Orlando. We were a diverse and ill-matched bunch, mostly single, though one or two had partners at home. I guess we were a group of misfits.

The majority of these people were 'into travelling'. Brian, a Canadian banker, had been toiling for fifteen years in his bank in Vancouver, his existence only made tolerable by taking annual holidays in very distant places. The Australians, all women, were doing the world. I hoped they might be quite good sources of information on deserts. Between them they had covered the Western, Gibson, Kalahari and Sinai deserts; but they didn't have much to say about them.

The daily life of an overlander is, in its essentials, not very different from that of any other kind of tourist. You go to visit 'sights', you look at them, take photographs, travel on, try to find an agreeable place to spend the night and an agreeable place to eat. The difference for the overlander is that the travelling is a little rough, the sights slightly off the beaten track, and the places to eat and spend the night will be isolated desert or mountain spots where tents are erected and barbecues lit.

The group dynamics between the nineteen of us were not unusual, but they became quite intense as we spent most of our waking hours interacting with each other in pretty much the same ways. Every day began early, involved a lot of travelling and had a crowded itinerary. This was good strategy. The fuller the day and the more exhausted the overlander, the less time he has to think, complain or act like a dissatisfied tourist.

I may as well admit that I found the Australian women on the trip very tough going. I had never been persuaded that travel broadened the mind; in these cases it seemed to have reduced the mind to the size of a small kiwi fruit. Not only that, travel seemed to have become a great flattener of experience. All things had been equalised for them: a felucca trip down the Nile, a climb up Ayers Rock, a five-day camel trek, a night in an authentic English pub all held exactly the same status. They were all really good. Their traveller's tales asserted that the world was easily travelled and easily known, and these women could give you the name of a good hotel, a decent restaurant and some tips to make sure that you didn't get ripped off by the pernicious locals. I'm sure that it isn't only Australian women who are guilty of this stuff, they just happened to be the ones I was stuck with in the back of the truck, and it drove me crazy.

One Australian, a teacher in her early thirties, asked me if I'd ever seen the movie *Midnight Express*. I said I had, though it had been some years ago.

'Well, you know,' she said, 'I think it must have been really exaggerated. I was in Turkey for two weeks and I never even *saw* a jail.'

I admitted I was a writer, not something I automatically do in mixed company.

'Are you going to write about us?' somebody asked.

'No,' I said. 'Nobody would ever believe you lot.'

I hoped that reply might divert further questions, but it didn't.

'But as a writer you must always be looking for ideas.'

'Well, sure.'

'So you must have had *some* thoughts.'

'Well, I did have one idea,' I admitted reluctantly. 'I had this vague idea about a character who's really boring and shy and ordinary, he works in a bank or something, and his father dies, and it's his father's dying wish that his ashes are scattered in the Sahara. So this very conventional, unadventurous man has to go to the middle of the desert and he goes by truck and meets all these weird people.'

'Is it a comedy?'

'It could be,' I said.

'Does he succeed? I bet he falls in love. Do they all die in the desert?'

'I've no idea,' I said. 'Maybe all those things.'

I didn't give that plot idea another thought for a good ten months.

From Malaga we drove to Algeciras, crossed to Ceuta in Morocco and began the drive south to the desert. We were involved in what has become known as overlanding. Quentin Crewe says that's a very accurate description of the process since it involved passing over the land without in any way touching the culture. I can see no reason to argue with that assessment. Yes, we travelled in a kind of bubble taking our own culture with us. We ate tinned corned beef for lunch. We wore Nike trainers. Thanks to the battery and the portable cassette player we were able to sit in the Sahara and listen to the Pet Shop Boys. I suggest you don't do this. Equally, of course, we could buy boot-legged cassettes in Morocco and take some Berber folk music back home with us.

I don't know exactly how I feel about this. I like my own culture. I am attached to it and don't want to deny it or be without it, just as a Tuareg tribesman wouldn't want to be without his. And yet there were moments on the trip when we did seem to be involved in some mad, reprehensible enterprise. One night as we sat in the desert round a camp-fire a lively conversation broke out about the merits and iniquities of the British tax system as opposed to the Australian. It must be said there was a splinter group who thought this was a bit inappropriate. We preferred to sit around and say 'Wow, look at those stars.' At one point we even discussed literature. A Dutch swimming-pool designer who looked like Martina Navratilova, though less so, asked me which modern writers of English I could recommend.

'J. G. Ballard's very good,' I said. 'And there's Anthony Burgess and Julian Barnes, and there's always William Burroughs.'

'Do all good authors in English have names beginning with B?'

'All except Paul Bowles,' I said.

I take a slightly less hard line against Paul Bowles now than I did then. I'd read *The Sheltering Sky* as 'background' for this trip and I'd found it a silly and clumsy book. Bowles has the problem that all novelists have once they put their characters in the desert. The plot options are severely limited. The characters can get lost in the desert, they can experience *cafard*, they can have weird sex, they can have revelations and they can die. That's about it. Perm any three of the above and you have a desert novel much like any other desert novel. Bowles, of course, perms the lot.

Writing about lofty themes doesn't guarantee a lofty book, so, although Bowles and his characters batter on about, for example, 'the proximity of infinite things', infinite things don't find their way into the novel. When Bowles writes, 'The landscape was there, and more than ever he could not reach it. The rocks and sky were everywhere, ready to absolve him . . . ' we know what he means, and we know that this sort of subject is the stuff out of which great novels are made, but that doesn't guarantee that the book we're reading is great. Bowles seems ham-fisted. He seems to be trying too hard.

And when Port dies, it just gets comical. 'Blood and excrement. The supreme moment, high above the desert, when the two elements, blood and excrement, long kept apart, merge. A black star appears, a point of darkness in the night sky's clarity. Point of darkness and gateway to repose.' Surely nobody writes like that once they turn seventeen. You notice the use of paradox, the use of imagery, the veiled reference to buggery. You could write a pretty good essay in practical criticism about it, but could you take it seriously? For myself, I was hoping that blood and excrement would stay unmerged during my desert truck adventure.

I went on to read some of Bowles' short stories about the inscrutability of the Arab mind and I enjoyed these a lot more than his posturings about desert angst. Despite our insularity, our enclosure in our own cultural bubble, we met and spoke to quite a number of Moroccans; in a superficial, touristy way of course, how else? But our Moroccans didn't seem so very inscrutable. Most of them made their intentions clear. They wanted to fleece the tourists, a perfectly reasonable desire, but they didn't seem to have worked out the best way of doing this. They hadn't understood the advantages of charm, of the indirect approach, of the soft sell.

If you sat alone at a pavement café one or two Moroccan youths would sit down next to you and say, 'Hello friend.' This only convinces the paranoid tourist that whatever else these guys want it definitely isn't friendship. In the souks we were touched and poked and grabbed, sometimes insinuatingly, sometimes roughly, to encourage us to look at some damned shop or stall. It didn't seem to have struck any of the locals yet that the Western tourist can be more easily fleeced if you don't invade his sense of personal space.

Even in the rural areas people tried to sell us jewellery, blankets, fossils, rocks, marijuana. They wanted our money. They wanted to make a living. The very young children had the same idea but they had nothing to sell so they would poke us gently but relentlessly in the arm or leg and repeat over and over again, '*Un cadeau. Un cadeau, monsieur. Un cadeau. Un cadeau.*' This could go on for a very long time indeed and you felt that if you didn't finally brush the kid away with a display of real or feigned anger it might go on forever.

Instead of a cadeau we were sometimes asked for a dirham, a bon bon or '*un stylo*'. The demands for the *stylo* completely baffled me. It didn't seem to me that the kids asking for ballpoint pens would really have much use for them. I mean, it wasn't as if they ever asked for writing paper. Similarly most of us don't travel laden down with large quantities of spare pens. However, the guide books to Morocco now tell you to be sure to carry a supply since you're bound to be asked for them. Thus a completely bogus medium of exchange seemed to have been set up. The Moroccan kids got what they asked for, but it was hard to believe that was what they really wanted. The tourist meanwhile had given what had been asked of him but couldn't feel that warm self-satisfaction that comes from distributing to poor children those things they really need. Occasionally children would throw rocks at the truck. That seemed to be a far more honest and meaningful exchange.

There in Morocco the word on Algeria was somewhat different from what it had been in England. Salman Rushdie didn't figure; instead, it was believed to have something to do with Algerian students. The British government had decided, or noticed, that not every Algerian claiming student status and trying to get into England was studious, bookish and academic, and had started getting particular about which ones they let in. In retaliation the Algerians, absolutist rather than particular, had decided they'd let no British in at all, at least not by land borders. There was a rumour that if you flew into Algeria they just might let you in, but then again they just might not.

The leader and main driver of the tour was a short, lean, darkly sun-tanned American called David Bosio. He hated being called Dave. He was in his mid-thirties. He had elegantly receding hair, high cheek bones, very white teeth, and he spoke with a quiet, unruffled inhibitedness that positively reeked of authority. After half a day's acquaintance I wouldn't only have trusted him to get me safely through Morocco, I'd have trusted him to get me to Hell and back.

On one of the early days of the trip the truck stopped for lunch and we all piled out for tinned meat and pasta salad, but instead of eating lunch with us David put on his running shoes and set off running along the road in the direction we were heading. The rest of us ate our lunch, washed up, packed up, got back in the truck and the co-driver set off driving in pursuit of David. I was in the cab with the co-driver and I was watching the odometer to see how far David had run. When it showed that we'd covered sixteen kilometres we both began to worry that David had taken a detour, got lost, fallen into a ditch or been kidnapped; although even then it seemed to me David was not the kind of man to whom such simple and banal misfortunes would happen. We were seriously thinking of turning back, imagining that somehow we might have driven straight past and missed him. And then we saw him. He wasn't running. He was just standing by the side of the road waiting for the truck to catch up. He wasn't sweating and he didn't have a hair out of place. He had run seventeen kilometres in the time it took lesser mortals to eat their lunch and he hadn't even got out of breath.

We got to talking. He had worked for his father's glazing company in Kansas until the company hit financial troubles. Even though he was the boss's son he had to go, so he started travelling and he hadn't stopped since. He had trained as a plasterer and as an auto mechanic; two pretty good ways of making sure you were never going to starve in this world.

'I'm not the regular kind of tour leader,' he said. 'I like to stand back and choose who I talk to. Like there's no way I'm ever going to have a conversation with that spoiled Australian bitch Melissa.'

Melissa was indeed a spoiled Australian bitch. She had recently graduated in English from Sydney University and was hoping to become an 'editor'. She managed the considerable feat of keeping a perfect manicure through the entire trip. Yes, David looked like a man after my own heart. And, of course, I was flattered that I was one of the lucky people he'd singled out as being worthy of his time and conversation.

'I was never what you'd call a people person until I started this job,' he said. 'This job has done me some good.'

David was so profoundly and conspicuously *still* not a people person that you were kind of glad you hadn't met him in the old days. He kept a considerable distance from the group, though there was nothing stuck-up or aloof about him. I'm sure this distance was good for his sanity. It was certainly good for maintaining his authority. A tour round Morocco was not his usual route and he obviously in some way found it a little beneath his dignity. What he really felt at home with was a four-and-a-half-month trek across Africa.

He had great pride in his work and in his truck. When we met other overland trucks he would look them over and declare them to be 'a piece of shit'. And his driving, which appeared to my untutored eye to be pretty good, was not to be criticised. When someone, one of the Australian girls inevitably, suggested he was driving too fast, his silent fury and his subsequent glowering sulk knew no limits.

We were driving along a brown, unsurfaced desert track. David said he loved driving as an activity in itself, he didn't much care what he was driving. When he was a mechanic he'd worked on Porsches and Ferraris and got to drive them afterwards.

'What's it like driving a Ferrari?' I asked.

'It's fun. It's fast.'

'Is it difficult?'

'The gear change is a little stiff. But Porsches, they're nice cars.'

Then I asked him about driving in the desert. Was it easy to navigate? Was it hard to avoid getting stuck in the sand?

He said, 'You just follow the tracks. And there's no reason to get stuck. It's just a matter of technique.'

I knew it would have been foolish to ask him to divulge what the technique was.

Then he added, 'You know, I think I could live really happily in the desert if I had some interesting work to do there. A lot of people can't take the desert, but I think I could.'

This was all looking very good. This looked like real material. Here I'd come across a real desert character, someone lean and spare and detached, disciplined, a little cranky. I was thinking David might make a 'my most interesting character'. I knew I'd have to quiz him about this need to live in the desert, but I waited a day or two to pick my moment, also giving myself time to weave some literary nonsense around the man.

'So tell me about this need to live in the desert.'

'Oh,' said David, 'I couldn't really say that it was a need. I mean it's not something I'm working towards.'

Which was a shame because obviously I'd been desperately hoping that it was. It seemed, in fact, that his ideal would be to settle down somewhere on the coast in Australia. David had let me down. He wasn't the desert rat I'd been hoping for.

Late in the trip he went to get a haircut at a local barber. He had always looked clean cut, but after the barber had done his work David looked for all the world, and despite wearing shorts, thongs and a running vest, like the popular image of a CIA agent.

'Hey David,' I said cheerily, 'nice haircut. Very CIA.'

David froze. This he didn't find funny. I had clearly said the wrong thing, but it seemed almost as though I'd hit the nail right on the head. It all made sense to a lover of conspiracy theories. This was surely why he preferred the four-and-a-half-month trips through Africa with their added scope for information gathering, extra opportunities for fomenting unrest and destabilisation. My fantasy of David the desert rat was over, but a new one was instantly available. He was the kind of man it was easy, perhaps unavoidable, to weave intrigues around.

Later I wondered if David's inhibition, detachment and lack of enthusiasm for social interaction mightn't be more easily explained by some repressed and all-consuming sexual preference, but such a theory was too boring by half.

Even the most ascetic of travellers seems to like to bring something back from his travels. We all despise 'tacky souvenirs' but that implies that we don't mind tasteful, nicely made souvenirs. It hadn't occurred to me that 'overlanders' would do a lot of souvenir buying, whether tacky or otherwise. I was naïve. When you have nineteen people, most of them pursuing their idea of the perfect souvenir, that adds up to a lot of shopping. Most of our number were entertained by the chance to haggle, and even I enjoyed it on occasion, but God, how it slowed us down. And when anyone had finally bought anything we all had to hear what a good price they'd paid for their silver teapots and their Tuareg scarves and their Berber blankets.

We were in a brown, unlovely stretch of desert somewhere near a town called Rich; a long flat gravel plain with low undramatic mountains behind it, when we came across a market. It seemed to be miles from anywhere and it was huge. Donkeys and goats were being traded and there were stalls selling colourful baskets of spices, but essentially it was very unexotic. Most of the market was selling the kind of goods you'd find in a good hardware store: washing-up bowls and buckets, packets of soap powder and folding step ladders. There was a man making wrought-iron gates to order and another recycling tin cans to make small portable stoves. Tourists were perfectly welcome but there wasn't much that a tourist would want to buy. Consequently nobody was trying to coerce us into buying anything. That in itself was a breath of fresh air, but more importantly it was a chance to see what Moroccans bought and sold outside of the tourist economy. I loved it. As we got back on the truck after looking round the market quite a few overlanders complained about how disappointed they were by the lack of good craft items on sale. They'd found nothing worth haggling for.

Steve, the electrician who'd been in South Africa, had taken one or two steps towards going native. He had started wearing a jellaba and a blue Tuareg head-dress. It looked utterly unauthentic, not least because Steve was very tall and had a big, white, totally unArabian face. However . . .

He was a motorbike enthusiast and every now and again he'd say wistfully that this journey would be so much more exciting if only he was on a motorcycle. We were at Meski Oasis on the edge of the desert, also known as the Blue Springs. In some ways it was very much the way you would expect an oasis to be: palm trees and shade and a flat-roofed café. On the other hand there was a swimming-pool with changing-rooms and showers, and these didn't quite fit the picture.

Two Norwegian men arrived at the oasis while we were there. They came riding chunky, modified, dust-clad BMWs. Steve went over to talk to them, to ask them about their bikes, but they wouldn't talk to him. They wouldn't even give him the time of day, wouldn't even acknowledge his existence. This puzzled us for some time and then we realised the reason why they wouldn't talk to him was because they thought he was some damned Arab, and they knew the only reason an Arab would talk to them was to try and sell them something. We felt, briefly, slightly morally superior to the Norwegians.

All the way through the early part of the trip I was sustained by the knowledge that I was 'on the way' to the desert. Travelling hopefully is fine. But knowing exactly when you've arrived in the desert isn't so easy. There is no signpost, no border crossing to tell you you're now officially there. I would constantly look around at the landscape and ask myself, 'Am I there yet? Is this really the desert?'

A series of absences pointed to the approaching desert. Things disappeared, ceased to be present. Vegetation reduced, until there was almost no flora, just big rocks. And there were fewer and fewer sightings of people and buildings, and eventually the big rocks disappeared and there were only much smaller rocks, and the road faded away and we were on a dirt track, and sometimes not even that, just a series of tyre tracks about a hundred yards wide. There was nothing very scenic about these things.

I tried, with a certain amount of success, to convince myself that the true connoisseur of deserts enjoys these absences, these blank stretches of rock and earth, these defiantly unpicturesque elements. They were not easy to like. They were not by any stretch of the imagination tourist attractions. That was why they were especially to be savoured. I still more or less believe this. Nevertheless, the Merzouga Sand Sea can be enjoyed by those who make no claim to connoisseurship.

Arrival there coincided with the moment when all doubts ceased about whether or not we were truly in the desert, the moment when the sand dunes appeared, rising in rippling waves out of the flat gravel plain over which we were driving. There they were, the real thing, as advertised, the stuff of cliché as promised by the brochures. They were even dotted with camels. They were, despite or because of the clichés, completely, overwhelmingly beautiful. We all cheered with delight at seeing them. This was perhaps not the most sophisticated response there's ever been to the desert, but it was deeply felt.

Since then I have seen other sand dunes with as much to recommend them as these, but none have ever made quite the same impact. These were my first dunes. They were a rich orange, silky yet solid looking, like great frozen billows. They were full of compelling contradictions: soft curves and sharp edges, monumental yet impermanent and fragile, inviting yet forbidding. It was a landscape to make you weep, but whether with joy or sorrow I couldn't have said, and still can't.

Suddenly as we drove, like an hallucination, four boys on bicycles appeared out of the heart of the dunes. They were in their early teens and wore jellabas over Western clothes. They seemed almost to spring from the sand itself. They were an amazing sight and a photo stop was obviously required. David stopped the truck and the boys pedalled their bikes up and down the dunes while we photographed them. We needn't have been so eager. They were with us for the next twenty-four hours.

We camped in the dunes. We had arrived about four-thirty in the afternoon, about an hour and a half before sunset. The boys offered their services as guides. This was not their forte. The service they offered was to take us in small groups to the top of a highish dune which they would assure us was the best possible place from which to see the sunset.

Finding myself with a guide and two terrible Australian girls, I deliberately fell behind, waving them on, saying that I'd catch them up later, though having no intention of doing so. Sitting atop a sand dune with this guide and a little clutch of tourists was not my idea of a good time. But I wasn't allowed to fall very far behind. The guide came back to hurry me along, to bring me back to the fold. I decided this was absurd. I didn't need to worry about hurting this guy's feelings. I waved him away and set out on my own in a different direction. With some reluctance he let me go.

I found a dune of my own. I was only a short way into the Sand Sea, but it was a spot where I couldn't see the truck, and if I angled myself properly I couldn't see anyone else in the group. I could hear them, of course; the desert silence wasn't much in evidence. The space and the openness were, however, as advertised. There was great distance and flatness and the big sun going down. It was just possible to imagine oneself alone in this vast, magnificent landscape, although to have been in this spot completely alone might, of course, have been terrifying. The giant dunes were reduced to ripples, the sand appearing orange where the sun fell directly on it, creamy light and dark greys where in shadow. But it was already apparent that this wasn't going to be one of the great sunsets.

Climbing up Saharan sand dunes is crippling hard work, for me anyway – the moment we arrived in the Sand Sea, David had run barefoot into the distance, taking the direct route up the highest possible dune. I sat on the top of my own dune. My mouth and lungs ached with the effort of having climbed up it. I drank some warm water from my water bottle. My guide reappeared.

'Hello friend,' he said.

'Hello,' I said.

'American?'

'English.'

'Ah,' he said. He said it as though this was a great shame but it explained everything. 'I am Hassan. You?'

I said my name was Kevin.

'Good. This is best?' he asked, indicating the spot I'd picked from which to watch the sun going down. Both he and I knew it wasn't.

'It's best when you're left alone,' I said.

He smiled uncomprehendingly. I had already noticed that he was carrying a little metal box made out of an old oil drum. He tapped the box.

'You buy fossil?'

'No, I shan't be buying any fossils,' I said.

He took the lid off the box and displayed a selection of highly polished souvenir-shop fossils.

'Not for me,' I said. 'They're not really what I'm looking for.'

He looked at me blankly. Perhaps he hadn't understood what I'd said or perhaps he found it totally impossible to believe I wasn't entranced by his fossils. I found his incomprehension peculiarly liberating.

'Look,' I said, 'there may be many and various reasons why a man comes to the desert, but surely some desire for tranquillity, silence and solitude must come into it somewhere. Here I am, I'm sitting happily alone on top of a sand dune. I know what you're going to say, you're going to say this solitude is illusory; the truck's only two hundred yards away, there are a dozen people behind the next dune, and perhaps you'll say that the whole notion of setting off to find tranquillity in the company of eighteen other tourists is a pretty naff one anyway, and I'd probably agree with you. *But,* I want to sit alone in the desert and even if I'm involved in some absurd illusion here, the illusion of being alone in the desert is better than nothing.

'And if I can't be completely alone in the desert, I suppose I would settle for rolling around naked with some gorgeous lovely. What I won't settle for, what I didn't come 1,500 miles and pay good money for, is to sit on top of a sand dune with some twerp who thinks I want to buy some of his fucking fossils.'

He nodded thoughtfully.

'You buy fossil?'

Next day in the dunes we went to gawp at a traditional Berber family encampment, or a traditional tourist attraction, depending on your point of view. The dwelling looked suitably authentic and not unpicturesque. There was a small conical Berber tent, a windbreak made from a Berber blanket, a wattle hut and a chicken coop. The father and four small children, all in Western clothes, showed us around, and we met the wife who wore traditional dress and had two small sick babies with flies round their eyes. The babies looked as though they didn't have long to live.

Even as we gawped another party of sightseers arrived; squeaky-clean German tourists in two squeaky-clean Land-Rovers. We felt we held some ambiguous moral ground by being sweaty and dirty and riding in an open-sided truck. We were told we were free to take pictures of the scene but it would cost us a couple of dirhams each. Some of our group lost the moral high ground here, handed over the money and began snapping their cameras. Others, myself included, felt this was a fairly unedifying spectacle. We had never expected much human dignity from tourists, but we'd hoped for more from the Berbers.

The P32 is the main road running across the south of Morocco. It ultimately goes into the mountains and on to Agadir, but for me it was a perfect road for observing the desert. It was a major route and yet for much of its length it was barely two cars wide, and it was possible to drive for long periods without seeing another vehicle.

Sometimes there was a petrol station and a café, or a village with red mud-walled buildings, but mostly it was a sampler of a certain sort of desert landscape. There were no dunes here, but there were mountains of sedimentary rock – sandstone – soft, easily corroded, mountains that were sometimes miles distant but which sometimes nudged right up to the road. In places the land had been carved into a series of miniature Grand Canyons. Sometimes the desert was a pale yellow, sometimes it was ash grey or bloodless brown. Often the desert was utterly naked but then there would be an oasis, a sudden explosion of greenery with lush crops cultivated in neat squares with date palms rising up to signal its presence from miles away. Then there would be more featureless desert, and there, in the middle of nowhere we suddenly would see a man walking through the desert, a man in a jellaba, carrying nothing, not even water; and we couldn't begin to imagine where he was walking to or from. Sometimes we saw herds of cows or goats or camels, and very occasionally there were wrecked cars that had had everything salvageable stripped from them.

And there were graves in this desert, not graveyards exactly, nothing so organised, but little clusters of pointed stones, set a little way outside of the villages, very close to the road and the traffic. Each stone was small, about a foot or fifteen inches high, and each one indicated a grave, but it was a grave without any name or marking. I thought that if you have to be buried somewhere, this wasn't a bad place. There was nothing pompous or falsely pious about graves like these.

I suppose it's possible that all writers are condemned to find characters in their travels whom they think they might have created. No doubt Graham Greene couldn't turn around without stumbling over a Graham Greene hero, and even Nicholson, it seems, occasionally encounters a Nicholson character.

We were in a place called Alnif, a parched, dessicated two-café village attached to an oasis that grew dates, maize, coriander and giant radishes. We had stopped for a drink in one of the cafés and were setting off again when there were loud shouts and a disturbance, and a well-to-do Moroccan marched purposefully towards the truck. He was plump, had a rugby-ball-shaped head and was wearing a clean white shirt with a tie.

'Excuse me, please!' he called out in barely accented English. 'Do any of you young people speak German? I have something here I need translating.'

He held what turned out to be the instruction book for a photocopier. The text was in German. He owned the village photocopier and this seemed to make him quite a big wheel around Alnif. It also seemed, however, that photocopiers in Alnif are much like photocopiers anywhere else, and this one wasn't working. Not only that but a strange yellow light kept flashing. The man knew just enough German to see which paragraph of the instruction book told him what to do when the light flashed, but he didn't know enough German to understand what that was.

He was delighted therefore to come across a group of travellers with lots of languages between them, and two Dutch girls knew enough German to be able to translate the relevant paragraph. As they translated, the man's delight seeped away. The manual was perfectly clear. When the yellow light flashed there was nothing that the owner could do to the machine for himself, and it was imperative that he consult his local dealer. This owner's local dealer was in Marrakesh – some two hundred kilometres away.

So, if I didn't manage to find silence, isolation and tranquillity in the desert, did I manage to find sensuality and romance? Did I get any oats in the desert?

Well no, after all, this is only the first chapter, but what happened was this.

Her name was Ursula and she was the doctor from Nottingham. She had demoted herself to specialise in casualty, or A and E, accident and emergency, as it is apparently known in the trade. She was twenty-seven, tall with very pale skin and bright-red hair. She was slightly gawky, had the fruitiest upper-class accent I'd ever heard, and was as far away from being 'my type' as I could imagine. I thought she was great.

She had heard of Edward Abbey, which nobody else on the trip had, she read books, and she was appreciative of my Jamieson's whiskey and didn't want to pour Coke in it, which was the way the others on the truck seemed to take their whiskey.

As the truck drove through the desert we passed a semi-derelict Kasbah where, rumour had it, the movie *Jesus of Nazareth* had been filmed. Ursula said she couldn't imagine which scene had been shot there.

'Me neither,' I said, 'but then I'm not all that familiar with the story.'

'Oh, it's a good read,' she said. 'A twist in the tail and a happy ending.'

Perhaps this ought to have made me suspicious.

Ursula and I got on very well but romance hadn't arrived by the time we got to the desert, and anyway I wasn't sure I wanted to 'get involved' and I wasn't at all sure how much she liked me nor in which way. An ill-timed and unwelcome proposition in the desert threatened to put the mockers on our dealings with each other for the rest of the trip.

We slept out without tents in the sand dunes. So did a lot of other people, and we all stayed close together in case of sandstorms, but my sleeping-bag was adjacent to Ursula's, and although this seemed like fairly adolescent stuff, lying there in the Sahara, staring up at the Milky Way with a woman you quite like only an arm's length away, well, it didn't seem like the worst hand anybody had ever been dealt.

In the night I put out my arm and stroked her hip through her sleeping-bag. She squeezed my hand. It was a very articulate squeeze. It was affectionate certainly, appreciative, but sharp, brief and no-nonsense, as if to say, 'that's enough of that, at least for now, and I wouldn't want to make any great commitments for the future either.' I really didn't mind too much. I was never a man to force himself on a woman in the desert. Maybe I was relieved.

Anyway, our flirtation continued throughout the desert stage of the trip but nothing had been decided, much less consummated, by the time we left the desert and got to Marrakesh. Detaching ourselves from the rest of the group, never the easiest thing to do, we went out and had coffee in the Place Djemâa el Fna.

The Place Djemâa el Fna is *the* tourist attraction in Marrakesh. It is full of acrobats, snake charmers, story-tellers, stalls selling fish and chips and cooked snails, water carriers who want to be paid to be photographed, touts who squabble with each other to have the privilege of guiding you round the souk where you don't want to go, pickpockets, performing monkeys, tacky souvenir stalls, beggars, teenage gangs, some heavy-handed uniformed police. A thick cloud of dust and petrol fumes hangs over it. It is about as much fun as skin disease. It is definitely no place for a romantic assignation. Nevertheless, I tried.

'Can I ask you a personal question?' I said.

'Yes,' said Ursula.

'Do you have a boyfriend?'

'No.'

'Would you like one?'

'Well, that depends.'

'What if it was me?'

'Let's say I wouldn't rule it out.'

'Good. Okay, the only thing you need to know is that I have a wife who I'm getting divorced from. That's not a problem, is it?'

'Well, it is actually. It's totally impossible actually. You see, I know it sounds wet, but I'm a Catholic . . . '

I'm not sure what I would have said next, nothing very positive I'm sure, but I didn't get the chance to say anything as a dozen or so of our fellow desert-truck adventurers descended on the café and we were surrounded by talk of who had bought blankets, leather goods and teapots in the souk that day and how well they'd done at haggling.

I never did get to discuss with Ursula the full implications of her Catholicism. I wasn't very interested and there didn't seem much point if it was 'totally impossible'. I returned to England with as many condoms as I'd set out with. Waiting for me at home were the first bits of paper concerning my divorce from Tessa. I felt wretched. I felt ready for some serious desert.

2

Mad Max and Me (Australia)

Eight months later I was standing in the Budget Car Rental office at the airport in Kalgoorlie, Western Australia. I was divorced and I was with Sue, the one with whom I would eventually share Room 206 of the Desert Villa Motel in Barstow. I didn't know Sue very well but I liked her very much. We would be together for some time, but I wasn't sure of that then. We were in Kalgoorlie, in the Budget Car Rental office, because we wanted to pick up a Toyota Land Cruiser and head off into the desert of Western Australia for a couple of weeks. The guy behind the desk asked where we were intending to go.

'Oh, just touring around,' I said briefly and vaguely. I had already learned that brevity and vagueness went down pretty well in this part of Australia. 'I guess we might get as far as Laverton, or maybe Wiluna . . .'

I tapered off. I wasn't sure whether he'd think that going to these places was an incredibly stupid and insane thing to do, or whether he'd think it was tiresomely tame and predictable.

'Well, you'll be okay in this thing,' he said, nodding towards the bright red Land Cruiser parked outside the office. 'You probably won't even need the four-wheel drive, but it's always good to have it. And you won't have much difficulty getting diesel or water out that way either.'

He seemed to be coming down on the tame and predictable side. Fortunately the map we had of the area made it sound considerably more adventurous. 'Desert roads: WARNING,' it said. 'The area shown on this map is uninhabited except for very infrequent towns and station homesteads. All rivers and most lakes are dry and the area is waterless except during rain. Spares for all cars can be hard to obtain even in Kalgoorlie. Traffic is almost non-existent except on main roads.' Maybe it wasn't going to be so tame and predictable after all.

The man at Budget gave us a small jerrycan to carry extra water in, even though we probably wouldn't need it. He showed us the woefully inadequate tool kit that came with the Land Cruiser, and sketchily explained how to change a wheel. And that was it. We were masters of our own fates and were free to go off and get lost in the desert; which is more or less exactly what we then did.

Kalgoorlie is a gold-rush town. Gold was found there in 1893, and by 1902 it had a population of thirty thousand, with ninety-three hotels and eight breweries. Things have calmed down a little since then. Today there are twenty thousand people, twenty-eight hotels and just one brewery, but Kalgoorlie manages to promote the feeling that it is simultaneously a rough border town and yet a place of permanence and prosperity. It has a long, well-heeled main street, wide enough for a camel train to do a U-turn in; and in the early gold-mining days many a camel train did make U-turns there. The camel was vital in the opening-up of the Australian desert.

The main street, called Hannan Street, has two-storey hotels, imposing civic buildings made of stone, and a life-size statue of Paddy Hannan, the man who first found gold there. The statue holds a bronze waterbag that has a shiny silver tap attached to it, so it doubles as a drinking fountain.

These days sheep-rearing and tourism are every bit as important to Kalgoorlie as gold. Gambling and sex are held in high esteem too. Even the tourist postcards show the bush two-up school and Hay Street, where the tarts line up in little brick cubicles that look like changing-rooms at an English municipal swimming-bath.

Not all the region's gold-rush towns have enjoyed Kalgoorlie's continuing prosperity. Elsewhere the gold has run out, and many places that were once centres of mining, wealth and population are now deserted ghost towns. We thought we'd take a short trip to one of these ghost towns in our newly rented Land Cruiser. We were planning an easy jaunt to get used to the feel of driving the thing. We didn't think we were doing anything very ambitious. We certainly didn't think we were in any danger of getting lost; which, I have learned, is precisely when you're in *most* danger of getting lost.

We went to the local K-Mart and bought some cheap, basic and disposable camping-gear that we could ditch at the end of the journey. Then we went to Woolworth's to stock up with enough food for the next couple of days. Our first, unambitious foray was going to take us to the ghost town of Kanowna. After that we were planning to drive on and find somewhere to camp. Failing that, if it was getting late, or if we couldn't find a good camping-spot, or if we simply didn't feel like it, we might even go back to the Sandalwood Motel in Kalgoorlie where we'd spent the previous night. We weren't in a hurry. We had no worries. We had nothing to prove.

Kanowna was just twenty-two kilometres away from Kalgoorlie, north-east along a fairly solid dirt road. In the days when Kalgoorlie had its thirty thousand souls, Kanowna had twelve thousand of its own. Today there is nobody and nothing in Kanowna, really nothing. The hotels, breweries, churches and railway station are all gone, and not just abandoned but completely obliterated. You could drive through and think it was just an ugly stretch of land where some low-lifes had thrown their litter and dumped some builder's rubble, if it wasn't for a metal sign on the end of a pole that proudly says 'Kanowna'. We had arrived. We parked, got out of the Land Cruiser, and began to look around. Even from a ghost town we had expected a little more. There were a few other signs that had been put up for visitors, signs that said 'Court House' or 'Post Office' but they seemed to be marking nothing more than piles of old bricks. From our map we were able to see where the hospital and one of the churches had been, but it took more data and more imagination than we possessed to even begin to picture what this place must have looked like in its prime.

The ground was littered with tin cans that might have been fifty or sixty years old. They were old-fashioned designs, and had started to decay to the extent that their surfaces had turned black, but they showed little sign of rusting away and returning to the earth. In the wettest areas of Western Australia they say it takes ten to twenty years for tin cans to decompose, and Kanowna is not one of the wettest areas. These tin cans were going to be around for a while yet.

A couple of hundred yards away from the road was a tailings dump, the place where they dump the waste from mining. In these parts that had to qualify as a major 'sight'. We went to look. We were being real tourists. We didn't bother to lock the Land Cruiser. We weren't wearing hats. Obviously we didn't bother to take any water with us. Why should we? We were only going two hundred yards from the road. All I had with me was my camera.

We looked at the tailings dump. There were two hillocks of white sand about twelve feet tall. There were tyre tracks where off-roaders had come and gone. There was an open mine shaft about a yard square and of uncertain, though I suspected enormous, depth. We had soon exhausted the possibilities of Kanowna and its environs.

We set off walking back to the Land Cruiser. After a while we had not arrived. We stopped. We had obviously walked in the wrong direction. We looked around. We couldn't see the Land Cruiser or the road, nor any of the street or building markers. In all directions the land undulated gently; brown earth, low scrub, a few gum trees, nothing that qualified as a landmark. Still, we obviously weren't far away, and we obviously weren't lost. We set off in another likely-looking direction, and after a while concluded that was wrong too. In the distance Sue saw something that looked like a telegraph pole. She felt that had to be the road, but I wasn't at all sure there had been telegraph poles along the road.

From looking at the sun we could, I suppose, have got a vague idea of where north, south, east and west were, but we didn't know which direction we'd walked in when we left the road. We hadn't known that we were going to need to.

This was getting silly. It was one thing to get lost in the middle of say, the Simpson or the Great Sandy Desert, that would have had a certain grandeur to it, a certain scale. That would have been under-standable and forgiveable. But to get completely and utterly lost when you were only a few hundred yards from a road meant that you were a grade one idiot. But that didn't mean you weren't lost.

I started to worry. I surveyed the territory. The land was big and desolate and empty in all directions. Of course we knew there was civilisation out there, not more than twenty-two kilometres away, but we didn't know in which direction. The stupidity and danger of our situation started to come home. The literature and mythology of the Australian desert, perhaps of deserts everywhere, is full of stories about unwary travellers who died just a short distance away from a waterhole and salvation. Why shouldn't two dumb English tourists do much the same sort of thing just a short distance away from their Land Cruiser?

I looked down at the ground and there gazing up at me was the bleached skeleton of a sheep; right on cue. I tried hard to stay calm. I tried to collect my thoughts. I looked at Sue and she looked at me, and although she didn't say anything I could tell she was thinking, 'How the hell did I get myself into this?' There was no very simple answer.

In November 1989, having recently returned from the Morocco Desert Truck Adventure, I was invited to read a short story of mine at a 'literary party' given by *Ambit* magazine. *Ambit* is edited and run by Martin Bax and includes J. G. Ballard and Eduardo Paolozzi among its contributing editors, and they had been publishing what might be called 'experimental prose' of mine for about ten years.

I had long felt that being able to read my work in public would somehow be 'good for my career', so when asked I agreed to read a bit of work in progress called *The Food Chain*. Also reading was Sue Jackson; in fact the party and reading was taking place in her gallery cum shop, a place in Covent Garden called Cabaret Mechanical Theatre.

As I discovered when I arrived to do the reading, Cabaret is Britain's most important collection of contemporary automata; wonderful small wooden machines that spring to eccentric life when a button is pressed or a coin put in a slot. In one a group of sailors sit at a refectory table and bang their fists up and down on the table in anticipation of a meal. They are about to eat the last dodo. In another automaton a man sits in a bath full of spaghetti while parmesan and tomato sauce pour into the bath through the taps. In another, Anubis, the Egyptian jackal god of the mummy wrappings, removes his jackal head to reveal a bandaged, mummified head beneath. The automata were exquisitely made, fun and funny, and yet the best of them, which were made by someone called Paul Spooner, had a seriousness, a philosophical quality and plenty of 'edge' about them.

Sue read a prose poem called *The Other Woman*. Sue was, and is, an attractive, short, blonde, pear-shaped woman with a lot of bustling, good-humoured energy and a big smile. I didn't know then, but Sue was a little bored with running Britain's most important collection of contemporary automata, and was looking for something different. One of the things she was contemplating was becoming a full-time writer. She was impressed that I made a living from writing, not a *good* living I pointed out, but she was still impressed.

Ambit readings, and I seem to have been to a great many of them, are good because the reading is kept to a minimum. This leaves lots of time to pursue lady poets. I pursued Sue. In the course of the evening she told me, and anyone else who happened to be listening, that she had been married for thirty years to an antique dealer, who had died of cancer two years earlier, in much pain and in a terrible physical state. I was at the stage of thinking this sort of thing only happened to other people. The marriage had been successful enough to produce three children, all of them now adult (she had married young). In the course of the marriage she had had fourteen lovers, she said, but had never let any of them see her naked because she was ashamed of her pear-shaped body. Gallant to a fault, I assured her she had nothing to be ashamed of. After a lot more drink, a meal in a Greek restaurant and a visit to a club with a transvestite stage show (not my idea) I found myself in bed with Sue Jackson.

We both agreed that we were not the kind of people who normally did this kind of thing.

'What do you really want from me?' Sue asked.

I, very drunk, said, 'I want to take you to the desert. We'll make love in the dunes, we'll get tattooed, we'll get married in a chapel in Las Vegas.'

This was a line, but I thought it was quite an original one, and in some ways I meant it. She received the line in the spirit it was intended and I told her my plans, still not very well focused, for writing about the desert. I don't think she was entirely convinced.

'But what is there to say about the desert?' she asked.

'Lots of things,' I said, and I told her my traveller's tale about the man in Alnif with the photocopier.

I have always thought that laughter ought to be the way to a woman's heart, but I have found it seldom is. This time I was better rewarded. Sue found the anecdote funny. It seemed to convince her that I wasn't a complete charlatan.

'Would you really like to make love to me in the desert?' she asked.

'Yes,' I said.

'Which desert?'

'Any old desert,' I said.

'When are you setting off?'

'It'll be some months yet.'

'If I still know you in some months, maybe I'll come with you.'

In June the next year we still knew each other and set off for the desert together. We got on very well in London. Whether we'd get on well in the middle of Australia was another matter, but there was only one way to find out. I was glad to have someone going with me. I felt perfectly able to travel on my own, but exploring deserts completely alone is not recommended, and in certain circumstances can be suicidal. Having a companion meant that even if I got into trouble, say by being injured or having a vehicle breakdown, I was in with a chance of survival.

'This is all perfectly safe, isn't it?' Sue asked. 'I'm not going to get bitten by a funnel-web spider, am I?'

'No.'

'And I'm not going to die of thirst or heat exhaustion?'

'Definitely not.'

'And we're not going to get lost in the middle of the Australian Outback?'

'Of course not,' I said. 'Trust me, I'm a writer.'

I had always known, indeed had revelled in the fact that the desert is a place of exaltation, self-discovery and revelation; but it is none of those things when you're lost. When you're lost it's just a big, frightening, dangerous place without any water.

Inevitably this is not one of the great 'lost in the desert' stories. We did not wander for days, dehydrated and hallucinating. They did not send out teams of desert trackers to find us. We did not suffer savage hunger, thirst and madness. In reality we simply wandered around for an hour or so, utterly lost, getting truly frightened and panicky, until very suddenly, for no good reason, we saw something we recognised. It was nothing much. It was just some particular configuration of scrub and earth that told us we'd been in this spot when we first wandered from the road. It therefore followed that if we could retrace our steps from here, we could get back to the road, to the Land Cruiser and salvation. Which is what we did. I realise this doesn't make for a particularly gripping anecdote but I am happy to sacrifice the anecdote for the sake of being alive.

In one profound sense we were there simply because I had succeeded in getting myself commissioned to write a book about deserts. I don't know if you've ever tried to get commissioned to write a travel book. It's a rum business. Clearly you need to do some research, so you talk to people, read books, look at maps. You get very excited by all this. So you write a proposal and send it to an editor, in this case to one I knew fairly well. Of course, it's hard to believe that anyone is going to cough up money so that you can wander round the world looking at deserts, but by now, having squandered quite an amount of effort thinking about and planning this trip, you start really, really wanting to do it.

My editor's initial response was good; or at least good enough that he wanted me to discuss it with his editorial director. My job was simply to go into his office and sell him the idea of a desert book, and more importantly, sell him the idea that I was just the man to write it.

I had put together a chapter about why I liked deserts, a description of my visit to Morocco (a shorter version of the first chapter of this book), and an outline of what the rest of the book might entail;

namely three separate trips to three separate deserts in Australia, Egypt and the United States.

So I went to see the editorial director carrying a selection of 'materials', maps, of course, showing possible routes, newspaper clippings, photographs, postcards. I knew I needed to convey bound-less enthusiasm for this project but by now my enthusiasm was actually quite real. I really did want to write this book about deserts for him.

I walked into the office and I was so keyed up, so bursting with conviction and wanderlust that I felt I would do *anything* to make this book a reality. I would sell my car, my flat, my soul, anything. At the same time I had to make it quite clear that I wasn't *actually* going to sell my car, my flat, my soul. What I was actually going to do was ask this man for money, and if he didn't give it to me the whole project would go down the pan. He knew all this too.

Hodder's editorial director is Ion Trewin. I had an unusual and very oblique connection with his father J. C. Trewin, the theatre critic. The first 'proper' job I had after leaving university was working for Bertram Rota Ltd, a bookseller specialising in twentieth-century first editions but also dealing in authors' letters, manuscripts and other more ephemeral items. Very shortly after starting at Rota's I spent an afternoon arranging several thousand theatre programmes into alphabetical order by title of play. They had belonged to J. C. Trewin and he was selling them to clear his study and make some money. However, the day before my interview with Ion Trewin his father died after a long illness. There was talk of the interview being cancelled but in the end it went ahead. I was too embarrassed to mention either the fact of the death or that I had once sorted thou-sands of J. C. Trewin's theatre programmes. I like to think I wouldn't be so embarrassed today.

Ion Trewin knew a great deal more about the business of travel writing than I did. He knew Geoffrey Moorhouse though he couldn't offer an explanation as to why he referred to his ex-wife as 'J'. He also knew Paul Theroux and remembered meeting him shortly before he set off on the journey that became *The Great Railway Bazaar*.

'Do you really think there's a book in it?' Ion had asked Theroux.

'I'm sure there is,' said Theroux.

'What *kind* of book?'

'I don't know,' Theroux had replied, 'I just know there's a book.'

That was how Ion Trewin felt about my proposal. He thought that probably I was right, probably there *was* a book in it, and though he wasn't quite sure how it would work he was prepared to take a risk. When the offer and the advance came through it became obvious to me, if not to him, that he wasn't prepared to take a very *big* risk, but still . . . He talked positively and encouragingly about the project.

'If I have a worry,' he said, 'it's this. You'll be in the desert in Australia and in Egypt and in the United States, but what will be the connection, the link between them all?'

'*I* will,' I said.

He seemed to like that answer and so I was commissioned to write *Day Trips to the Desert.*

So that, in one sense, explained what I was now doing in Australia. But why Australia? Well, if you're looking for desert, Australia has it in spades. You can't turn around without running into the Tanami, the Simpson, the Great Victoria, the Great Sandy, the Sturt Stony or the Gibson. There are also lots of little deserts, such as the inventively named Little Desert between Adelaide and Melbourne, or the Pinnacles Desert north of Perth. Although by certain definitions most of Australia might not be called true desert at all, by other definitions almost *all* of it might.

The Australian desert comes by many names, most of them colourful. Most frequently, of course, Australians speak of it as Outback or bush. I am told it can be referred to as the Never Never, as sunset country or 'beyond the black stump', but I never heard anyone use any of those expressions. I have heard it called 'the great buggerall' and I suppose it's the very fact that there's buggerall in the Australian desert is what most attracted me to it.

Australians are proud of their Outback. They like to identify with it. They think it confirms their rough, tough, pioneering origins. They like to compliment themselves on living with this great void at their back. But they want to make sure it *stays* at their back. They don't actually want to go to it or live in it. They just like to know it's there.

If the population of Australia was spread evenly over the whole country they'd have half a square kilometre each. This compares favourably with the UK, where everybody would have 1/229th of a square kilometre each. But, of course, the population isn't spread evenly throughout Australia, and the West and the centre of the country offer an overwhelming emptiness and vast quantities of un-inhabited land. Western Australia, where Sue and I were to do most of our travelling, has an area the size of Algeria ($2\frac{1}{2}$ million square kilometres) and a population the size of Birmingham (1.3 million).

However, since about a million of these people live in Perth you can see that once you get out of the city you're in for some serious underpopulation.

Australia is short on archetypal desert features. There are no palm trees there, no cacti, at least not naturally. Sand dunes are comparatively rare and where they do occur they are limited in height and are surrounded by vegetation. There are dunes in the Simpson Desert and on the coast at Eucla. I have only seen photographs of these but they look like magnificent sand dunes. More often the Australian desert is made up of stony or sandy plains, clay and salt pans and thin savannah. There are all sorts of rock features poking up through the desert: mountain ranges, buttes, mesas, Ayers Rock. The most striking thing about much, though not all, of it is the redness of its sand. This is particularly apparent in the centre of the country. Windblown sand passes over the ground and picks up iron oxide as it goes, and this luscious, burned scarlet stains the heart of the country and anything that passes through it.

It is said that Australia's prehistoric isolation from the rest of the world turned it into a sort of evolutionary laboratory. Marcus Clarke described it as 'the strange scribblings of nature learning how to write'. But this is insulting as well as inaccurate. Kangaroos and emus, for example, may at first seem curious or grotesque, but when you see a kangaroo bouncing effortlessly through harsh terrain, or an emu's long legs enabling it to clear all obstacles of scrub and bushes, you realise how perfectly these creatures are adapted to their environment. They are not 'scribblings' and nature could not have learned to write any better.

For a long time I fretted about the flora of Australia. I thought that if I was going to write a travel book I ought to be able to identify and describe every bush and tree that I saw. Then I could write the sort of sentence beloved by some travel writers: 'We passed through a cluster of grevilleas and there spread before us was a dazzling array of red mallees, mulgas and quandongs.' Of course, I realise now that this means nothing at all to most people. But I bought a book that enabled me to identify the trees and bushes of Australia, and I tried to identify the ones I saw, but I really had no talent for it. That bush over there could well be a mulga, but it might be a mallee and it just possibly might be a quandong. For a while this worried me. Then I thought, why do I want so desperately to be able to name every tree in Australia when in England I can only name about three? So I stopped worrying. However, before abandoning the handbook I had learned to identify desert oaks, certain sorts of wattle, desert peas, wild tomatoes and, of course, eucalyptus.

The other plant I took to in Australia, largely because it was easy to identify, was spinifex. Spinifex is the common name for the group of grasses that forms in a hummock in the desert and then has long, spikey stalks shooting out of its centre. Aboriginals weave this grass into twine which is then used to form intricate nets of great complexity and craftsmanship.

The Aboriginals are the true heirs of the Australian desert. Before the white man came to Australia they were not uniquely desert dwellers. Some were coastal fishermen and others lived in the colder climates of what is now Victoria and Tasmania. But many did live in the desert, and lived in places and climates where no white man could have hoped to survive, and despite impossibly forbidding conditions the desert Aboriginals seldom experienced serious hunger or starvation.

Heirs to the desert or not, the desert is all most of them have ended up with. Australia is a rich country and feels able to afford a liberal conscience at the moment. The Aboriginal population is minute and they have been 'given back' massive areas of land. They say it is not enough, and in one sense it will never be enough. The Aboriginal belief that every rock, tree, hill and plant is holy, will inevitably not be satisfied until all the land is in Aboriginal hands.

Pat Dodson, an Aboriginal who was once a Catholic priest, has written, '. . . we come to them. No, they say, you can't have the land which we own. You can only have the land which no white man wants. The Land Council helps you. You go to the Land Commissioner. You tell of your love, duties and relationship with your land . . . You bear the secrets of your soul to total strangers. You are given back the land that no one wants. The land you cannot leave. The country you call father.'

There seems to me an obvious problem here. If *all* the land is holy then I don't see how he can talk of a land that no one wants. Surely he must want any and all of it. But you see what he means. The white man seems to be saying you can have lots of land, just so long as it contains no mineral deposits or is unusable for agriculture. And certainly I get the feeling that if, at some later date, the white man suddenly found a use for the land he currently doesn't want he wouldn't have too many qualms about taking back the land that's been given to the Aboriginals.

*   *   *

All the time I was in Australia I kept thinking of that song 'The Tender Trap'. It contains the line about hurrying to a spot that's just a dot on the map. I would sit in London, in my small room, looking at maps of Australia and more or less everywhere looked like 'just a dot'. In fact, the size of the dots tended to exaggerate the status of the places. Even quite a modest map of Australia is likely to show such places as Coolgardie, Menzies or Agnew. But these places are only marked because they're all that's there. A big dot doesn't necessarily mean a big place. Coolgardie has a population of nine hundred, Menzies of ninety, and when I was in Agnew the population was described as 'less than ten'.

However, one place on the map kept catching my eye, and it had nothing to do with the size of the dot. In fact it wasn't a town at all. It was a lake, a dry lake I assumed, and I was much taken by the name: Lake Disappointment. It sounded like my kind of place. It was situated almost dead centre of Western Australia, in the Gibson Desert. A trip to a place called Lake Disappointment appealed to me. I expected to find it dry, barren, utterly desolate; though I suppose to have been genuinely disappointing it would have needed to be full of water, well stocked with fish, and with elegant birds skimming across its surface.

My problem was that there didn't seem to be a road to Lake Disappointment, or rather, some maps seemed to indicate a road but others didn't. So I spoke to a woman at Western Australia House. I asked her was there a road to Lake Disappointment or not?

'Well, I wouldn't call it a road exactly,' she said.

'No?'

'More kind of a track. I mean, what do you want to go there for? Are you part of a television crew or something?'

'I'm a writer.'

'Have you been to Australia before?'

'No.'

'So what is it you want to do exactly?'

I mumbled something about wide open spaces and deserts and hiring a four-wheel drive. I tried to make this sound reasonable.

'Look,' she said, 'you don't want to go to Lake Disappointment. Nobody goes there, not even the Aboriginals. Once every few years a convoy maybe goes out there. But you don't want to go on your own. For one thing, it's awful expensive getting back the bodies.'

That was the first time I'd heard that line, but in Australia I heard it several times. It seems to be a classic of its kind.

'Well, how about Laverton and Wiluna? What's it like there?' I asked, naming a couple of dots I'd seen on maps.

'That's more like it,' she said. 'Yeah, that ought to be enough desert for anyone.'

'Really? Are you sure?' I said. 'You see I don't want to get there and find millions of tourists and it's all like Trafalgar Square.'

'Trafalgar Square it isn't,' she said. And I later discovered she was right.

So I trimmed my ambitions somewhat. After all, I had nothing to prove. I was just a guy taking a look at the desert. I wasn't some kind of he-man adventurer. When I got to Western Australia I'd hire a Land Cruiser, just drive around, forget about Lake Disappointment, and yes, that would be plenty of desert for anyone.

There was, however, one pressing, indeed overwhelming, reason why I might not have made it to Australia at all. About two weeks before I was due to leave, it was a Sunday afternoon, I got a phone call from my mother at home in Sheffield.

She said, 'Geoff, you've got to come home. Your father's dying. You've got to come home.'

When your mother says something like that you tend to drop everything, pack a bag, get in your car and head for home. Only as you drive do you start trying to make sense of it.

I knew that my father had been having some trouble with his back. Since taking early retirement he had gone back to being a jobbing carpenter, putting in fitted wardrobes, cupboards, shelves, dormer windows, new doors. The simple explanation for the pain in his back seemed to be just that he was getting old and had been working too hard. His GP had diagnosed arthritis but hadn't been able to give him anything that eased the pain. My father, who had no respect for doctors at the best of times, had been to an acupuncturist. In retrospect this looks like a very desperate and uncharacteristic thing for him to have done, and should have alerted us to the seriousness of his concern. The acupuncture, if anything, seemed to make the pain worse.

I knew that on Friday, two days before my mother called, he had gone into the local orthopaedic hospital for tests, but that appeared to be a sign that he was being helped, rather than a cause for alarm. After all, I thought, nobody dies of arthritis. So I thought my mother was being melodramatic and that my dash up the motorway, though necessary to show what a good son I was, would be a bit of a waste of time. I hoped so. I hoped that my father wasn't really dying. Next day at the hospital it appeared my mother wasn't being melodramatic at all.

We spoke to an Indian doctor whose accent my mother couldn't understand, and he told us that my father's blood contained debris from a tumour somewhere in his body. A tumour, we knew instantly, was a codeword for cancer. The doctor said by the time debris is detectable things are very serious indeed. The prognosis, he said, was very bad. I wondered how many relatives of Sheffield hospital patients knew what the word prognosis meant.

We saw my father. He was in bed, half asleep yet obviously in pain. He had spilled food down his pyjamas and on to the sheets. He was heavily drugged, came round briefly, managed a little confused conversation and dozed off again. I got the impression he already knew how bad things were even though no doctor had told him anything, and my mother would certainly not have wanted him to know. He looked resigned, defeated. He didn't look as though he had much heart for a fight. My mother and I went home shaken and tearful.

My parents lived in a three-bedroomed semi-detached house in a suburb on the south side of Sheffield. It was neat, clean, well behaved; not well-off but comfortable. Everybody had a newish car and PVC double glazing and adult sons and daughters who had moved away and were supposed to be doing well. But recently the street had become a street of widows. Husbands had died of cancer and heart attacks and the wives, in their sixties, were left behind supporting each other by means of evenings out, coffee mornings, and a little gentle gardening.

My mother's neighbour had lost her husband too. He had died on Boxing Day. She and my mother had become reasonably good friends, and she told me how sorry she was to hear about my father.

'I don't know, Geoff,' she said. 'It's happening all over. There's no sense to it. I can't understand it. None of it makes sense to me these days.'

I did my best to agree in the right places but I couldn't really accept the proposition that there had once been a time when everything *had* made sense to her. She had seen the world as safe, orderly and comprehensible until her husband died, she seemed to be saying. Now he was gone she was surprised to find that the world was cruel, dangerous and painful. I was surprised by her surprise. The suburbs are, perhaps, our idea of a safe place. Yet the widows in my mother's street had found that death and misery could burst out there too, just like everywhere else. The problem was that death and misery didn't suit the landscape. One might expect, say, the desert to be a pitiless, lethal place, a place of death, but surely not the suburbs of Sheffield.

The next day we got a phone call telling us that my father had been moved to the big teaching hospital. This seemed reasonable enough. If he had cancer there didn't seem much point keeping him in a bone hospital. We visited with some trepidation and found, to our astonishment, that my father seemed fine. He obviously didn't like being in hospital and he was obviously feeling some pain, but he was alert, talkative, and as cheerful as circumstances permitted. He was not the drugged, defeated man we had seen in bed the previous day, and although there was no reason to believe that the prognosis had changed, it was hard to remember or justify the terrible gloom we'd felt the previous day.

We said nothing to my father about our conversation with the Indian doctor. My mother was adamant that we should tell him nothing, because if she was in that situation she wouldn't have wanted anybody to tell her. Since I, in that situation, would have wanted to be told, I felt very differently. But it was an argument I was content to let her win. In any case, it seemed to me my father must surely know how bad things were. There was no point rubbing his or our own noses in it.

There were things to be done. Relatives had to be told, hospital visits organised and co-ordinated. At that time I found myself quite likely to burst into tears if anybody rang up to ask how my father was. It is one thing to know your father is dying, quite another to have to tell that to people half a dozen times a day. Being a writer and not having a real job meant that I could be at home with my mother for as long as necessary, or until I went to Australia, whichever came first; that was assuming I went to Australia.

The way the Indian doctor and my mother had spoken, indeed the impression I got when I first saw my father, suggested that he might have days rather than weeks to live. Now, only a day later, he looked so much better that we felt surely we must be talking about many months, with luck, who could say, maybe even a year or more. The worst possibility was that we might be talking about a few weeks, in which case he would die while I was in Australia; in which case I surely had a duty not to go.

'You've got to go to Australia, Geoff,' my mother said several times. 'Of course you've got to go. But what if he died while you were away? You'd never forgive yourself, would you?'

I didn't know. At the time I thought I might have forgiven myself quite easily. In all sorts of ways it would have made my life infinitely easier to be somewhere else when the worst happened. I didn't admit that as one of my reasons. I merely adhered to the fact that I had been commissioned to write this book, that it was a job, that writing was what I did with my life, and that I really did want to go to the Australian desert.

In retrospect I'm not entirely sure why it seemed so important to me that I should make the trip precisely then and not postpone it until later in the year. Certainly the tickets had been booked, but they could no doubt have been changed. I could have said the question of climate was somewhat pressing. I wanted to go to the Australian desert in winter, while it was still bearably cool. Certainly Sue had gone to a lot of trouble to take time off from her business and it might not be possible for her to get the same amount of time off later. But mostly I think I was so determined to go because I was so determined to *start*. This idea of a book about deserts had been with me for what seemed like a long time, but until I actually set foot in the Australian desert I would feel like a fake, a pretender.

Each day in Sheffield was moulded around the evening's visit to the hospital. The ward was long and densely populated, but subdivided into small units each containing four beds. The floor was lustrously smooth and polished and there were tall, slender windows which could not be opened but which gave a spectacular view over the city. My father was not much interested in views.

I have some trouble remembering the exact order in which things happened. I know our conversations were banal and repetitive. We talked about how the food was, the people in the other beds and what was wrong with them, the garden at home, how various relatives were, how my car was running. I saw my father getting thinner every day, the bones in his face becoming more jagged, the teeth becoming more prominent, his features adopting a permanent expression of discomfort and disgust.

There was much talk about tests: blood tests, X-rays and bone scans. These seemed to be designed to track down the exact location of the cancer, its whereabouts being somehow elusive and uncertain. It might have been in the liver, it might have been in the kidney, it might have been in the bone.

I remember my father sitting on the edge of his hospital bed eating his evening meal from a tray. His back was bent, his head was down. He was trying and failing to eat some sort of sliced, tinned meat with salad. It looked terrible. He said this was one of the best meals he'd had in hospital.

In the next few days my father lost the ability to walk, but he didn't accept the fact. One day when we visited he told us he'd fallen and hurt himself trying to get to the toilet. He would not use a bottle or a bed pan on the grounds that they were 'humiliating'.

My mother developed a way of talking about him in the third person while he was there. 'He doesn't look as though he's enjoying that salad very much.' 'He's looking a bit rough today.' 'I don't think he's very comfortable in that bed.' It wasn't so much that she thought he was helpless and deaf, but rather, I think, because she felt a glass wall had come down between my father and the rest of the world, between the living and the soon to be dead.

At home my mother and I tried to stay sane and coherent. Once in a while we had a good cry together, but most often we sat with the television on. It was much easier to do that than to talk about the situation. When we did talk we tended to argue, though not, of course, about anything real.

I remember my mother saying, 'I'll have to wash his pyjamas because he seems to mess them up every day and he's only got two pairs.'

I said, 'Why don't we buy him another pair?'

She said, 'I would, but would they be of use to anybody?'

'Well, they'll be some use to him.'

'But how long will he need them for?'

'It doesn't matter how long he'll need them for. He needs them now.'

'But what's the point of buying a pair of pyjamas he's not going to get any wear out of?'

In order to be doing something in the long days in my parents' house, I tried to do some gardening. The garden had always been my father's province, not because he wanted it to be, but because he thought of it as a hard, manly domain. My mother, he'd say, wouldn't have been able to cope with it. He grew a few roses, a lot of runner beans and kept the lawn trimmed. This year the beans hadn't been planted. The garden had never been a place of great colour or fertility, and certainly not a place of enjoyment. The garden was a place of back-breaking toil where you weeded and dug trenches and hacked back the hedges. It was not a place you experienced pleasure. But then, it seemed to me, my parents had never been very good at experiencing pleasure.

Meals, for example, which might have been a source of some enjoyment were joyless occasions, grudgingly necessary to support life but certainly not to be enjoyed. Meals created a lot of washing up and so had to be eaten quickly in order that the washing up could be done and the whole business of the meal got out of the way. Only when the washing up was done could my parents 'settle'. This meant sitting in the living-room watching television. Apart from occasional visits to the local pub this was their only joint leisure activity. But if you asked them if they'd enjoyed a particular programme or asked if they wanted to watch something specific on television, my father would say, 'It's all a load of rubbish, anyway,' and my mother would say, 'I'm not bothered about television.'

The only activity my father positively seemed to enjoy were his occasional visits to one or other of the Sheffield casinos; but he went alone since my mother didn't enjoy gambling.

It sometimes horrified me to discover that, despite my best attempts to be otherwise, I had inherited my parents' ability not to have a good time.

I felt I had to phone Tessa, who was now my ex-wife. She had always liked my father and got on very well with him. She cried when I told her the news.

'You're not going to Australia, are you?' she said.

'Well, yes, I suppose I am.'

I could feel that she disapproved.

'I could come up and see you,' she said. 'I could come at the weekend. We could go for a walk or something.'

I thanked her, said it might be a nice idea and that I'd think about it, but I knew I wouldn't ask her to come. Of course I hadn't told her that Sue was coming to Australia with me, or that Sue even existed. I was still playing the part of the wounded husband.

Sue, however, did come to visit. I wanted her there for a couple of reasons. First, I was finding it hard to cope. Secondly, sentimentally, I thought Sue would be important in my life for some considerable time and I wanted her to meet my father before he died.

The circumstances of the meeting were not those anyone would have chosen, but Sue and my father certainly got on well enough. Until now I hadn't even told my father that Sue was coming with me to Australia. I didn't really know why. Possibly it was because I was still prepared to abandon the trip if my father asked me not to go, and if he knew Sue was going as well it would be that much harder for him to ask. More likely I was just very bad at discussing anything that mattered to me with my father. Now I told him. He was surprised yet relieved. He was glad that his thirty-seven-year-old son wasn't going to be all alone in the desert, and, of course, his thirty-seven-year-old son was glad too.

We sat at my father's hospital bedside and Sue talked about the dangerous snakes and spiders in Australia and my father told a story about being in India in the war and seeing a local boy catch a cobra using a forked stick, then smashing its fangs out on a rock and taking the snake away to be sold. We told him our route through Australia, said we'd be doing some travelling by bus, some by train, but that the high point would be hiring a Land Cruiser and driving into the Outback.

'Blimey,' he said. 'I hope you don't get lost.'

He asked me what the most impressive sight I'd ever seen was, the most spectacular piece of landscape, and I had to say the sand dunes of the Merzouga Sand Sea in Morocco. How about him? He said it was sunset over the sea, seen from on board ship; space, emptiness, stillness in all directions. We reckoned there might be some connections between these two things.

My father and I shared the same name. It caused endless confusion throughout our lives together. The worst was when he was known as Big Geoff and I was known as Little Geoff. My father said, 'I've been thinking and I know what name I'd use if I was going to write a book. I'd take half of my first name and half of my second name, so instead of being Geoffrey Nicholson, it would be Frey Holson.'

It had never occurred to me that my father would spend much time thinking about what pseudonym he'd use in the totally unlikely event of him writing anything, but in hospital I suppose he had time to think about all sorts of things he didn't normally think about.

'Never mind Australia,' he said, 'I suppose you could write a book about going on a day trip to Rotherham.'

'You could write a book about anything,' I said, 'but I don't think I could have got commissioned to write about Rotherham.'

As we left that night he told me to take care of Sue and he told Sue to take care of me. Sue, who claimed some expertise in these matters having watched the slow death of her husband, said there had been a period of about nine months between her husband being in my father's state and his death. My father seemed quite strong, quite alive. I had every reason to want to believe her. Certainly it was hard then to imagine that he would die in the next few weeks. There seemed to be no real reason to cancel the trip.

Of course, in these situations you hear the advice you want to hear, but I spoke to my mother's neighbour, a man called Ernest who had retired from a job with the railways. He was one of the few surviving husbands in the street, but he was a widower, his wife having died of cancer.

'Of course you've got to go to Australia,' he said. 'Your Dad would want you to go. More to the point. what can you say to him if you don't go? "Hey Dad, I've changed my mind. I'm not going to Australia. I'm going to hang around here until you die."'

When my mother had been in hospital with a heart condition some years earlier, my father had been a very reluctant visitor. He recognised, as everyone surely does, the difficulties of sitting at someone's bedside for an hour or more and being forced to make conversation. So he would only turn up for the last half hour of visiting time. My mother wasn't very pleased but she accepted that was his way. However, when it was his turn to be visited he demanded more than half an hour of attention. Visiting ended at eight o' clock, so my mother and I tried to arrive at about six-fifteen which we felt gave us time enough, but he always managed to imply that we were late and failing in our duty. One day he was particularly upset when we arrived.

'I thought you weren't coming,' he said. 'I just rang up the house to see if you'd left. The doctor wants to see all three of us.'

We suspected this was going to be the big one. A doctor and nurse arrived at the bedside and the curtains were drawn around us. My mother and I sat on either side of the bed on plastic chairs, the nurse sat to attention at the foot of the bed, and the doctor sat casually on the bed itself. The doctor looked young, slim, athletic, had blond, spikey hair and a bluff Midlands accent. We sat waiting for him to utter some wisdom, to deliver some thunderbolt, and he confounded us all by saying to my father, 'Well, what do you think's wrong with you?'

My father didn't know what to say. He had prepared himself to listen, not to speak.

'Well,' he said after a long time, 'I feel rubbish. Every day I feel a little bit worse. Whatever it is you're doing for me, it's not working, and I feel I need building up, and I think if I was at home I'd feel more like eating and I'd get some of my strength back.'

I don't think this what was what the doctor had expected. I think he was expecting a tougher response, something more John Wayne, something like, 'Sure Doc, I know it's the Big C, but I'm going to fight it and I'm going to win!' The doctor was going to have to approach this differently.

He said, 'There are two basic reasons why people get back pain. One is mechanical, it's like carpentry, something needs fixing and we can generally fix it. If it's not mechanical then it's usually something nasty. Yours isn't mechanical. Yours is something nasty.

'You're an intelligent man,' he continued, 'you must have worked out for yourself that you've got something more than arthritis. You've probably worked out for yourself that it's a tumour, and that's basically as far as we've got as well. We're trying to find out exactly where that tumour is and what we can do about it. Now, I've got to tell you that even when we work out exactly what's wrong with you there's a very fair chance that we aren't going to be able to do anything about it.'

My father's face showed, more than anything, surprise. This was all new stuff to him. He *hadn't* worked out for himself that he'd got something worse than arthritis. He wasn't the 'intelligent man' of the young doctor's imagination. He was a sick, frightened man who until then had believed that if there was something wrong with you, you went to hospital and got it put right.

'You're saying I might not make it,' my father said tentatively.

The doctor nodded. I wondered how often he had these kinds of conversations with patients. He started to talk about what they would do next. They would take a piece of bone and see if the 'tumour' had spread there. Treatment, if any, was likely to be via drugs or radium. There would be no point operating. By then, however, we were too upset to be able take this in. Eventually the doctor and nurse left, the doctor giving my father a manly punch on the knee as he went. I asked my parents if they wanted to be alone and they said yes. I waited outside the ward, in the vestibule by the lifts. After a while my mother came out and said he wanted to see me.

I went back to the ward, pushed through the curtains and looked at my father. He was lying back in a nest of pillows, looking forlorn, desperate, in pain. He lifted his arms towards me. It was a gesture of love but also one of submission. He was distressed by what the doctor had told him, and, I think, doubly distressed that I should see him in that state. I bent over the bed and we hugged each other. I felt the tremor of a sob go through my body. We soon released each other. We were not comfortable with this physical nearness, this display of feeling. I squeezed his hand. It was a handshake as much as anything else. There was nothing at all to be said.

'I'll see you tomorrow,' I said.

He nodded, too choked to speak.

The next day my mother and I visited the hospital with far more than the usual, generalised dread. We walked into the ward. My father looked fine. In some bizarre way it was as if yesterday had never happened. We sat down beside the bed. We talked as before about clean pyjamas and hospital food and how my car was running.

At the time I thought this was pathetic and absurd. Today I'm not so sure. At the time I thought we should have talked long and hard about what the doctor had said. I thought we should have tried to deal directly with death by talking about it. Today I don't know what we could have said. I can imagine no way of 'dealing with' the imminent likelihood of my father's death.

My father said, 'Tell me again about the route you're taking through Australia. I know you've told me before, and I know I'll have forgotten again in about twenty minutes, but tell me anyway.'

So I told him again.

'Look after Sue,' he said. 'I liked Sue. Yes, I liked Sue. I know it's wrong to compare people, and I liked Tessa, but yes, I liked Sue.'

He let that one hang in the air for a while and then he said, 'You know, I never thought I'd finish up like this.' That was as much as he ever said about death.

One popular way of describing cancer is as though it were a rapacious, virulent invader, a corruption that spreads, multiplies, annexes the body and makes it foul. Yet it seemed to me that nothing invaded or multiplied in my father. Rather it was if he was slowly evaporating. Each day he was less substantial. Each day there was less and less of him. And yet there was still enough of him that I felt able to leave Sheffield, make my trip and feel confident that there would still be plenty of him that had not evaporated by the time I got back.

I felt guilt and relief in more or less equal quantities as I left Sheffield, heading first for London, then for Australia. I was very glad to be freed from the drudgery of hospital visiting and the almost equal drudgery of trying to be a tower of strength for my mother. I was sorry to leave her to cope on her own, but I had been going quietly mad sitting for two weeks in that sterile semi-detached house, trying and failing to be the caring, sympathetic, capable son.

I phoned Tessa before I left to tell her the latest news on my father and to say that despite her advice I was going to Australia. She was depressed. She said that everyone was telling her she was wasting her time and talents in her job, that she should hand in her notice, travel, see the world, 'find' herself. I said I couldn't see any necessity for that. Her life and her work didn't look so bad to me.

She said, 'If I was still married to you I'd give up my job and I could come with you to the desert.'

I snorted down the phone.

'When I'm feeling really down then I wish we'd never split up,' she said. 'And sometimes when I just feel okay, I still wish we were married. But when I'm feeling good, then I'm glad, very glad, that we're not together.'

I believe this is known as giving contradictory signals. I was glad to be going away. I wasn't hoping to 'find myself'. Travel can take you away from difficult situations, and if you're lucky it may take you away from yourself.

I know of no better lines to describe the ambivalent feelings that accompany even the most modest journeys than those in Eliot's *Dry Salvages* about faces relaxing from grief into relief, about being between the hither and the farther shore, of not faring well but of faring forward. And certainly, following Eliot's advice, I could not think 'the past is finished'.

The other literary source that was with me was Patrick White's *Voss*. The eponymous hero says of Australia, 'In this disturbing country, so far as I have become acquainted with it already, it is possible more easily to discard the inessential and attempt the infinite.' I was not wholly convinced of my ability to judge what was and wasn't inessential, and I certainly wasn't planning to attempt the infinite, but I thought I knew what he meant. England had always seemed to me an unlikely country in which to attempt the infinite.

Later in the book Laura Trevelyan says of Voss, 'You are so isolated. That is why you are fascinated by the prospect of desert places, in which you will find your own situation taken for granted, or more than that, exalted . . .' I thought that described my own situation reasonably well.

The members of Voss's expedition die horribly, lost in the desert. People in literature do not go to the desert and live happily ever after; but personally I still had hopes.

*   *   *

The plane journey to Australia was a bore. The food reminded me of hospital food. I thought of myself trapped in my seat much as my father was trapped in his hospital bed. I was ministered to by hostesses in fancy uniforms much as my father was ministered to by nurses.

We arrived at Darwin International at four in the morning. I suppose International is as International does, but this title seemed a little grandiose for a building that looked like the kind of English bus station they pulled down and replaced in the early eighties; bare walls, cream paint, ugly overhead strip lighting. The immigration men really did say 'G'day' and wore collar and tie with shorts, long white socks and sensible shoes. This, I understand, is called Territory Rig.

Darwin is not in the desert but it is in the tropics. It had the misfortune to be more or less blown away in 1974 by Cyclone Tracey. Surely if your town was going to be blown away you'd prefer it to be done by a cyclone with a more epic name, like Theresa possibly, or Tallulah. After the cyclone they rebuilt, with the result that almost everything in Darwin looks incredibly new and shining. It is all glass and concrete with pastel colours and post-modernist flourishes. The city centre is also, to an Englishman, staggeringly, bafflingly clean. Where is the dog shit? Where's the litter and the beer cans? Where are the signs of life?

In England I had kept my eyes open for Land Cruisers, knowing that I was going to be hiring one. In a month I saw two. This is not the case in Darwin. Toyota has colonised the Outback. The Land Cruiser comes in many forms and with many accessories; with long and short wheelbases, as station wagons, as personnel carriers, as table tops, with roo bars, scrub bars and bull bars, with rows of spotlights, with metal meshes to protect the windscreens, with winches and snorkels, with 'Desert Dueller' tyres. All these variations could be found on the streets of Darwin. Even the number plates in Darwin looked serious. They were marked 'Northern Territory Outback Australia'. Some of these vehicles, despite all the rugged paraphernalia, looked suspiciously spotless and unabused, but most were undoubtedly the real thing. And the same could be said for the men who drove them.

They looked wild. They had lots of hair, lots of beard, lots of stomach, and quite a few tattoos. The tattoos showed a lot of Asian influence, with serpents, dragons and wild cats. One young guy had a tattoo that said AC/DC but I'm pretty sure that was a reference to the Australian rock band rather than an advertisement for his sexual catholicism. They looked like bad guys, at least like bad-assed guys. That was the image they wanted to show and they succeeded admirably. They looked like they were just back from the bush where they'd been wrestling crocs and biting the heads off geckos, but when I saw them they were happy to hang around in the Smith Street Mall and look mean.

Feeling tired, jet-lagged, a little sick, we ventured out into Darwin. It was hot, tropically hot, although the humidity was low. Walking down the street with Sue presented certain problems; the kind you might have walking down the street with someone who'd just taken a lot of acid and was starting to get cosmic. She had always been an enthusiast but this was ridiculous.

'Oh wow!' she kept saying. 'Look at that! Look at that sky. Feel that heat. Smell those bougainvillaeas. Look at those Land Cruisers and those mean men with the amazing tattoos!'

I didn't feel that these mean men with the amazing tattoos would take kindly to this show of childlike wonder at their expense, so I assured her it was all 'very nice, dear' and hurried on.

Darwin provided us with our first glimpse of the distress of some Aboriginals. They too sat around in the Smith Street Mall looking lost and confused and drunk. They did not look like anybody's idea of heirs to the desert.

Sue and I went to the nearest supermarket and bought some bread and camembert. We took them to a park by the harbour. The heat made my skin itch. The brightness hurt my eyes. Flies buzzed around us. We tore a hunk off the bread and found a thick black human hair woven through the centre of the loaf. We opened the box that contained the camembert and discovered it was in a tin. Until now I hadn't known, hadn't dreamed, that camembert came in tins. We did not have a tin opener. I did not feel so wonderful.

'I bet you wish you were here with your wife,' Sue said.

'My ex-wife,' I corrected. 'No, I don't.'

'I'm jealous,' she said. 'You'll go back to her. I always knew you would.'

'You don't know anything about it. *I* don't even know anything about it.'

'It's all right. I'm more mature than you. I don't blame you.'

'Well, thanks a *lot*,' I said. 'Thanks a lot for not blaming me for something I haven't done.'

We sat in sulky, jet-lagged silence. Maybe things would get better when we were in the desert.

Three days later we had made it up and were sitting in another mall, the Todd Street Mall, in Alice Springs. It was six in the morning and we had just arrived from Darwin by bus. We were sitting in the all-night café eating steak and eggs and I was reading a newspaper with the headline, 'Desert Women In Welfare Funds Alcohol Dilemma.' The story was that the Aboriginal women who lived in the desert were complaining about the way their men had nominated Alice Springs as the place for cashing their Social Security cheques. The men came into town from their tribal lands, collected and cashed their cheques, then drank away the money leaving their women and children penniless. A couple of weeks earlier two hundred Aboriginal women from desert communities in Southern Australia and the Northern Territory had held a bare-breasted march to Alice Springs in protest. In a way I was sorry to have missed that.

There were Aboriginal women sitting in the Mall right now, not bare-breasted, but wearing long skirts and tee shirts. They had strange, round, shapeless bodies, and ancient faces that gave no clue to their age. There was a pair of beautiful, skinny, naked Aboriginal children running around the Mall. They obviously belonged to the women but they had long blond hair that almost looked as though it had been peroxided. The women travelled with a huge soft cargo of blankets, bags and pillows. They sat on the tiled floor of the mall waiting for their bus, looking quite content and yet looking utterly out of place in this scrubbed, airless, covered mall.

We walked down to the Shell Ward petrol station and hired a Mini Moke. Our plan was simple. We were going to ride out into the desert surrounding Alice Springs and take a look around, not a very serious look, not in a Mini Moke, the serious look would come later in the trip. We hadn't been in the country very long and a nice jaunt in a Mini Moke would help us acclimatise.

The Moke was white and tatty looking and the tyres, far from being 'Desert Duellers' were labelled 'Motorway Remoulds'. The guy doing the renting wasn't exactly a ray of sunshine, but the rates were cheap, one Mini Moke was surely much like any other and ours seemed to go all right. So we drove off in search of some desert.

It was June, the Australian winter, but it felt like a good English summer's day to me. The sun was bright and a warm breeze flapped in through the open sides of the Moke. We felt good.

On the outskirts of Alice Springs there is a spot where road, river and railway line all converge through a gap in the hills. As we drove through it, a train, the legendary Ghan, which runs from Adelaide to

Alice Springs, was passing through as well. It was like driving into a travel documentary. It was great. This was surely the life.

We had driven a couple of kilometres from the hire place when I slowed the Moke to make a turn. I depressed the clutch pedal, tried to engage a lower gear and found that, despite any amount of grinding from the Moke's innards, the machine couldn't be coaxed into taking us any further. The drive shaft had broken. We coasted to an ignominious halt. Life suddenly didn't look so great at all.

I left Sue with the Moke and hitched back to the Shell Ward garage. The guy who had hired us the Moke became even less like a ray of sunshine when I told him what had happened to his vehicle. In fact, he became downright suspicious.

'I was driving it an hour ago,' he said, 'and it went just fine.'

I tried to explain that it had gone just fine for me too until the moment when it wouldn't go at all. He handed me over to the mechanic who, while still not exactly a bundle of joy, was older and mellower than the first guy. I told him my story. 'It's a worry,' he said. This was quite alarming in a country where most things were 'no worries', although I found it hard to believe he would really be losing a lot of sleep just because one of his boss's cruddy Mokes had broken down. It would have been far more of a worry for me if it had happened fifty kilometres later while I was out in the middle of nowhere.

We got in his jeep and drove out to the sick Moke. On the way we talked about the weather. They'd been having frosts in Alice Springs. 'It's all right,' he said, 'but you don't thaw out till ten o'clock in the morning.'

We arrived at the Moke. He started the engine, twiddled with the gear lever and announced, 'She's buggered.' I thought he might give me a hard time for being the one who'd done the buggering. I thought he might even try to get me to pay for the repairs, but no. He simply said, 'They take some hammer, these things,' and he towed us back to the garage and gave us a different Moke. This one was red but it looked no better than the first, and where that one had had two wing mirrors, this new Moke only had one. I did not feel one hundred per cent confident of my vehicle as we set off, again, to explore the desert.

From Alice Springs all roads, I felt, should lead to the desert, so it didn't seem to matter much which direction we drove. We headed out towards the airport, past the 'Floodway' signs and the Swagman's Rest Motel and the Arid Zone Research Institute. After Lindy Chamberlain's baby had (maybe) been eaten by a dingo at Ayers Rock, they slaughtered all the dingos they could find in the area and shipped them to this very Arid Zone Research Institute, and kept them in the deep freeze there until their stomach contents could be analysed. They found nothing in the dingos' stomachs, although experts said that even if the dingos *had* eaten the child, such is the rapid turnover in a dingo's digestive system, they'd *still* have found nothing.

Even when you'd like to claim to be vaguely knowledgeable about deserts, even when you know deserts aren't all rolling dunes, there still remains that nagging question as you look across the landscape from behind the windscreen of your Mini Moke, 'Is this really desert?'

It had been like this all the way. The bus journey from Darwin to Alice Springs had held considerable frustration. My map appeared to show that the Tanami Desert lay about a kilometre off to the right of the road we were travelling down. In my naïve way I had thought surely you ought to be able to see some real desert out there through the bus window. But although the vegetation had become more sparse, from tropical luxuriance around Darwin, to fairly thin scrub outside Alice Springs, it still looked remarkably lush for a desert. This didn't bode well for a man writing a book about deserts.

Fortunately, we were scarcely twenty kilometres out of Alice Springs in our Moke before we hit what looked like fairly authentic, fairly unarguable desert. The land was flat as far as the horizon, where there was a thin band of blue and grey mountains. The ground was sandy yellow, but not smooth creamy sand, rather washed out earth scattered with ballast. The vegetation was thin. There were some gum trees, but not many, little eruptions of spinifex and some scattered mulgas sticking up like fan-shaped bundles of dead twigs.

We parked off the road and walked into the desert. This was a great moment and a great feeling. You leave the car and the road behind you and you think you could walk for ever into the desert. But on this occasion we didn't intend to walk very far at all. There were some billboards along the roadside advertising motels and res-taurants, the most eye catching of which was for the Greenleaves Caravan Park. There was not a green leaf in sight. It's strange the way some desert establishments choose names that identify them-selves with the desert, like the Desert Oaks Motel or the Desert Rose Diner, while others name themselves in opposition to the desert, the Oasis, the Palms or Greenleaves. At the foot of these billboards was a row of very clear camel prints.

Sue, never having shown much sign of being a nature lover back home, became entranced by the spinifex and the gum trees and particularly by something that was hanging in the branches of the mulgas. It was a brown, sticky, dusty sort of bag, small enough to hold in the palm of your hand, and lodged about three feet off the ground. We were tempted to have a poke around and see what was in the bag. It looked neither wholly vegetable nor wholly animal. However we didn't investigate too closely and that was one of the smarter things we did in the desert. These bags, we discovered later, are made of the web laid down by the larvae of the bag moth. These larvae are known as processionary caterpillars. They shelter in the bag by day and come out in procession at night to feed. The processionary caterpillar is quite a cute little critter compared to some of the bugs you can come across in Australia, but their hairs cause powerful irritation if they come into contact with human skin, and the bag itself, which contains the caterpillars' excreta and cast-off skins, does exactly the same.

As we were wandering idly, aimlessly, probably lamely but perfectly contentedly across the desert, I heard a strange whistling. It consisted of two low, gentle notes that repeated from time to time at irregular intervals. As we moved, the whistling seemed to move with us. We looked for a source of the sound but we couldn't see anything, and it was very hard to tell how far away it was coming from. It could have been a bird's warning call and yet it sounded disturbingly human. It kept repeating; these two notes that were haunting, luring, profoundly lonesome. There was some element of threat about the sound. It seemed as though we were being tracked, watched, as if it was a signal conveying something about us, being transmitted to and from unknown sources. Even in that tame stretch of desert we felt very much at risk and very vulnerable. It scared the hell out of me. Having the hell scared out of you is, I suppose, another of the pleasures of the desert.

Back at the Moke it was easy to be brave and laugh at ourselves for being so easily spooked. No doubt there was a perfectly simple explanation for the sound. But on your first real day in the desert, lonesome, half-human whistles tend to send you scuttling back to security, and if you're me, you feel no shame about it. We headed back for Alice Springs.

Alice Springs was certainly at one time just a dot on the map. It was famous for being a waterhole in the middle of nowhere. It was only there at all as a staging point for the telegraph line. The Superintendent of Telegraphs in Adelaide was called Charles Todd; hence the Todd River, hence Todd Street and hence, eventually, the Todd Street Mall. Todd's wife was called Alice, and a spring nearby the telegraph lines was given her name, but there was no town at the spring itself until the 1930s. Today, however, Alice Springs is definitely 'somewhere'.

You can see why people would come to Alice Springs. You can see why some people, though by no means very many, would want to see what the centre of their country looked like. So Alice Springs is a tourist spot. And tourists like to spend money. Hence people will try to get them to buy, say, a piece of Aboriginal art. Alice Springs has plenty of Aboriginal art galleries, but frankly they looked as uninviting and snooty as any Bond Street gallery. But if you don't want to spend your money on art you can visit the camel farm and the aviation museum and the date garden and the auto museum. There is no reason why these things should be in Alice Springs except that a lot of tourists pass through, eager for something to do, and quite willing to risk a couple of bucks on a tourist attraction. If I was going to set up a tourist attraction somewhere in Australia I'd probably go for Alice Springs. Sue and I joked that it might be a great place to set up an important collection of contemporary automata, and the more we thought of it the less it seemed like a joke.

I enjoy a good motor museum wherever it may be. The Stuart Auto Museum in Alice Springs contained thirteen cars, four motorcycles, one wreck and one 1946 Nash Super 600 which was for sale. There were the remains of the first car to cross Australia. These remains consisted of a tyre and a wooden box. The wreck was of a 1923 Rugby, and it had been set up in front of a diorama showing the car's final resting place, which was the middle of the Australian desert.

The inhabitants of Alice Springs have to worry simultaneously about drought and flood. The average rainfall there is 246 millimetres per year, which qualifies it as desert, if only by a whisker. The problem is that when the rain comes it comes with a vengeance. They can expect a 'serious flood' in Alice Springs every six years. They had them in 1983 and 1988 and they caused millions of dollars of damage and took a handful of lives. And that figure of 'every six years' is only a prediction based on probability. The fact they had one in 1988 didn't guarantee that they weren't going to get one in 1989.

I knew that June ought to be a dry month, but I thought it would be just my luck to get to the desert and find it flooded. That would have been a real disappointment, and disappointments weren't hard to find in and around Alice Springs.

Next day we went to Simpson's Gap. I have a postcard of Simpson's Gap. It appears to be two great brown humps of rock, a hundred feet high, sliced in two by a creek that has had six million years to carve a channel through what was once one piece of rock. In the postcard it looks utterly forbidding, bleak, isolated in a sea of parched brown desert. In fact, Simpson's Gap is easily accessible from Alice Springs even in a rented Mini Moke that you don't have one hundred per cent confidence in. When you get there you find a clear footpath, a visitors' centre and a busload of tourists. When I was there the rocks didn't even look brown,

There's a story that Sidney Nolan took Benjamin Britten to see Simpson's Gap. It was sunset and two Aboriginal boys stood silhouetted on the skyline at the top of the Gap, their skins taking on a golden glow in the light. Britten turned to Nolan and said, quoting Henry Vaughan, 'Ah! the treasures there are on a boy's limbs.' But then I suppose Benjamin Britten would, wouldn't he?

Feeling disappointed by Simpson's Gap, feeling I wasn't living up to my responsibility to get out there and report back from the real desert, I thought we'd give the nearby Cassia Hill a try. It was an easy thirty-minute walk to the top of Cassia Hill, through red sand, dry riverbeds, past tea trees and I suppose past cassias, to a peak that gave a huge, expansive view. It was like standing on a small mound in the centre of a giant saucer. You could see mountains in every direction, the West McConnell Range, Mountain Gillen, and even Simpson's Gap which looked considerably more forbidding at this distance, considerably more like the postcards.

Despite its proximity to a tourist spot, in fact despite being a sort of tourist spot, it was possible to sit on top of Cassia Hill in spectacular isolation. It looked as though few people ever came that way. There was a road visible in the distance but little moved along it. There was space. There was sun and heat and there were colonies of ants and flies. Not much grew on the distant hills and mountains, and the red desert sand was visible in places beneath the vegetation. But something wasn't quite right. The books went on about the desert carvings and desert ecosystems in this area, and that was some confirmation that this was really desert, but everything looked distressingly green. It just didn't feel enough like a desert for my tastes. I wanted more. I began to think I might have come to the wrong place in the wrong season. I thought I might not find anything to write about. That scared the hell out of me too.

As I stood on top of Cassia Hill, looking at this magnificent land-scape that failed to satisfy me, I thought about my father. There was some horrible comparison to be made between me standing here in all this space, and my father lying immobile in the confines of his hospital bed in Sheffield. I wished he was here. I wished he could see all this, or something better than this, something more desert-like than this before he died. I wished we could be together in some wild desert place and I could say to him, yes, this is what I'm all about. And, of course, I knew that standing in some wild desert place was the very last thing my father would have wanted to do whether he was dying or not.

From Alice Springs I phoned home. I dreaded it. I dreaded my mother having to tell me that my father was dead. It took a long time to get through. The longer it took the tenser I got, the worse the possibilities seemed. And yet when my mother answered the phone she sounded cheerful and not at all dramatic.

'There's not much change,' she said. 'He's holding his own. He's bearing up. He's no worse. When I got there the other night he'd got a pain and he said, "I'm not going to get better" but while I was there the pain went and he felt all right. They're trying to build him up with milky drinks. He's got to get some weight on.'

I wasn't used to making international telephone calls. My mother wasn't used to receiving them. We kept it short. I asked about the tests. They were continuing and no definite conclusions had been drawn. I asked how my mother was coping. She said she was coping. I felt a little relieved, a little reassured. I allowed myself not to feel too guilty for not being there.

I never wanted to go to Ayers Rock. I didn't want to climb it or photograph it or worship it. I didn't even want to see it. It was just a piece of rock as far as I was concerned. Sure it was a *big* piece of rock, and it was a monolith, and it stuck out of the desert, and the Aboriginals regarded it as holy; but I thought it had been photo-graphed and captured too many times. I thought it must have been reduced to a cipher, to something no more spiritual than Blackpool Tower. On the other hand, it was going to be a long time before I was this way again, so we decided to go to Ayers Rock after all.

We took the standard bus tour in the company of a handful of other tourists, mostly young and not Australian. The bus was old and the driver thought he was a comedian. He had a favourite joke, in fact a whole routine, about a man with a hare lip. The bus wandered around the dirt roads between Ayers Rock, the Olgas and the resort of Yulara to ensure arrival at the Rock in time for sunset. Even in daylight the colour changes were wonderful, moving through cerise, angry purple, kangaroo brown as the light changed. But I still thought it was just a piece of rock.

Ayers Rock is five and a half hours by road from Alice Springs so we needed to spend a night there. Just one night, we were sure, would be enough. All the Ayers Rock accommodation was at Yulara, a good Aboriginal name for a place that was like Butlins without the charm and elegance. It was newly built and contained a campsite, a hotel, a lodge, maisonettes and a Sheraton. They were all ruinously expensive. Yulara, they'll tell you, was built to combat the vulgarity and bad taste of unbridled private enterprise. They'll tell you it was designed to harmonise with the desert which explains why it's painted pinky red. Less explicable is why it was built out of corrugated iron with rows of 'sails' that are set on the roofs of the buildings. They're there to give shade and deflect the sun, which is reasonable enough, but there's no way you can pretend they harmonise with the environment.

The Aboriginals are now the official owners of Ayers Rock, though it is permanently leased back to the government. Before there was Yulara there were a number of campsites and a motel nearby. These have been taken over by Aboriginals too. I think they got a good deal. Anything must be better than having to stay at Yulara. It was at one of these campsites that the dingo baby case had its origins.

I had always thought the death of Azaria Chamberlain, the dingo baby, had happened in the wildest, most inhospitable part of the desert. Certainly Ayers Rock is a long way from most places and yet the area seemed safe, civilised and well populated, not the sort of place to breed myths about desert sacrifice.

The Chamberlain story is at heart a simple one, made infinitely complicated by legal process, scientific evidence about dingo behaviour, obfuscated by the unsympathetic personality of Lindy Chamberlain, distorted by misconceptions about the desert, stoked by a secular suspicion of religion.

Imagine you were camping at Ayers Rock. You've been walking, taking photographs, having family fun, and at the end of the day as you're relaxing with a beer and a barbecue, suddenly a woman nearby starts screaming that a dingo has pushed its way into her tent, grabbed her baby and run off into the desert with her. Imagine too that this woman has a husband who doesn't seem too concerned about the disappearance and is muttering some stuff about it all being the will of God. Days go by and although the baby's bloodstained clothes are found, the baby never is. Well, would you think that's just a normal scene from family life?

Had I been on the jury that tried Lindy Chamberlain for murder I think I would have found her not guilty, which is not to say that I would have been wholly convinced of her innocence. Whether the dingo really took the baby, whether Lindy Chamberlain really did murder the child, or whether something quite different happened, I suspect we're never going to know for sure. At different times I have believed each of these three possibilities. However, it is significant that a certain proportion of press and public opinion actually *preferred* to believe that Lindy Chamberlain killed the baby rather than believe the dingo story.

The people who were familiar with the desert and with the behaviour of dingos had no great trouble in believing that a dingo carried off and killed the baby. But such people are as much a minority in Australia as anywhere else. The popular urban imagination liked to believe that something pretty strange had gone on in the desert. It appeared to have something to do with religion (Lindy's husband was a Seventh Day Adventist preacher), something to do with fertility (she admitted she'd visited the Aboriginal Cave of Fertility), possibly something to do with witchcraft, paganism, madness and human sacrifice. I think people who believed this stuff were crazy. How, in God's name, could any of that stuff seem more likely than believing that one of the half-tame, half-wild dingos round Ayers Rock had somehow got its instincts confused?

The fact that a Judicial Commission granted Lindy Chamberlain a pardon doesn't resolve anything. One hopes it makes her life a little easier to live but you don't feel the next Lindy Chamberlain will be treated any more charitably. The urban imagination sees the desert as a place of evil, lawlessness and death. Who was a better desert rat than Charles Manson? I *don't* perceive the desert as a place of evil, lawlessness and death, and yet I admit it's the desert setting that gives Lindy Chamberlain's story its resonance, its creepiness, its thrill. If a Rottweiler had apparently taken Azaria Chamberlain from a suburban garden, however strange the circumstances, I'm sure the story would not have lived on the way it has. The dingo baby case is a story of the desert, but it is a story told in the cities.

Lindy Chamberlain's husband was an enthusiastic, not to say obsessive, amateur photographer. He would have found himself in much like-minded company at Ayers Rock. Light bounces off the rock and into millions of clicking, whirring cameras. The rock becomes the subject of a million snapshots. Of course, it won't look as good in the prints as it does in real life, and surely we prefer it that way. We show the photographs to our friends and say, 'This only gives you the vaguest idea. You really need to be there.' That's because we're amateurs. Photographs by professionals make places look better than they do in real life.

I think we take photographs because we believe looking is not enough. Looking is an idle, passive, inert business. To take a photograph is to be active. It is an act of participation.

So there we all were, coachloads of people all ready to participate in Ayers Rock. The sun was going down behind the Olgas, making a wonderful, orange-stained sunset, and as it descended Ayers Rock started to come alive.

As we watched it changed colour continuously from moment to moment like something pulsing and glowing. There was orange, vermilion, silky scarlet. Ayers Rock stood over the landscape, simple, majestic and holy. Even with our bus tours and our fully automatic cameras and our cries of, 'Oh wow!' we still couldn't belittle it. I had come expecting nothing much, but by the power of the thing itself I had, like some ancient tribesman wandering through the desert and confronting this phenomenon, been turned into a worshipper. Nobody was more surprised than I.

Climbing is the other way of participating in Ayers Rock. You can buy tee-shirts with the slogan 'I climbed Ayers Rock – Impressed?' and others that say, 'I didn't climb Ayers Rock – So what?' I think there is a great deal of wisdom in those tee-shirts. I had no intention of making the climb.

There are plaques attached to the face of Ayers Rock commemorating those who attempted to climb up it and died in the process, either by falling off or by having heart attacks. The plaques try to assert that climbing Ayers Rock was a lifetime's ambition for the dead ones, that dying in the process was the way they would have wanted to go. None of them says that the beloved didn't really give two hoots about climbing the rock and was only talked into it by his glib-tongued friends or family. They would have you believe that only those who really love Ayers Rock die on it. Something told me this probably wasn't true.

I am not the first to notice that if you tell people what a good time you had on your travels they instantly glaze over. They'd far rather hear about the rip-offs, the pesky Arabs, the buggered Mini Moke and getting lost in the desert. To make these people happy I talk about bus travel in Australia.

I intend to keep on calling it bus travel but the locals would probably call it coach travel and they wouldn't speak of bus drivers but of coach captains. Our first glimpse of a bus driver came at about four-thirty in the morning on arrival in Darwin. I suppose he wasn't entirely to know that we'd just arrived from England and hadn't had any sleep for the last thirty-six hours, but I think at four-thirty in the morning, any morning, a driver, any driver, might have worked out that we weren't all that keen to have the local tourist attractions pointed out to us. But our driver was keen that we should know where the fish feeding took place, fish feeding being one of the peak activities in Darwin apparently. And it was with true pride that he pointed out the new flyover, saying, 'We used to have some rare old traffic jams before that flyover was built.'

There are a number of major bus operators in Australia. We decided against going with Greyhound because it sounded too American. We eschewed Deluxe because it sounded too deluxe. We went for Pioneer because we were trying to maintain some bogus notion of ruggedness. Connoisseurs of deranged advertising copy should read what Pioneer have to say about their bus drivers. They say, 'Philosopher, mechanic, leader, planner and friend, your coach captain is a true professional. Your enjoyment is his concern.'

I'm not sure how much leading and planning is needed to drive a bus from, say, Alice Springs to Coober Pedy, our next destination. There is only one road. True it is a very long road, about nine hundred kilometres, but it's not a road on which many executive decisions need to be taken. You basically point the bus and drive. Friend? Well, how intense a relationship can you have with the back of someone's head? Personally I'd call it nodding acquaintanceship rather than friendship. And philosopher? No, I didn't think I'd be able to saunter down to the front of the bus and engage any of my drivers in lively dialectic, but maybe I was being a snob. Perhaps I should have tried and been surprised.

Philosophers then, they might possibly have been. Mechanics they definitely weren't. At night between Katherine and Tennant Creek we got a flat tyre. We all piled out of the coach in manly fashion to watch our two drivers (there were two on this trip, one driving, one resting) while they changed the wheel. We were only able to watch because somebody on board had a pocket torch. The bus itself wasn't equipped with one. Using a jack and a block of wood they found lying by the road, our friendly leaders and planners, our philosopher-mechanics had the job licked in barely two hours.

The bus drivers I met were mostly quiet, self-assured, polite men, but they did tend to think of themselves as 'characters'. They would have been harmless enough but these guys had the means of expressing their character. They had a microphone and a P.A. system. This enabled them to point out items of interest as we drove along, and you couldn't complain about that. It also, however, gave them the chance to express their opinions; that having laws against drunken driving was the first step towards Australia becoming a police state, that Australia was becoming a colony of Japan, and that Elton John was the greatest singer in the history of the world and here was a tape of Elton John's greatest hits and we were all going to sing along.

In the way that if you give a child a hammer everything suddenly needs hammering, give a bus driver the means of playing music, and music has to be played *the whole time*. The drivers seemed to be able to choose what they played, but the company had obviously warned them not to play anything that might offend anybody. Thus we had hour after hour of 'inoffensive' music. The Carpenters figured largely here. After the first twenty-four hours I was ready to kill something, anything.

Of course, you tried to escape by putting on your personal stereo and playing something you actually wanted to hear. This didn't quite work. The muzak was just loud enough to leak past your headphones so that you heard your own music but the Carpenters seeped through in quiet moments. And what if you didn't want to hear anything at all? That was not an option. Hell, they'd got a P.A. and tape deck, they weren't going to waste it. The only break from the music was the video entertainment.

This was the real hardship. Never mind the heat and dust and flies and lack of water. You try travelling through the desert while watching multiple episodes of 'Bill Peach's Video Express' and you'll soon discover what real privation means.

The bus driver slips a video cassette into the machine. The screen bursts into life. Bill Peach, a pudgy man who tries hard to look outdoorsy and trustworthy, appears on the screen and introduces a documentary about the history of Australia. This lasts about an hour, then Bill returns and introduces a feature film. The chief problem here is that at any given time there only seem to be about three feature films in circulation on the Video Express. Therefore, if you do a lot of travelling, and we did about five thousand kilometres, there is a likelihood, call it a dead certainty, that you'll see the same film more than once. I'm sure *Battleship Potemkin* or even *The Big Sleep* are the kinds of movie that might benefit from this kind of repeated viewing. The same can't be said of Michael Caine in *Surrender* or Shelley Long in *Troop Beverly Hills*. We saw these films three times each. But at least the soundtrack of a movie was a little easier to ignore than the sound of the Carpenters.

I did my best to look out of the window, to be fascinated by the vast expanses of desert and to have lofty thoughts. And, if I say so myself, I did a pretty good job.

All whinging aside, there were some great moments on the bus. Frequently the buses were not full and the driver would encourage passengers to spread out and have two seats to themselves. For whatever reasons, Sue and I preferred to sit next to each other and not to spread out. The driver walked past us for the second time and said, 'You know, there are plenty of seats in the back if you want to spread yourself out.'

'No, I'm all right, really,' said Sue.

'I know,' he replied, 'you'd rather snuggle, wouldn't you, you little devil.'

This was true.

I remember the bus journey back from Ayers Rock to Alice Springs as being particularly wonderful. The sun was very low, going down at exactly right angles to the road, and the shadow of the bus was distorted to look like a truncated pyramid on wheels, or like some sort of flying saucer. As the sun set, the sky was filled with a brocade of violent orange and purple clouds. There were mountains on the horizon and from behind them rays of light fanned outwards and upwards like searchlights in shades of pale blue. There was something cinematic, uplifting, climactic about it. The driver, responding in his own way, put on a tape of the Eagles performing 'Hotel California'. The opening line starts, 'On a dark desert highway . . .' and you could see how it might have been appropriate. It seemed pretty stupid to me, but even so it couldn't spoil the sunset.

I remember the drive to Coober Pedy. Cattle, both alive and dead, were scattered along the sides of the road, and there were metal cows made out of oil drums, with signs painted on their sides saying, 'Please Don't Hit Me.' I remember the distant, flat-topped mountains, and I remember approaching a place called Marla and the clouds in the sky ahead of us, in neat lines, like the receding planes of theatre scenery as we headed upstage.

There were also the stops. At Marla I tried hard to fall into conversation with two guys who were driving a Mitsubishi jeep that had been competing in the Alice Springs to Finke desert race. The vehicle was covered in advertising stickers and the windscreen had cracked. One of the guys was hard-looking, tanned and tattooed. The other was wearing a silly sombrero and Bermuda shorts.

'Were you in the race?' I asked needlessly.

They nodded.

'How was it?'

'It was a pisser.'

That was as much as they wanted to say about it. At a place called Erldunda we saw what claimed to be Australia's biggest corrugated-iron canopy, and I guess that being the biggest in Australia would make it the biggest in the world. We were as impressed as anyone is likely to be by a corrugated-iron canopy.

But mostly what I liked about riding on buses was the sense of being suspended, of being in the middle of nowhere. The bus ploughs along the road, the only road through the desert. The sun is sinking and there's no sign of civilisation (whatever the hell that is) in any direction as far as the eye can see, and further. It's getting late. It's starting to get dark. It will be many hours before you arrive anywhere that has a name. You sit there, doing nothing, not talking, not really thinking, just looking out of the window at the desert. You are in the driver's hands. You are not responsible for your own fate. You feel that nothing will or can happen to you. It feels perfect.

But most people would rather hear about rip-offs, the pesky Arabs, the buggered Mini Mokes and getting lost in the desert.

It was largely because of the lack of barrenness and desolation around Alice Springs that we decided to go to Coober Pedy. The landscape around Coober Pedy is described as 'lunar' and one of our bus drivers said, 'It's a great place, especially when you see it through your rear-view mirror.' So we thought it couldn't be all bad.

The town is an opal-mining centre. It is in the desert, beset by wild extremes of temperature, by dust storms, and it is chiefly famous because most of its inhabitants live 'underground' in dwellings known as dugouts. In fact, they're only underground in a limited sense. Most of the dugouts have been burrowed into the side of the hard sandstone hills, but they haven't been excavated out of the earth.

The building regulations in Coober Pedy are less than rigorous. If you want a new home you buy a hillside, hire a tunnelling machine and carve as many rooms as you need out of the rock. If at some time later you need an 'extension' you tunnel some more. The fantasy is that while carving out a home you will hit a seam of opal, which could mean you're suddenly a couple of million dollars richer, in which case you won't have to live in Coober Pedy at all.

When I was there, the going rate for a dugout was about 55,000 Australian dollars, which, at two dollars to the pound, made it a lot cheaper than most English holiday homes. My urge to own a little patch of desert was still with me, but it would have been a long way to go for a weekend. You could buy a bungalow for about half that price but how could you ever live in it when the temperature rises to fifty-four degrees on a good summer's day? Dugouts stay a nice eighteen degrees winter and summer. Of course, the simple answer to that question is that the whites live in the dugouts and the Aboriginals live in the bungalows.

On the outskirts of town the land is dotted with cones of white and cream earth. This earth has been sucked out of bore holes in the search for opals, and left behind when the search proved futile. They certainly scar the view, although in themselves they are extremely neat, symmetrical and ordered. But in Coober Pedy nobody seems to worry much about the view. Prospecting within the town itself is now officially forbidden but officialdom doesn't count for much here and the town still buzzes with the sound of drilling and digging and this couldn't be accounted for simply by people adding extra rooms to their dugouts. The whole town is messed up with the detritus of past mining activity. White, dusty rubble is abandoned where it was first deposited. The streets are littered with mining machinery that has either ceased to work or to be of value. And in this mass of rubble and machinery what could it possibly matter if people decide to dump some old cars or fridges or oil drums? The view doesn't matter because dugouts don't have many windows and nobody goes out much.

Nobody ever came to Coober Pedy for the views, except possibly me. Most people look at the earth and they see money, or at least a dream of money. There are (they hope) opals in that earth, and all they need do is shovel them out. The 'environment' counts for nothing. It's a means to an end. People can put up with any amount of ugliness so long as they can keep in view the promise of untold wealth.

So Coober Pedy isn't pretty, but neither would I have called it lunar. It is wide and open. The earth's surface is a pale, dessicated beige. The sky did contain a few clouds, fleecy clouds at that, but you absolutely knew it wasn't going to rain, not today, and not for a very long time. A dust storm was far more likely.

All up and down the main street miners loaded up their trucks and utes (utility vehicles). A lot of the vehicles had the word 'Explosives' painted across the back, which I took at first to be some kind of boisterous, laddish joke, but it wasn't a joke. You could buy explosives at the local supermarket. There was a sign hanging up over the tills giving the prices of gelignite, detonators and fuses. There was a discount for cash. You needed to have a permit before you could buy explosives, but a permit wasn't a hard thing to come by in Coober Pedy.

In fact, some of the cars had the word 'Explosvies' painted across them, poor spelling being no handicap to opal mining nor to getting a permit. Whether they spelled the word right or not you got the message. This was not a car you wanted to run into the back of, and I'm sure those signs were a lot more persuasive than the 'keep your distance' or 'baby on board' signs that you sometimes see.

The day before we got to town someone had blown up the local Greek restaurant. The charred shell of the building was cordoned off and there was a man inside sifting through the debris. Local opinion was that whoever blew up the restaurant and whatever his motives, he was a pretty pathetic amateur. He'd used fifteen sticks of dynamite and only four had gone off. The restaurant was called the Acropolis and the sign outside showed a drawing of Greek ruins. If all fifteen sticks of dynamite had detonated there wouldn't have been any ruins left at all.

To get the spirit of Coober Pedy we stayed at the Radeka Dugout Motel. The façade was Spanish hacienda style. The interior was pure Flintstones. The walls and ceilings showed where a tunnelling machine had created the room out of solid rock. The surfaces showed circular scars from the cutting gear, the surfaces then being coated with some kind of sealer to keep the dust in. Our only access to fresh air was by way of four circular ventilation holes, about three inches in diameter, bored in the rock above the bed, up through twenty feet of rock to the top of the hill, out of the side of which the motel had been carved. A fine mesh of spiders' webs crisscrossed the holes.

The Aboriginals in Coober Pedy seemed more despairing than those we had seen elsewhere in Australia, perhaps because in Coober Pedy they had easier access to alcohol. Mostly they sat by the roadside (there being no pavements in Coober Pedy) and created litter. But every now and again one of them would get up and stagger unco-ordinatedly into the road, barely avoid being hit by a car, and then curse the driver at considerable and often very articulate length. 'I know where you live!' one young Aboriginal guy shouted after a Holden saloon as it swerved to avoid him. This being Coober Pedy he probably did.

There is not much to do in Coober Pedy if you're not an opal miner. I found that a great relief. There was an 'international standard' hotel called the Underground Resort, consisting of a series of dugouts that included the Crystal Cave, Umberto's Restaurant and something called the Underground Theatrette. You could drink cappuccinos in this complex, look at the 'visual display' on the history of Coober Pedy, but we, like a good many other out-of-towners, went to the Level Bar and drank. We sat on a plush banquette consuming glasses of Fosters and bags of Nobby's nuts and got pleasantly sozzled and watched the other people.

The out-of-towners were not desert folk, but they did belong to some strange tribe. They had streaked hair-dos, wore expensive trainers and padded bomber jackets. They had clipboards and designer sunglasses. They were movie people.

Wim Wenders was in town. He was making some sort of post-nuclear-holocaust-type movie so naturally (and a little facilely I'd have said) he chose the desert as one of his locations. He had built an aircraft hangar just a couple of weeks ago and it was highly visible on the edge of town and looked as though it had been there for ever. William Hurt was starring in the movie and he was in town too, but there was no sign of him in the Level Bar, nor of Wim Wenders, which was a pity I thought because I'd have been prepared to take a small role as a post-nuclear extra if asked.

But watching the antics of film crews is still not really 'doing any-thing'. We went to look at the visual display. It was good. We learned about a character called 'Iron Man' Jim Shaw, also known as the Human Buckjumper. Jim Shaw would walk into a bar, get down on all fours, and challenge anybody to sit astride his back while he tried to buck them off. He was pretty good at this. He made a lot of money out of it. In 1920 he set off across the desert to walk two hundred and fifty kilometres from the town of Tarcoola in South Australia to the opal fields. He was pushing a wheelbarrow full of tools, and when he hit the sand hills he had to keep unloading it, carry it up and over the crest of each hill, then carry the tools over, reload, and so on when he reached the next hill. He kept going for eleven days, through dust storms and thunderstorms, across the gibber plains, until he finally reached the mining camp at Bolshevik Gulf. The miners came out to meet him and organised a celebration at which, despite what he'd been through in the last eleven days, Jim Shaw got down on all fours and challenged the other miners to sit astride his back while he tried to buck them off.

When a bystander first saw the size of the load Shaw was carrying he said that he was trying to do a horse out of a job. Shaw replied that a man couldn't call himself a horse until he could walk and crap at the same time, a feat he'd never managed, though you get the feeling he'd probably tried.

There was a golf course in Coober Pedy. I've found that lots of desert places attempt to create golf courses. I suppose it's a way of saying they're not really desert places. The course at Coober Pedy is on the flat, featureless side. Its greens are small and I guessed they were made out of some sort of fake grass. Making bunkers there in the sandy wastes would seem a little superfluous, so they've built sandy humps here and there, and the odd bush has been planted so that it isn't one straight, flat punt from tee to hole.

The most obvious things for tourists to do in town are either to fossick for opals or take a tour of the town in an air-conditioned minibus. I didn't want to do either of these. I wanted to go to the Moon Plain. The Moon Plain is about thirty kilometres out of Coober Pedy, out by the Breakaways Reserve and the dingo fence. The Moon Plain too has featured in movies, notably in *Mad Max 3*, and it is, I was told, utterly unworldly, a vast, featureless stony expanse littered with fossilised shells. It sounded a lot more interesting than a guided tour of the opal mine and the Big Winch. It was the kind of thing I was in Australia for.

The problem was getting there. We had no car. Two companies in Coober Pedy offered to take you to the Moon Plain, but these tours were 'by arrangement', and it was an extremely difficult arrangement to make. A funny little Italian squirt in one of the companies told me, 'You don't want to go there. Nothing there. What you want to do is take the town tour and go fossicking for opals.' You don't need to be Marco Polo to get pissed off when some Italian squirt starts telling you where you do and don't want to go. We left the office with a bit of a flounce.

The guy at Opal City Tours was more optimistic. He'd be happy to take us to the Moon Plain but he needed four people on the trip to make it viable. In fact he'd had two people come in the day before who were interested in going to the Moon Plain. If they showed up again in the course of the day we'd have a party of four and there'd be no problem. We wandered the streets of Coober Pedy looking at people. Did any of them look like the sort of people who wanted to go to the Moon Plain? We called back after an hour but the couple hadn't returned. We called back an hour later, and an hour after that. It was now afternoon. Should we try hitching? Should we hire a car? Suddenly it seemed terribly important to get to the Moon Plain. But would it really be all that wonderful? Would it really be worth the effort or the expense? Or would it be another strip of disappointing desert?

We looked at the Underground Catholic Church. We went inside. The architecture of a church or a house or a motel is all pretty much the same in Coober Pedy. They all use the same kind of tunnelling machine. But the church had some stained glass and there must be a lot of metaphoric satisfaction in building a church out of (or into) solid rock. There was a little hollow scooped out of one of the walls, a place for people to drop notes asking for prayers for their family's health. I thought of dropping one in for my father but couldn't bring myself to do it.

Sue and I never did get to the Moon Plain. I was disappointed and irritated with myself for not having the ingenuity to get there. I told myself I'd hire a video of *Mad Max 3* when I got home. I did. It looks like I missed something.

There are reasons why you might think that a train ride across Australia would be one of the world's great railway journeys. The times and distances involved are epic. Perth is 4,348 kilometres away from Sydney. The rail journey is scheduled to take sixty-five hours. And the name of the train is impressive: the Indian Pacific, so called because Perth faces the Indian Ocean and Sydney faces the Pacific. Certainly the guy who wrote the Railways of Australia brochure, who may be some relation of the guy who wrote the Pioneer bus brochure, thinks it's pretty hot stuff. He calls the train a 'flagship' and goes on to say, 'Train travel lets you enjoy a closer understanding of the environment in a quite unique way. No other mode is quite the same . . . bringing the real Australia close to you and still surrounding the traveller with the most desirable creature comforts.'

I had made a couple of long but unchallenging train journeys in my time. I had travelled to Athens partly by Orient Express when it was still a real train. My clearest memory is of a middle-aged Greek woman who wanted to feed me on condensed milk and meat balls, and who became abusive when I resisted. My other long train journey was from Vancouver to Toronto, a journey that is only memorable to me now for being the first occasion on which I tried to read *Gravity's Rainbow*. Neither trip had taken me through the desert.

Our trip on the Indian Pacific was not going to take us all the way from Sydney to Perth. We were in Melbourne and therefore had to take a different train to Adelaide where we joined the Indian Pacific, already into its run. And we weren't going all the way to Perth. We were stopping off at Kalgoorlie so we could hire the Land Cruiser from the Budget office and get lost in the desert. But even the journey from Melbourne to Kalgoorlie is epic enough and it includes a crossing of the Nullabor Plain.

'Nullabor' is bad Latin for 'no trees' and the Nullabor Plain is a flat, featureless expanse that runs for the best part of a thousand kilometres along the south-western part of Australia. The Eyre Highway skirts the southern edge of the plain, but the train track scorches right through the middle and contains the world's longest stretch of straight railway track; 478 kilometres between Ooldea and Wurina.

We had been to Melbourne to visit Sue's adult son and his girl-friend. They were living in the seaside suburb of St Kilda, and he was working for a firm called Motherarts who made offbeat props for advertising shoots and TV commercials. We went to their premises, a vast shed on an industrial estate, and saw a showreel and a stills portfolio of their work.

One of the stills showed an ad for a vacuum cleaner. The machine was set amid vast sand dunes and a woman was pushing it along, vacuuming up the desert.

At Motherarts we met a man called Brendan who was carving horses in clay that would be used to make a low-relief mural for the race-track. He'd crossed the Nullabor Plain by the same train we were taking and had two things to say about it. One, that he'd spent the whole trip drunk, and two, that he'd been so bored he'd taken his watch to pieces and put it back together again. These two stories didn't seem to mesh. Sure there'd be enough time to take your watch apart, put it back together and *then*, get drunk, but I doubted that anyone who was drunk the *whole time* would be in any condition to reassemble anything, let alone a watch. You have to make sure your traveller's tales are consistent. Brendan, inconsistent or not, had travelled first class with a sleeping berth, in fact something called a 'roomette'. Sue and I were going to be 'sit-up' passengers.

Sue's son and I talked about the fact that my father was dying and that I had thought, even if only briefly, about abandoning the trip. He had had a similar problem. With his father, Sue's late husband, dying of cancer, he'd been presented with the chance of going to live and work in New York. He'd gone and his father had died while he was away.

'I can't really regret it,' he said. 'I suppose a part of me would have wanted to be there when he died. But you know, you picture some touching deathbed scene and let's face it, that just doesn't happen.'

From Melbourne I'd rung my mother.

'Some days he's smashing,' she said. 'Other days he's not so clever, but he's no worse, shall I say that. Kathleen and Oliver came to see him but he didn't want to see them. He was glad to see the back of them.

'On Monday they took that piece of bone. They haven't got the results yet and I'm frightened to death of what they might find. But now they're talking about giving him some radium treatment, which they said they weren't going to do, so it sounds like they don't know *what* it is. Do you think that's right?'

'I don't know,' I said. 'The way the two doctors have talked, there doesn't seem to be much doubt.'

'But if they don't know what it is then there must be some hope, don't you think?'

'I don't know,' I said. 'I suppose there's always some hope, but I don't know.'

As she talked I rapidly jotted down what she said. Partly it was because I wanted to be able to tell Sue the latest news, perhaps also so that I could chart precisely the course of my father's illness, but chiefly because by then I knew that my father's death was going to figure in this book and that I needed to take notes. I needed to use my mother's words as material. I felt some guilt about this but not enough guilt to stop.

We boarded the train from Melbourne to Adelaide at nine o' clock on Saturday evening. This train was called the Overland. It looked very modern in a fifties sort of way, all shiny metal and moulded contour lines on the outside. Inside, the seats looked like they were part of a three-piece suite. In the lavatories the sink and toilet bowls were made of stainless steel and could be folded up into the walls. There was a ladies' 'Powder Room', and the sign for the gents showed the head and shoulders silhouette of a man with a trilby hat and a pipe. The Indian Pacific, when we eventually boarded it, was identical except for the colour of the seats.

After the days on the bus it was a great comfort not to have music, videos and coach captains. Having a little more leg room was good too. In fact, had we been travelling first class we would have had videos and, as well as a roomette, we'd have had the chance to sing along with the electric organ. This was what the brochure told me.

Sit-up class, or coach class to give it its semi-official name, is for those too cheap to pay for a sleeper. Not that you need to be as cheap as all that not to be able to afford first class. A first-class sleeper, Sydney to Perth, cost 836 dollars. We were paying 150 dollars, and the Railways of Australia didn't want us to forget it.

Meal sittings in the dining-car were announced over the loud-speaker system that broadcast throughout the train, but sit-up passengers weren't invited. There was a little dining-area adjacent to the snack bar, hardly ritzy but the kind of place you might want to linger with your toasted sandwich, but a notice informed the likes of me that sit-up passengers had to take their food back to their seats and eat it there. I am pleased to say that this notice·was ignored by everybody the whole time, but it was the principle of the thing.

We killed a long day in Adelaide and caught the Indian Pacific on Sunday evening. It set off two and a quarter hours late. Of course, in England two and a quarter hours is a long time, time enough to make what we would consider a long train journey. But on a sixty-five-hour journey both passengers and staff tend to be philosophical about a little delay like that. If you're not philosophical you probably become demented.

Boarding the Indian Pacific in Adelaide at night means that it's dark and you don't see any scenery at all until early the next morning. So we missed the legendary silos of the wheat country, but at six o' clock on Monday morning I got my first glimpse of what I thought might be the Nullabor Plain. I awoke to see sunrise over a desert covered in frost. The red sand and the low scrub sparkled with the sun and ice. But something told me this might not be the Nullabor Plain because there were still plenty of trees around. The country-side wasn't lush with foliage but it wasn't exactly treeless either.

Running alongside the track were telegraph wires on extremely short poles. They looked short enough that you could stand beside them and reach up and touch the cables. There was also a dirt road parallel to the rails, and piles of wooden sleepers that had been replaced then tossed aside like matchsticks.

On the bus, the landscape had been viewed through tinted glass. On the train it was seen through dirty double glazing. The two layers of glass were an inch and a half apart. Thick dirt had settled along the bottom of the window and there was a fabric Venetian blind set in the gap between inner and outer panes of glass that could be wound up and down by turning a little silver handle.

It was two hours before we reached anywhere that could be described as a 'place'. The place was called Barton, consisting of a handful of extremely neat bungalows, painted pale yellows and blues. They all had the 'galvo' roofs that had already become familiar on this trip; shiny, unpainted corrugated iron that glistened in the sun. Stretches of galvo were also used as fences and water tanks. Each bungalow had a rigidly demarcated plot of land around it, an amount that was surprisingly similar to an Englishman's idea of a 'manageable' garden. These gardens, and the verandahs on the bungalows, looked towards the railway track, not towards the desert. They looked towards travel and maybe escape. As we left Barton we saw a dry river bed that had become a dumping ground for scrap metal, includ-ing abandoned cars. But this was not Barton itself. This was outside. This was just the desert. It didn't matter to the people of Barton what got dumped there.

Around me on the train people were now awake and eating their breakfasts. A majority of the passengers were in their early twenties. Some were undoubtedly part of the international backpacking brig-ade, but others seemed to be genuine Australian travellers who were using the train beause they needed to get from one place to another. One wildly disreputable-looking guy in a Triumph tee-shirt said he was going to Kalgoorlie to get a job in a gold mine. But there was also a father and daughter pair, a middle-aged couple who said they made this trip fairly often, and plenty of big healthy-looking boys who kept falling into conversation with each other about rugby and Australian Rules football. They didn't have a lot to say to me.

I looked out of the window and saw a vista of dense forest all the way to the horizon. There was no sign of bare sand or even scrub, just lots and lots of trees. Then we got to Bates, a place that made Barton look like a throbbing metropolis. Bates consisted of one railway siding and a series of mobile homes on railway flat cars. The train slowed down to walking pace as we reached Bates. Why was not clear, and we never actually stopped.

By nine-thirty I had to admit I was beginning to feel bored, not bored by the desert, but bored by the train. It was slow, sealed, air-conditioned, insulated from the outside world in a way that the buses somehow hadn't been. The telegraph poles started to get taller and the service road disappeared for a while. These felt like major events. I fitfully tried to read more of *Voss*. I thought about putting on my personal stereo but there was nothing I wanted to hear. The sun was scorching through the double glazing. Sue was being a writer and making copious notes on the journey so far. I envied her concentration and industriousness.

Outside the window the forest had now gone. Instead there was a flat, grassy plain interspersed with little, low grey bushes, and there were only a few scattered trees, though still not a complete absence. The train speeded up. Now we were moving, now we were getting somewhere. The discarded railway sleepers were now in neat stacks held together by wire. The telegraph poles were short and stocky again. The service road reappeared, now further away from us, deeper into the desert, perhaps thirty yards to the north, cutting through the grass and bushes, with stones set along it marking its edges.

We didn't slow down again until we reached Watson. In Watson there were just four bungalows and an adventure playground, though the bit of land fenced off as the playground didn't look any more or less adventurous than all the desert around it that hadn't been fenced. Outside one bungalow there was a strange desert vehicle constructed out of sheet metal and tubular steel, and shaped like a wedge. There were some empty water tanks and one or two quaint, curious little railway buildings. And as we left Watson the name Nullabor was, for a second, literally correct. We were on a plain without a single tree. I thought I had arrived. Then, to my irritation, trees appeared again, but I consoled myself by saying they were only small, stunted trees this time. This went on for some time; stretches of bare plain then suddenly a tree or two and then nothing again. This, I told myself, had to be the Nullabor Plain, and even if it wasn't, it was a pretty good stretch of bare desert and it was more than good enough for me.

It was by no means beautiful but neither did it have the bleak ugliness that creates a sense of danger or awe. No doubt it would have been perfectly easy to die out there; the sun was burning, there was no water, no shelter, no people, yet it didn't look especially bleak or hostile, and I don't think that was only because I was looking at it from the safety of a train. The view was featureless yet the greenish-grey vegetation looked much friendlier than bare rock or sand would have.

Then the low, grey bushes began to thin out, sometimes replaced by parched grass or stretches of red sand. It was not the true, sumptuous red of the centre but it was red sure enough.

Then the train slowed down and stopped, and we were in Cook. Cook is about as real a place as you could wish for in these parts. It had a whole housing estate, a repeater station, two historic, wooden lock-ups, and a caravan that had been converted into a postcard and souvenir shop. There was also a post office but it was closed. Closing time was eleven-thirty. Since the train had pulled in at eleven-thirty-two you felt this had to be more than just coincidence. Someone was trying to avoid us.

Everybody piled off the train, stretched their legs, elbowed each other in order to buy postcards from the caravan. We all had a passionate need to do something, anything. I hunted around beside the track to see if I could pick up any interesting-looking rocks. Sue did the same and came up with much more interesting rocks than I did. 'It's good to have a purpose in the wilderness,' Sue said archly.

Cook is on that 478 kilometre stretch of dead-straight track and that is one of its three claims to fame. The second is that it has a hospital and visitors are encouraged to contribute to its upkeep. A large metal tank stands beside the track and on it is painted, 'Our hospital needs your help – get sick,' and 'If you're crook come to Cook.' You can put money into the tank through a slot. The third claim is that Cook has *trees*. They were planted by some group of benefactors known as 'The Men of Trees' and there is a monument to them in the main street of Cook. The monument is a large rock with a metal plaque on it. You feel they might have commemorated these men by planting another tree. The trees of Cook are fine but another one wouldn't come amiss.

The general torpor of the train journey affected even the stop in Cook. It was announced that we would stop for fifteen minutes but we stayed for forty-five. Nobody seemed to mind. There wasn't another stop scheduled until Kalgoorlie, our destination, still some twelve hours away, and the vast majority of the Nullabor Plain still lay ahead of us. I felt rather good to think I'd be staring out at that plain from now until the sun went down. That was what I'd come for.

The last place we passed through in South Australia was Hughes. Long before we reached the place we knew it was approaching because for several miles we saw wrecked cars in the desert, dozens of them, some piled into big heaps. I began to imagine Hughes must be a sizeable town if it could produce so many wrecked cars. Then we arrived in Hughes and saw that it consisted of three bungalows.

Once into Western Australia the plain became even more barren. Only the lowest, toughest grasses survived and whole areas had been baked brown and bare. The earth looked overcooked. The service road here looked so neglected, so little used, that it had huge rocks strewn all across it. The sun was hot and high now and nothing on the plain was tall enough to cast a visible shadow. In the sky to the south, long strings of ash-coloured cloud ran parallel to the railway line, soft, pale-blue sky behind them.

At one-forty-five the train stopped dead. Given the general slow pace of progress this didn't in itself come as much of a surprise. We had already stopped a few times for no apparent reason. We were in an unlovely bit of desert. Immediately beside our carriage there was a ruined bungalow. Its galvo roof and wooden frame were intact, but every panel in every wall, all the doors and windows, had been systematically smashed. There was a railway workers' camp visible a few hundred yards away, with bulldozers, heaps of ballast and all sorts of railway jetsom lying dejectedly in the sand.

Then the guard made an announcement. It was not in the cheerful style that coach captains used to make announcements. It was an announcement to tell us that a ballast truck working further up the line had derailed itself. The railway line was a single track, therefore there was no way we could move until the truck was back on the rails. He apologised convincingly and admitted that he had no idea how long we were going to be there. But he was good enough to point out that the train was currently two and a half hours behind schedule. Around me in the carriage sages were offering the opinion that we were talking about hours not minutes. The man travelling with his daughter said he'd made this trip once or twice before and the record for being late was nine hours, and that had been without a derailment.

I turned the little silver handle and lowered the Venetian blind to keep out the sun. Stripes of shadow and light stretched across the compartment like something from an over-obvious TV commercial. A girl with long ginger hair walked up the aisle wearing a tee-shirt that read, 'I don't want a vacation. I want an adventure.'

Nearby two young athletes were discussing the joys of skiing. As the girl passed they stopped talking and one said, 'You see her? She's strange.'

'Yeah? How?' asked the other.

'I don't know, but she's strange.'

A pick-up truck drove over from the railway workers' camp. The guys in it were curious about why we'd stopped and knew nothing about the derailment, but as soon as they worked out the situation they came up with a scheme for making money out of us. They knew how much beer cost on the train, so they loaded a palette of cold beer into the back of their pick-up truck and they sold it to us through an open window in the train's door at fifty cents less than the bar price. They got plenty of custom.

It was tough sitting there in the desert on a stationary train. I tried telling myself that I'd be sitting there in much the same way even if the train was moving, but there is something reassuring about a train in motion, and you know that however vast the distance you are getting closer all the time to your destination. When the train stops you're not only not getting any nearer, but each moment you're not moving is an *extra* moment you're going to have to spend on the train.

I had the growing realisation that I wasn't going to see very much more of the Nullabor Plain. The sun was already starting to sink. I knew it got dark in these parts as early as five p.m. If it took us a couple of hours to get moving again it would be four o'clock and I would barely have an hour left in which the plain would be visible.

The shadow of the train grew and stretched to monstrous length, becoming fifty or sixty feet long, putting the smashed bungalow into the shade, casting a long swathe of land into gloom. The sky was too cloudless for a spectacular sunset. The sun was a hot white ball, sinking matter-of-factly to the north-western horizon. At four-thirty, with still no indication that the train was ever going to move again, the sun slipped out of sight completely and there was a band of hot orange colour across the sky, pink at the edges, above a skyline that might have been drawn with a ruler.

At five o'clock the train finally began to move and there was a brief, eerie half hour of travelling through the desert, the sky fading orange and darkening blue, with the telegraph poles parading relentlessly, rhythmically, across the field of vision.

Before long there was no light at all in the sky and as I looked into the window all I could see were ghost images, reflections of the inside of the compartment. The vastness of the Nullabor was out there on the other side of the glass and I wasn't going to be seeing any more of it.

We arrived in Kalgoorlie many hours later, at about three in the morning. The train was six and a half hours late. After a night at the Sandalwood Motel we were well placed to go to the Budget Car Rental Office at the airport, hire the Land Cruiser, drive out to Kanowna and get completely lost.

Our spell of being lost in the desert, paltry and trivial though it seemed once we were safe, taught us how very easy it was to become totally disorientated in this vast, unchanging country. From then on we made damn sure that we took every conceivable precaution to make sure it didn't happen again. So far it hasn't.

We felt pretty good when we got back into the Land Cruiser after getting lost, good enough to decide we didn't want to spend the night in a motel. So we needed somewhere to camp. We didn't have a tent or anything wimpish like that. We had two sleeping-bags that we were simply going to unroll in the back of the Land Cruiser and sleep there. So all we really needed was somewhere to park, somewhere preferably attractive, certainly somewhere well off the road where there were no people. This was harder than we thought.

We knew from our experience on the train that it would be dark by five o'clock, so we drove hastily around the outskirts of Broad Arrow and Ora Banda, ghost towns, though still inhabited and not nearly so ghostly as Kanowna. We came across a lot of slag heaps. This was mining country and mining is a very messy, ugly activity whether it's in Coober Pedy, Ora Banda or Pontefract.

We were on unsurfaced roads and as we drove we threw up a very satisfying cloud of dust that trailed behind us and hung for a long time in the dry air. The few other vehicles we encountered were doing exactly the same. It wasn't too bad if the vehicle was coming towards us. The dust cloud enveloped and blinded us for a couple of seconds but then we had driven through it. Far more troublesome were vehicles travelling in the same direction. Three Land Cruisers driving in convoy appeared in my rear-view mirror. They were from a mining company and the drivers were used to making much more rapid progress on these roads than I was. They rapidly overtook me. I was duly blinded by dust, but this time I was driving *into* it and could see nothing at all. I slowed and hung back, waiting for the three Land Cruisers to pull away and for the dust to settle. But although they pulled away from me, they didn't pull away from each other. They continued in tight formation, tailgating each other, and you could be absolutely certain that the drivers of the two rear vehicles couldn't possibly see anything but dust.

The low sun and the floating dust made a great spectacle. The bushes and trees stood out in hazy silhouette, in different shades of blurred, hazy grey as they receded into the distance.

We picked a camping spot as far from slag heaps as possible and as far from the road as we dared. Hell, we didn't want to get *lost* or anything. We took care to avoid ants' nests and overhanging trees as recommended in the manuals. As we put down the rear seats of the Land Cruiser to make our bed it was nearly dark. We opened the evening's first bottle of Jacob's Creek. In the darkness we could see nothing, but we heard strange sounds all night, though perhaps they were not so very strange considering we were in mining country. There were trucks and trains moving, there was a peculiar toy-like electronic bleeping, and there were plenty of barking dogs. We had finally made it to the desert on our own. It was not Lake Disappointment, but we were not disappointed.

That night Sue had a dream so real that when she woke up she wasn't sure it had been a dream at all. She dreamed that as we slept a group of Aboriginals surrounded the Land Cruiser and began a kind of war dance. They frugged and shrieked and beat on our windows. They had bloodlust in their hearts and they were planning to drag us out of our sleeping-bags and kill us in some sort of fertility rite. This was what they did to all unwary travellers in this area. Just in case you think this dream might be fuelled by racist paranoia, she then realised in the dream that these people weren't real Aboriginals at all but white Australians posing as Aboriginals in order to give the Aboriginals a bad name. It turned out to be a white liberal dream after all.

She woke up before the sacrifice but even awake she still half-believed there were people out there in the darkness ready to slaughter us. Such is an urban response to a night in the desert. Daylight, which did not come quickly, made this nightmare laughable, but we still felt uneasy when we checked the map and found that we had been sleeping in the shadow of a peak called Mount Carnage.

That day we drove to Menzies. Once again, Menzies was a place that had formerly enjoyed prosperity and today enjoys very little. This change of fortune is neatly emblemised by the town hall, a distinguished Victorian stone building with a clock tower but no clock. The ship bringing the clock over from England sank, the money ran out before they could afford a new one, and the tower now has smooth, blank, blue faces where the clock ought to be.

I was still carrying a lot of uptight English mental baggage with me, and Menzies looked like *Deliverance* country to me; the tight, enclosed, isolated community that just hates strangers and just loves to kill 'em. The day was hot and clear. The main street was wide and sun-baked. There were shuttered, disused buildings, a railway station that was barred and fenced as though it was Fort Knox. An Aboriginal man sat on the pavement in the lean shadow of a tree trunk. The shadow was exactly the same width as the man. Another Aboriginal walked down the street doing a very authentic 'pimp roll'. He looked at us with what I took to be suspicion.

I was expecting the people of Menzies to be hostile to outsiders, especially to a couple of English tourists, and I wouldn't have blamed them. But I was being too paranoid. The guy in the grocery store called me 'mate' and seemed to mean it. The kid at the petrol station went to some trouble to help us fill up our gerry can with water, and as we left he said, 'Have a nice day.' I wasn't sure what movie these people had been watching but it wasn't *Deliverance*.

In the continuing spirit of hurrying to a spot that was just a dot on the map we saw there was a place nearby called Lake Ballard. I had always liked the writing of J. G. Ballard even before he started accepting my 'experimental prose' for *Ambit* magazine. So, for no better reason, we decided to go to Lake Ballard.

Lake Ballard is actually rather more than just a dot. It is a long stretch of wet and dry salt lakes, mostly the latter. There are huge expanses of flat, crusted sand, a few distant sheets of still, glassy water, and at intervals there are rocky and sandy outcrops. There was one particular hill, very symmetrical, triangular in profile, that stuck up out of the dry lake bed like a cone.

On the dirt road out of Menzies a flock of green parrots flapped above us as we passed, and the lake bed showed evidence of all kinds of wild life; the footprints of emus, camels, kangaroos. And then we saw some real kangaroos. They were standing on a red, sandy hillock, completely motionless, looking at us as we looked at them. After a while they ran away, although it was less of a run than a spring-loaded lollop. It was comic yet beautifully fast and effective.

The lake bed also showed tracks where someone had attempted to take their four-wheel drive. The tracks ended not very far across the lake, in sand that was softer, deeper and wetter than it must have appeared. There were signs that the vehicle had got stuck and a frantic effort to free it had taken place. There were tree branches, old carpets, even a sheet of corrugated iron, that had been used in the struggle. The struggle had obviously been successful since the vehicle was no longer there, but these signs told us that a four-wheel drive vehicle was far from invulnerable in these parts.

We were being obsessively cautious now. When we left the Land Cruiser and set off walking across Lake Ballard, we made little piles of stones and drew arrows in the sand so we could find our way back. Having done this for some distance we looked behind us and saw the Land Cruiser was perfectly visible, sticking out like a sore thumb on the gravel edge of the lake. And yet we walked another twenty yards and it had completely disappeared. The thought that we were being absurdly careful coexisted with the thought that we couldn't be *too* careful.

Even here I had doubts about whether or not this was 'proper' desert. It was dry and it was barren, but it was still a *lake*. However, by now I was feeling so good I didn't really care. There was a staggering, wonderful amount of space at Lake Ballard. There was no noise of anything human. There was the noise of wind, which was cold and salty, but nothing else. We had the feeling that we might stay there for ever and never be bothered by people again.

I wondered how this place might feel if I was there with a truckload of eighteen overlanders. I think I would still have been awed by it, but I would have wanted to wander off and be alone. Clearly I was not alone at Lake Ballard because Sue was with me, and I thought that I was much happier being there 'alone together' than I would have been simply alone. Quite apart from all the sensible reasons why you don't want to be completely alone in the desert, it was good to have someone to share this experience, to share, paradoxically, the joys of loneliness.

It was at Lake Ballard that I kept my promise to make love to Sue in the desert. I kept my promise on the red hill where we had first seen the kangaroos. It will, and did, seem absurd, but I couldn't shake the feeling that perhaps we were being watched. I don't know whether I imagined some sort of eye in the sky, or whether my superego was at work, but it wasn't the most relaxed experience of my life. Sue said she was not entirely averse to being watched anyway.

'You see,' I said, 'Geoff Nicholson, the kind of writer who keeps his promises. You were right to trust him.'

Deserts make you aware of skies, both by day and by night but it is the nights that are truly spectacular. In England I had never really known what people meant when they talked about the Milky Way. In the desert there was no doubt. The sky was cloudless so the nights were cold and the stars hung densely as if sprayed thickly on to the inside of the black velvet dome.

Sitting in the back of the Land Cruiser, a little drunk, looking at the sky, is not the worst way of experiencing the desert. But in a way, having once been there you can never entirely stop experiencing it. The cliché is that you can take the man out of the desert but you can't take the desert out of the man. Wordsworth knew all about this, but he talked about daffodils rather than deserts. When on my couch I lie, I reimagine the desert. It is still with me. It is distorted and knocked about by memory but it is still there, recollected in tranquillity.

'If this is the best night of our trip I won't complain,' said Sue at Lake Ballard.

I said I agreed.

'In fact,' she continued, 'if I died right now I don't think I'd mind at all.'

I couldn't entirely go along with that. There were still one or two deserts I wanted to visit, still one or two books I wanted to write.

Sue said, 'When my husband was dying he kept complaining, "But I haven't done anything with my life." I don't want to feel like that.'

Neither did I. I don't suppose anybody ever does. I thought of my father and wondered how he might feel. Perhaps he hadn't done very much, and yet he had done all that he had ever wanted to. He enjoyed his work. He enjoyed a quiet life. And after all, what had I done that was so much better? I'd been a not very good husband. I'd written a few novels that I was glad to have written but was essentially dissatisfied with. I'd been to one or two places that interested me, but I had never seriously thought that travelling was *doing* anything. But I thought I had experienced more pleasure, more fun, in my life than my father had, though I knew that was a difficult and absurd calculation for a son to make about his father's life.

I certainly experienced pleasure at Lake Ballard. I had finally made it to the desert on the terms I had wanted to. I had done what I wanted to do, though I remained vague about why exactly I wanted it. This was the important part of the trip, the part beyond the confines of the bus and the train. This was what I had come for, and I was aware then as now, of the difficulty of saying what the pleasures of that were. I know the recipe but I'm not sure what the finished product is called.

You drive off a dirt road into some sparse, lean vegetation. You get out of your vehicle, you just look around, and although you know you are hardly in mortal danger, there are still risks, there is edge. You have to know what you're doing in the desert. This rough country doesn't suffer fools gladly and it is all too willing to make a fool out of you.

You keep walking, or you stand still, or sit, or maybe take photographs. You would like to feel a part of it and yet you know you don't belong. You are not a desert rat, just some English tourist with a notebook and one or two half-baked ideas. There is either nothing to see or there is everything to see, depending on your point of view. There is certainly, in one overwhelming sense, nothing to do and nothing to be done.

Now that you're here you realise, of course, that there is no revelation to be had in the desert, and in any case that maybe isn't why you came. You couldn't seriously expect revelation and perhaps you were wise enough not to . There is no self-discovery to be made here, and maybe this is as near as you can get to feeling at one with it all. Maybe there are some valuable moments when the internal and the external emptiness combines. There are, if you're lucky, times when you can cease to feel or think anything, when you can escape from ideas or theories or interests, from personality and aspiration and loneliness. You confront a supreme indifference and in so doing you escape from the tedium of the self.

After a few days camping at Lake Ballard we decided to spend the night in a desert motel. We drove to Leonora. Leonora (population fifteen hundred if you include the neighbouring town of Gwalia with which it merges) has an annual rainfall of 203 millimetres, and its main industries are gold mining and sheep farming.

We selected the Leonora Motel because it was there, the first place we saw on the road from Menzies. There was a long terrace of motel rooms going back from the road. There was a large square of red earth for parking and a small, improbably green, lush square of lawn by the office door. A young but raddled woman, with frizzed hair and a tired manner, was behind the desk. She seemed surprised that we, or anybody, would want to stay there. She wanted to be paid in advance but I'd left my wallet in the Land Cruiser. Would she trust me with the key to the room, then we'd unpack and be right back with the money? A hesitant yes. When I went back ten minutes later the office door was open but the woman was not to be seen. I rang the bell on the counter and became aware of the sound of running water inside the living-quarters attached to the office, and then the woman's voice called out, 'Is there anybody there?'

'Yes, it's me, I've come to pay.'

'I'm in the shower right now,' she shouted. 'Will you come back later?'

Hadn't these people seen *any* movies? Didn't she know about the dangers of taking showers in motels, especially while leaving the front door to the office wide open? It was another indication perhaps, that feelings about the dangers and general weirdness of the desert don't worry the people who actually live there.

I went back when she'd showered and asked if there was a laundry room or at least a clothes drier in the motel, so we could dry some tee-shirts and underwear we'd washed in the sink.

'No, we don't have a drier,' she said. 'When it only rains once every four years you don't find much use for one.'

I smiled. I tried to show that I appreciated desert jokes. I felt some obligation to make conversation. I felt the need to explain myself and what I was doing in Leonora. I thought she would have expected that; but I didn't have to say much.

'You're touring around, right?' she said.

'Yes,' I said. 'We're just on holiday.'

I didn't think it would be very useful to say I was writing a book about deserts and would she please be colourful for me so I'd have some material.

'On holiday. Right,' she said. And that was enough. That was all she needed or wanted to know. She had satisfied her curiosity. I could go now.

People complain that the English are cold and not outgoing enough. I think this is largely because English people have too much respect for others to want to impose their own views, personalities and problems on them. The people I met in desert places in Western Australia didn't want to engage in lively, revealing conversations, but that wasn't because they were cold or unfriendly or dismissive. It was because they respected other people's right to be left alone. I liked that very much.

The main street of Leonora had an old canopied sidewalk, like in a cowboy movie. There were kids playing and there was a big ice-making machine about ten feet high and ten feet wide, with a slot to insert your two dollars and a door, like the door of a safe, which you opened to get your ice. There was a community supermarket that was worried about shoplifting, and had big handwritten signs up designed to promote guilt. Six months ago they'd had twenty-five shopping trolleys. Now they only had six.

American culture, in the form of hip hop and graffiti, had also arrived in Leonora. 'We came, we saw, we whipped your ass,' was scrawled on one building. Another graffito with a poor grasp of rhyme, said, 'Hip hop, suck my cock.' They both seemed profoundly unAustralian and out of place.

We were sitting in our hotel room at about six o'clock that evening when all the lights went out. I, and a couple of other motel guests, wandered out of our rooms and lumbered about in the darkness asking ourselves and each other whether it was a power cut, a blown fuse, or what. The manager, the husband of the shower-taker, now appeared out of the office. In the darkness he had a look of Jesus about him; long straight hair parted in the middle and one of those trim little beards so favoured by the son of God in so many pictures of him.

'Is this a power cut?' I asked.

'Reckon so,' he said.

'Do you have them often?'

'Yeah, I'd say we have 'em fairly often.'

'How long do they usually last?'

'Well, you know, how long's a piece of string?'

In Leonora a piece of string is about fifteen minutes long, and that was the length of our power cut.

There was a bar in town where the miners were drinking and shouting very loudly, but they *had* to shout to be heard over the sound system which was playing a lot of very emotive sixties songs. The Trems figured largely. I was well aware that a certain sort of travel writer would go into this bar and fall into conversation with a few miners. He'd arm wrestle them, drink them under the table, probably get into a fight, and at the end of the evening he'd be accepted as a blood brother. I went in there, had a beer, looked around, didn't talk to anybody and nobody talked to me, and after a while I left to get some fish and chips.

I understand why people think there is something very erotic about motels. It's the anonymity, the transience, the looming presence of the bed. Others in the Leonora Motel apparently felt the same way, and the thinness of the rooms' walls meant we had to share the precious moments with them, at least aurally.

A little after midnight the couple in the adjoining motel room began making loud, deeply felt, sexual noises, but these were short lived. On the other side of us was the bedroom belonging to the shower-taker and her Jesus-like husband. Now, these people could *perform* and they wanted you to know it. Shrieks, gasps, and peals of dirty laughter drifted through the plasterboard for a while, and then the gymnastics started. The bed springs clanged in powerful but ever-changing time signatures, and then we could hear that the bed had started to move, and the bedhead was being slammed against the party wall, and the bed itself was being bounced upon with such vigour it sounded as though it was taking flight after each stroke.

When it finally subsided we were tempted to think it was now our turn and we ought to do our stuff for the benefit of the listeners at either side. I have always known that I'm more of a voyeur than an exhibitionist and I found the thinness of the walls and the nearness of other people completely inhibiting. Making love in the desert was one thing. Making love in a desert motel while people on both sides listened in, was another. This was not at all the promise I'd made to Sue.

A couple of miles down the road from Leonora was the town of Gwalia. It must be one of the most extraordinary-looking places on earth. It too was a ghost town. Once there were twelve thousand people living there and today there are about eighty, almost all of them connected with the Sons of Gwalia Gold Mine. What set it apart from other ghost towns, or any other sort or town for that matter, was the fact that it was constructed almost entirely out of corrugated iron.

Some of the buildings were very traditionally proportioned, with gable roofs and canopies and chimney stacks that looked like they'd be at home in any self-respecting suburb. Others were much more eccentric, more makeshift and cobbled together. But either way, everything about them, walls, roofs, fences, even some of the doors, were made of corrugated iron. Because the town was largely deserted many of the buildings were no longer in use. Some, like Petroni's Guest House or the old general store, still looked sturdy and usable, but many of the smaller, odder buildings were collapsing and falling in on themselves. They had been painted pale-yellow or terracotta and these colours had been bleached by the sun. Porches, doorways and floors had sunk or fallen. Rubble and scrap metal surrounded the abandoned buildings.

In some places cacti had run wild from what must have been somebody's attempts at gardening, cacti being indigenous only in the Americas. And (talk about J. G. Ballard!) there was an empty, abandoned swimming-pool with its steep-roofed, corrugated changing-rooms collapsed all along the poolside.

But not every building in Gwalia was in a state of distress. People were living in some of the houses. Phone lines ran to them. Television aerials were perched on the roofs. It must be hard to stay houseproud in that sort of environment and, as in Coober Pedy, many had decided not to bother. The houses had big yards full of old caravans and cars, a trail bike, maybe a couple of chained-up dogs.

But that wasn't the whole story either. One or two of the houses were made of shiny, new, unpainted corrugated iron. They were clean and solid and they dazzled where they reflected the sun, and looked as though they had been built very recently. Some, unlikely as it seemed, looked as though they were being used as weekend retreats; nobody was living in them and they were securely locked and bolted, with corrugated shutters pulled down over the windows.

As we walked down the quiet, hot, open main street we certainly felt out of place. But who wouldn't have felt out of place here? The arrival of almost anyone or anything would have looked odd, but I was tempted to believe I was seeing things when three little girls on bicycles appeared, all wearing immaculate girl-guide uniforms. They rode down the empty street, turned at a junction, and rode towards one of the houses with the messy yards. We walked in the same direction. Halfway down the street that led to the little girls' house, three dogs of varying sizes and shapes, but of a shared viciousness, trotted into the middle of the road and stopped. They confronted us like gunfighters in a cowboy movie, and there was some confusion in their canine minds about whether or not we were good guys. They weren't taking any chances. We kept walking and the dogs started barking at us. The three little girls watched with interest. This was as much entertainment as they were likely to get today, or any other day in Gwalia. We decided we didn't really need to walk down this particular street. We stopped, changed direction, chose another street to walk down, and came across some art.

It was at a house that looked new and well cared for. Nobody was home but it certainly wasn't abandoned and the inhabitant did a nice line in naïve metal sculpture. The yard was full of his work.

There was a link chain that had been welded together so that it stood upright like a rearing serpent. It had been painted matt silver, and a golden horse mascot sat atop the chain. Another piece was made up of a girder, bogie wheels and a plant pot. Others, more abstract, featured car bumpers, plaited pieces of wrought iron, and metal wheel rims attached to a flagpole.

We hung around looking like tourists, hoping that somebody might come along and explain the spectacle. But what was there to explain? Somebody here in Gwalia liked making things, liked welding one piece of metal to another and painting the results matt silver. It didn't require much psychological probing to understand that urge. It was a reasonably pure and uncommercial urge too. Rents in Gwalia surely could not be high. If ever an artist wanted a spot in which to live cheaply and be free of market forces, Gwalia is surely the place.

There was a cemetery outside Gwalia. It was off to the east of the Menzies/Leonora road. We went there in the early morning as the caretaker was arriving to start the sprinklers. They didn't seem to be working properly. A number of sickly-looking saplings sat in deep pools of water while the sprinklers added more and more water to the pools.

I don't know if it was just mawkishness or ghoulishness that made me want to visit the cemetery. I had always found desert graves moving, whether it was in the Mojave or in Morocco. And yes, I was much possessed by death, and my mind was full of thoughts about my father as I walked between the graves here.

It was a large, well-tended cemetery. There was a fence that separated it from the surrounding desert. Some money and some care had been needed to create its present form. Somebody cared and yet there were still signs of decay and neglect. It was a square patch of land, maybe a couple of acres in area, divided into four distinct sections by two crossing paths. Where they intersected, at the very centre of the cemetery, there was a gazebo with benches where you could sit and shelter from the sun.

Each of the four sections belonged to a different religious denomination. The graves were divided into Presbyterian, Catholic, Methodist and Anglican sections. Each was denoted by a blue and white sign. The Anglican section was the least cared for.

Inevitably the graves belonged to miners and their families. Generally the miners had been 'accidentally killed' down the mines. The gravestones and the messages on them had nothing desert-like about them. They spoke of the dead being at rest, of being gone but not forgotten, of reunions in the afterlife.

It would have been absurd to put fresh flowers on these graves. They would scarcely have survived half an hour in the heat. The solution was for many of the graves to have elaborate artificial flowers, usually carnations, their petals made of thick porcelain, their stems and leaves made out of metal. These were then put into small glass cases, either hemispherical or cruciform in shape. The desert air and the changes in temperature had made short work of the glass. The cases were cracked or shattered, even though the artificial desert blooms inside them remained impervious to decay.

I realised I had no idea whether my father wanted to be buried or cremated, where he might want his grave to be or where he might want his ashes scattering. I suspected that my mother wouldn't have much more idea than I did. These were not the kinds of things my family talked about either.

From Gwalia we headed to Laverton and the start of the Warburton Range Road. This is one of the great dirt roads, that plunges through the desert for six hundred kilometres, through vast emptiness to arrive at the Warburton Mission, a place you are hardly likely to want to go, a place that's hundreds of kilometres from where most people would want to be. It is a road without water or fuel, and with very little traffic.

I wanted to drive along it. Not all the way along it, of course, but far enough along it to be able to hold my head up and say I had driven along one of the great dirt roads.

Laverton was a hundred kilometres from Gwalia, a hundred kilometres nearer the centre of Australia. We drove through spinifex country. It was also bush-fire country. We drove along one stretch of road where all the bush to the right was black and burned, while all the land to the left was untouched. This soon changed and we entered an area where fire had consumed the vegetation on both sides of the road. This was real desolation, real ugliness, although bush fires are not ecologically a bad thing. In fact judicious burning of the bush to form a sort of fire gap in which new, not too flammable, growth can occur, is a technique now used to preserve desert habitats. The Aboriginals had been doing this for thousands of years before the white man developed an ecological consciousness.

Laverton was clean, orderly, suburban. We saw a mobile home being delivered to its site, and met a woman who kept a pet sheep on the verandah of her bungalow. She said it was an interest of her husband's. In the town centre, which was mostly an open, landscaped shopping-area with a few stores and a staggering number of litter bins, men ambled at intervals from the bar of the Desert Inn Hotel across the car park, to the TAB office to place bets. The TAB office was a white hut on short stilts, exactly similar in size, shape and design to the Winky's Unisex Hair Salon, a white hut on short stilts that stood right next to it. The TAB office was getting all the business.

I went into the local supermarket to buy something cheap so that I'd have change to make a phone call home to England.

'Do you sell pens?' I asked the woman at the checkout.

'I'm sorry,' said the woman. 'I did order some from the guy, but you know what he's like.'

I nodded to show that I did. I believe this was the first time in my whole life, anywhere in the world, that I had been mistaken for a local. It was all the better for that reason. I bought a bar of chocolate instead of a pen.

Phoning home no longer filled me with the dread it had at first. By now I felt that I was simply going to have a conversation with my mother. There was no reason to expect any terrible development in my father's state. A phone call from Australia to England was becoming routine.

The phone booth smelled of tinned meat, and as I tried to make the call I got a recorded message telling me that all lines to England were engaged. I tried again. This time the message told me that all the dialling codes for London had recently changed. I already knew that but since I wasn't trying to dial London it seemed irrelevant. I tried again and got a number that rang and rang without being answered. By my calculations it was eight in the morning in England and my mother ought to have been at home, but something told me I hadn't got the right number anyway. So I kept dialling and redialling and getting different messages and different tones, and I never got through to my mother. Finally I called the operator. She could connect me, but only if I put seven dollars fifty into the box. I went through my pockets, assembled my change, and came up with six dollars eighty. Ah well, I told myself, it was no big deal. It wasn't imperative that I speak to my mother right this moment. The call could wait a day or two until I found a more congenial phone box.

There were wrecked cars to be seen throughout the Australian desert. In fact there have been wrecked cars in all the deserts I've seen. I have always found them a melancholy and disturbing sight. Some have no doubt broken down and been left where they stopped because it would cost more to rescue them than the car was worth. Others appear to have been taken to the desert specifically to be dumped there.

The archetypical story of the Aboriginal and the motor car is as follows: a group of black fellahs get enough money together to buy a secondhand car. They leave the mission or the lands where they live, and make a long journey into town on foot. There they meet an unscrupulous white car dealer who sells them a useless heap of tin. They don't realise this and set off for home, driving their new possession. They haven't gone more than a few miles into the desert before the car judders to a halt. They lift the bonnet but they don't know anything about cars, and the car is such a lemon there's nothing they could do to repair it anyway. They leave the car where it is, abandon it, and set off on the journey home, on foot again, with no money, no car, but also with no regrets. They are completely able to shrug off the loss but they don't want to go home completely empty handed so they siphon off the petrol and put it into jars so they'll have something to sniff on the way home. The story is usually told to demonstrate that the Aboriginal has no sense of values and is as happy with a jar of petrol to sniff as he would be with a new car to drive.

I have no idea how true this story is or how often it repeats itself on the outskirts of Laverton, but there were enough wrecked and abandoned cars along the start of the Warburton Range Road, to suggest that it might be an almost daily occurrence.

A lot of these cars hadn't just been abandoned, however. They'd been systematically attacked and destroyed. Everything had been smashed and yanked off and ripped out. Items hadn't simply been removed for spares; they'd been pulled apart with an extraordinary violence. Cars were turned on their sides or flipped upside-down, their innards eviscerated and strewn around the desert; yet some of the cars still contained engines. I didn't do any bench tests, but there were some quite usable-looking V6 engine blocks lying in the sand. I suppose they were too strong to be destroyed and too heavy to be thrown very far. The worst of the cars had been shot at and bullet holes scarred their doors and body panels. Car wrecks in the American desert sometimes have bullet holes in them too, but I never saw one that had been as gleefully shot up as these Australian ones.

There was evidence that a certain amount of partying had accompanied this manic vandalism. Wherever we saw a mutilated car we also saw a heap of lager cans. Emu Export was the lager of choice for those who had a mind to perform automobile mayhem in the desert.

We passed the signs that told us there were no services for 570 kilometres and headed up the Warburton Range Road. The first few kilometres were surfaced but the road soon became dirt, and there was a feeling that we were now entering some more profound form of desert. We were going to drive for as long as it felt good and then we were going to stop. We'd know when we'd had enough, then we'd pull off the road, drive a couple of kilometres into the bush, camp for the night, then the next day we'd head back for Laverton and begin another journey, this time to Wiluna. It sounded simple, and yet . . .

As I drove along that corrugated dirt road, with a cloud of wicked dust blowing behind the Land Cruiser, with all that desert and desolation ahead of us, with no prospect of people or habitation, with only space and silence and loneliness, *I wanted to keep driving*. I wanted to be a he-man, a desert rat, a Mad Max. I wanted to tackle and conquer these mean desert roads and spaces.

Of course, I didn't. I wasn't insane, and only an insane person would have tackled the whole of the Warburton Range Road with the inadequate amounts of diesel, water and equipment we were carrying. All I'm saying is, I wanted to. I wanted to do more and be more than my limited horizons had so far allowed. I had only ever wanted to be the unadventurous urbanite, sticking his head out of the car window, looking at the desert and saying, 'Hey, that looks sort of interesting.' Now I wanted to be something else.

So in short, yes, all we did was drive along the Warburton Range Road for a while, and then we stopped and we camped, and the next day we headed back. Yes, a sensible part of me made sure I knew when it was time to make camp, when it would have been silly to go any further, but in another sense I never wanted to stop at all. I might know when I'd had enough, but then again I might not, and I certainly hadn't had enough yet.

*   *   *

June nights in Western Australia were freezing cold. Each morning when we got up to build our fire to make breakfast there was ice on the roof of the Land Cruiser. But the sun soon warmed us up and we forgot how cold we had been; at least until the next night.

After bacon and scrambled eggs and coffee, it was my custom to take a trowel for digging a hole with, disappear behind a bush, and 'go to the toilet'. There are few things more likely to make a man feel philosophical and at peace then to squat in the sand with the desert breezes playing round his bare buttocks.

The desert, we're constantly told, has a very fragile ecology. Merely walking, driving and camping in it can have profound effects, usually harmful. What then was the significance of mounds of rich human faeces suddenly being dropped in it?

Imagine you are a worm crawling through the earth. Some of you will have more trouble with this than others. Imagine the earth suddenly parts around you and vast quantities of dung are suddenly dumped on your head. (This is an experience most of us can imagine quite easily.) However, if you're a desert worm, I would guess you're rather pleased to receive this rich, fertile burden. It must be like several Christmasses all at once. In the world of the desert worm this must be the sort of event that could give rise to a cargo cult.

Thus you can squat in the desert with a fairly clear conscience, feeling like a nature boy, believing you're doing good for the environment. I'm willing to believe this feeling is totally self-deluding.

The need to ring home was becoming more pressing. Somewhere off the Warburton Range Road is nowhere to start looking for a phone booth. We knew, of course, there was the phone box in Laverton that smelled of tinned meat, but I didn't want to go through all that nonsense with the recorded messages again, and there was no guarantee that I'd get through. So we went to Kookynie, a dot on the map if ever there was one.

Our guide book to the area described Kookynie as an 'interesting ghost town with a surprisingly good hotel'. We didn't especially want to see another ghost town, but where there was a hotel there would surely be a phone. If we liked the look of the hotel we might even stay the night.

It was a Sunday and there were one or two Sunday drivers on the dirt roads; the kind of people who pulled over once in a while to look at the view and take some photographs; people like us. On our way we saw wallabies and parrots and emus, and I experienced a driving phenomenon without which no desert trip is complete.

They say that men can't stand to be criticised for their performance in bed or their performance behind the wheel of a car. I like to think I can take criticism of my driving. I was probably driving too fast at about seventy kilometres per hour along a dirt track. There were some deep, parallel ruts running in the same direction as the road, so I was correcting the steering from time to time to avoid the deepest of the ruts and keep the journey comparatively smooth. However, I obviously overcorrected, turned the wheel too hard, and the back end of the Land Cruiser started to 'fishtail'. This was a wild and frightening thing. The front of the vehicle kept pointing in the right direction, straight ahead, while the rear end flapped around frantically from one side of the road to the other. The classic advice when you're skidding is to turn the wheel in the direction of the skid, but this won't work when you're fishtailing. The other piece of advice is not to brake, and this I followed. I had absolutely no control over the Land Cruiser. I was just hanging on and wishing it would stop.

It seemed to go on for a very long time, time enough to envisage the Land Cruiser spinning, rolling, crashing in any number of spectacular ways. But it didn't. As I held on, the flapping of the rear end gradually subsided and I got control again. When it was all over I laughed a little hysterically. At least I could say I had done another archetypical desert 'thing'.

There was only one road that lead to Kookynie so it was hard to believe we could get lost, nevertheless Kookynie proved very hard to find. We came to a crossroads. There were a couple of derelict brick buildings, heaps of rubbish, an abandoned 1940s car that had been there long enough to actually start rusting. There were road signs pointing to other local places; Leonora, Malcolm, the ironically named Niagara, but no sign for Kookynie. Then, of course, we realised why there was no sign; because we were already there. This flat brown expanse of rubble and dirt road was Kookynie, and the surprisingly good hotel had to be that weird building over there surrounded by old cars and with a vintage bus parked outside. It was called the Grand.

Sure enough there was a phone box at the hotel. I could see it outside the main entrance, under the canopy. But also right outside the main entrance were half a dozen parked utes and their owners; beefy young guys with bare chests and beer cans, and they were whooping it up this Sunday afternoon clustered round the phone box.

No doubt they weren't bad lads. Maybe they'd have been understanding, even sympathetic, if I'd explained to them that I wanted to phone England to talk to my mother to find out how my dying father was. But maybe not. And even if they were understanding and sympathetic, even if they let me in the phone box and lowered the volume of their whooping, I was still going to feel pretty uncomfortable. I reckoned I needed to find another phone box.

That was easier said than done. We looked at the map. We were, of course, in the middle of nowhere. Gwalia, with its corrugated-iron fantasies, was about 130 kilometres away. I clearly remembered seeing a phone box there. Gwalia was so utterly underpopulated there was no way a bunch of guys were going to be clustered anywhere, certainly not round the phone box. So we went there. A 130-kilometre journey through the desert simply to find a phone box seemed completely reasonable.

I got through without difficulty. My mother sounded worried. The hospital had taken a piece of bone from my father's hip but had then decided they couldn't waste time waiting for the results. This seemed absurd given how long it had taken them to get round to doing the tests. But they had transferred my father to the cancer hospital. I had heard him say, long before he became ill, 'They never come out of that place except in a box.' At the cancer hospital they were giving him blood transfusions and had begun radium treatment. The radium, my mother said, was making him feel sick and confused. He wasn't eating much, though he was trying hard to. He had been told he would feel much better once the treatment was over, and then they could decide whether or not to remove one of his kidneys. They seemed to be going to a lot of trouble and expense for someone they had already declared doomed.

My mother seemed to be glad that he was finally in the right hospital, even if being there signalled the worst. She said she was keeping her fingers crossed. My father had signed the papers to convert his building-society accounts into joint accounts with my mother. My mother said he'd done it 'just in case'.

*   *   *

We set off for Wiluna. There are comparatively few reasons why anyone would want to travel to Wiluna. Certainly you would have to go there if you had an urge to visit the Kalya Emu Farm or the Desert Gold Citrus Farm, but such urges are rare. More likely you'd go there if you were working in one of the mines, or more likely still you'd go to Wiluna to catch a plane that would take you away from all that.

You would certainly have to go there if you wanted to get on the Gunbarrel Highway, which I did, for much the same reasons that I'd wanted to get on the Warburton Range Road. Incidentally, you would also go to Wiluna if you wanted to get on the Canning Stock Trail, the road that would take you, eventually, to Lake Disappointment.

We weren't going to Lake Disappointment, of course, and this was as close as we were going to get; not very close, about five hundred kilometres away. Wiluna would be a sort of journey's end, and appropriately enough we didn't know what we'd find there. It sounded as though it would be another shrivelled mining town, where gold and cyanide had once been mined in a big way, but no more. It had once claimed to have the world's longest bar, in the Weeloona Hotel. Now, our sources said, the population was about fifteen hundred, 'mostly Aboriginal', but that was fine by us if it was fine by them.

It took us a couple of days to get to Wiluna from Gwalia but it needn't have taken so long. We were travelling slowly, in search of delayed gratification.

We travelled entirely by dirt road, a road that was a pussycat compared to some of the really challenging routes across Australia. Nevertheless, the bumps and corrugations and holes and floodways and cattle grids set the teeth on edge, threw the Land Cruiser around, and made me very glad that the suspension being hammered belonged to a hire company and not to me.

The red earth blew up in a long, ragged tail behind us, and billowed around the Land Cruiser, penetrating the tightly shut doors and windows. We could see it settling, building up, on the dashboard, on our clothes, on our skin. After an hour everything in the vehicle, including us and all our possessions, was gloriously red and filthy.

I was being very careful not to make the Land Cruiser fishtail again. I varied the speed, trying to get the juddering of the vehicle to tune into the same frequency as the ruts. I experimented to see whether the cattle grids were best taken fast or slow. None of it seemed to make much difference. It was still an exhaustingly rough ride.

We didn't see more than a handful of other vehicles. Sometimes the drivers would give a wave. Some of the waves were very discreet, no more than a hand raised from the wheel, sometimes just a finger. Sometimes, however, it was the meanest, toughest-looking drivers who gave the most extravagant and friendly waves. Sometimes the drivers pointedly didn't wave at all. Few things make you feel more like a hick tourist than giving a big cheerful wave to some driver who considers himself too cool to return it.

We stopped at Agnew, the place with the population of 'less than ten'. We went for a beer at the Agnew Hotel. It was a rickety but charming kind of hovel. We stepped into the completely empty bar and found that all the bar stools had been inverted so their seats were on the floor and their legs sticking up in the air. We didn't ask for explanations, just ordered two cans of Emu Export to take away. We leaned against the Land Cruiser, revelling in the dry, dusty heat, drinking the cold strong lager, feeling like part of an Australian beer advertisement.

Opposite the hotel was a fenced compound, maybe twenty yards square. It contained a display of old metal artefacts; a winch, a steam engine, a boiler, a bedstead. They were unpainted and had been left to tarnish. Pride of the collection was a ten-foot-tall tin man, made of oil cans and ducting, with brake pads for ears and mouth. A bow tie and a dinner jacket had been painted on the drum that made his body, metal handles made his ears, and iron rods sprouted out of his head to form hair. One arm raised a giant can of lager in salute. The piece didn't show the same confident surrealism of the unknown metal sculptor in Gwalia, but no doubt they were of the same school.

A dog belonging to the hotel trotted out to make friends with us. He was a big squat mongrel, dusty brown, sad eyed, and very trusting. He brought a stone which he invited us to throw for him. I threw it a couple of times before he lost it. That wasn't so surprising. There were a lot of stones to choose from lying on the ground outside the Agnew Hotel. So he brought a piece of wood which was much easier for him to spot and retrieve. Neither he nor I seemed richly entertained by this activity but we went through the motions until the beer was drunk. Had we been real desert folk I'm sure we would have tossed the empty cans casually aside, maybe trying to shoot them as they fell to the ground. As we got in the Land Cruiser the dog looked at us with infinite, weary sadness. I hoped I might have brightened up his day a little, yet I seemed only to have confirmed to him that even the slightest of pleasures ends all too soon.

We camped on the dry shores of Lake Miranda, a vast salty

expanse, yet nearby a rich, red hill of sand grew out of the ground. We spent a freezing night camped there. We were in our sleeping-bags, fully dressed, spare clothes draped around us, anaesthetised by a couple of bottles of Jacob's Creek, and we still couldn't sleep because of the cold. 'Never again. Never again,' I vowed, but I broke the vow the next night.

A little way off the road from Lake Miranda to Wiluna were a lot of small mines. The sites had been given optimistic names: Dominion Mining, Bellvue Gold Mine. There was even a sign pointing to Albion Downs. Again there was the visible aftermath of bush fires. Again there were emus and kangaroos. It was easy to get blasé about these, as blasé as you might get about seeing sheep in England, and there were plenty of sheep too. The sheep seemed quite smart, smart enough at least to run away when they saw and heard a car coming at them. The kangaroos were nowhere near as smart as that and the roadside was like a kind of slaughterhouse, scattered with dead kangaroos in various stages of decomposition. Some had been reduced to a pelt and a few bones. Others looked freshly killed, their guts spilling out of them red and steaming and very appetising to the ravens.

We saw a big truck tyre at the side of the road, held upright by rocks, and on it was painted the word 'graves' and an arrow. We had to look. The arrow pointed to a little-used path that led off the dirt road and passed between bushes to a small clearing, marked by a circle of tyre tracks. There were two graves. The first was just a raised mound of red earth and there was a simple metal 'headstone', again supported by rocks. There had once been words on the metal but they had been bleached out by the sun, leaving the grave absolutely anonymous.

The other grave was more elaborate. There was a shield-shaped headstone, cast-iron railings around the perimeter of the grave, then four metal posts set a little further out with barbed wire strung between them to keep out desert predators. The carving on the headstone read, 'In loving memory of Cecily. Beloved daughter of B and L O'Donohue, who died on June 20th 1920 aged 7 years RIP.'

It was June 27th when we were there. We had missed the seventieth anniversary by a week. It appeared that someone was still looking after this seventy-year-old grave, someone who cared enough to mark it so that people like us could stop and gawp.

At last we came, though without much sense of having arrived, to Wiluna. Wiluna had a wide main street, again suitable for turning camel trains, but in their absence a row of gum trees had been planted in the centre of the street to make a kind of dual carriageway.

The mostly Aboriginal population was out on the streets, little clusters of inert men and women. A child was about to run into the road ahead of us but was dragged back by her father in the nick of time. There were a number of community buildings and a handful of government vehicles parked in the street. There was an attractive old auditorium, now empty and covered with 'Keep Out' signs, but its name, The Moonlight Hall, was still visible. And there was an establishment called Club Motel Wiluna. It was an impressive two-storey building with verandahs and mosquito nets and the offer of TV and air-conditioning in every room. There was a general store, which on closer inspection we saw was called the Ngangganawili General Store. It looked closed but we wanted to make sure. We needed some food. We parked the Land Cruiser, got out, and were about to try the door of the store. There were maybe ten Aboriginals hanging around outside.

'Closed!' they all shouted. 'Closed!'

'What time do they open again?'

'One-thirty.'

It was noon. It wasn't going to be easy to while away an hour and a half in Wiluna.

'Garage!' they shouted and they pointed to a big barn-like garage a couple of hundred yards down the road.

I wasn't sure if these sons and daughters of the desert were being genuinely helpful or whether they were trying to tell us that people like me shopped at the garage while people like them shopped at the general store. I said thanks, and we drove to the garage.

We had passed it on the way into town. A big truck was parked outside making a bulk delivery but we couldn't see what of. It just looked like a garage. It really didn't look like a place you could buy food. I filled up with diesel and asked the guy if he sold groceries as well.

'Sure do!' he said proudly.

'Do you have any bread?'

'Yeah. No worries. Come inside.'

I paid for the diesel, moved the Land Cruiser away from the pumps so somebody else could use them, not that there was exactly a queue of motorists. Sue slid open the doors of the garage and we stepped inside. It was like entering Aladdin's cave.

Part of it was like a supermarket with shelves of tinned goods, and fridges and freezers containing chilled and frozen foods. But there were also children's clothes for sale, electrical components, books and magazines, all sorts of children's toys and games and, of course, spare parts for cars. There was very little organisation to any of this. Clockwork robots sat on the shelves next to tins of pineapple, next to light switches, next to the latest Jackie Collins novel. What united everything, made everything of a piece, was the thick coating of red dust that had settled over every object in the whole place.

But as well as being a shop, this interior was also living-quarters for the garage owner and his family. In one corner there was a sink with last night's dirty dishes still sitting in it. There was a dining-area and a stereo and a microwave oven. And when we discovered that all the bread on sale was frozen, the owner was happy to defrost it for us in his microwave.

He was in his forties, short, bearded, open faced. He wore a cap and a pair of overalls, both stained red by the dust. He was easy going, helpful, but definitely the boss around here. By now we were well used to people not being curious about us. As we started to leave he said to us, 'Enjoy your trip.' He could see we were on a trip. That was good enough for him. That was all he needed to know.

There were a couple of the local miners in the shop at the same time as us. They were stocking up with milk, cheese and razor blades. The owner showed a modicum of interest in them.

'How many of you guys are working out there now?' he asked.

'Oh, you know,' the more talkative of the miners replied, 'it varies.'

The garage owner nodded. He was well satisfied with that answer. It was good to know that terse conversations weren't reserved solely for strangers.

We left the garage and headed for the Gunbarrel Highway. There was a sign at its start that gave distances to the nearest places. The Northern Territory border was 1,163 kilometres away. Alice Springs was 1,886. Ayers Rock was 1,421, but the makers of the sign had misspelled Ayers as Ayre's.

On the outskirts of Wiluna there were the bleak, square bungalows of an Aboriginal enclave. They were surrounded by a sea of junk and sparkling broken glass. There were wrecked cars too. Why give yourself the trouble of taking your car to the desert and trashing it there when you can trash it in your own back yard?

We drove along the Gunbarrel for fifty kilometres or so. There was low scrub quite thick along the edges of the highway. The sky was a pale, empty blue. The air was hot and motionless. The road itself was wide, rusty red, scored with tyre tracks, yet somehow its surface looked soft and sandy. Certainly it looked infinitely inviting. I felt again that I could drive for ever. But again we didn't. Once we stopped, the impulse was to remain still and silent for ever. I felt as if I never wanted to move again.

We were a long way from home and very happy to be there. We knew that we would not be driving into the full rigours of the Gunbarrel Highway. We were deliciously suspended in the Australian desert, comfortably far away from the stuff of real life, like dying fathers, and businesses that needed to be run, and books that had to be written. It was real pleasure. Sue and I had, both metaphorically and literally, come a long way together. We had both taken a risk in making this trip, but her risk was far greater than mine. I was not at all sure that being able to travel successfully and harmoniously through the desert together would stand us in good stead for the rest of our lives back home, but for now it was enough. We felt very close to each other and a million miles from everyone else. Melancholy crept over me knowing it would soon be over. I knew that sooner rather than later we would turn the Land Cruiser round, head back the way we had come, along desert roads, back to the Budget Rental office, then a bus to Perth and a flight back to England. From now on we were 'on our way home'. The prospect filled me with dread.

We had two days in Perth. We knew that after our time in the desert, Perth might well be an anticlimax. To combat that we planned to visit the Pinnacles Desert, which is a tiny patch of desert on the coast about two hundred and fifty kilometres north of Perth. Photographs of it appear in all the guide books and tourist brochures. It looks completely unworldly. Imagine a standard yellow, sandy desert with rolling dunes, then imagine that great spikes, fingers and stalagmites of rock have pushed up through the sand from the earth's core. That was how the Pinnacles looked in the photographs. It was also comparatively easy to get to. Five hundred kilometres might seem like a lot of ground to cover on a day trip, but Australians pride themselves on driving further than that for a not-very-good party.

Of course we no longer had the Land Cruiser and we had thought we might take one of the several specialised tours that go to the Pinnacles, but in the end we hired a Suzuki jeep, one of the ones that comes with a government health warning since some nerds in America discovered they could be turned over if you drove round corners like a maniac. It was sporty enough and looked like fun, but after the serious solidity of our desert Land Cruiser it felt like a toy.

Shortly before we set off from Australia I phoned my mother. This, thank God, would be the last such phone call I'd have to make.

'How's my Dad?'

'Not very good.'

She said it abruptly, dramatically. She wanted me to know that those three words were carrying all kinds of meanings and overtones, but I wasn't sure what those meanings and overtones were. Before I could ask anything else she said, 'But at least he's coming home.'

'Coming home?' I said, completely baffled.

'On Monday. But he's not very good.'

'Why's he coming home? What does that mean?'

'Well, they're sort of controlling the pain, but not properly, not all the time. And he's so fed up in the hospital. Everybody's dying all around him. He's just dying to get home.

'We'll bring the bed downstairs and they're going to send a commode chair, not that I think he'll ever use it, and there'll be tablets to take at eight in the morning and eight in the evening, so that should be straightforward enough.

'He's so depressed in the hospital. He asked last night who was coming to see him and I said Ken and he said, "Oh no, I don't want him. I don't want him here." And he said, "I'll have to be careful driving the car when I come out." Because he thinks he'll be just like he was but he won't.'

'How about the radium?' I asked. 'Does that seem to have done any good?'

'No. They were supposed to give him seven treatments but they stopped after five. I suppose it wasn't working. I had a word with the sister and she said I've got to take every day as it comes. She says there are far worse things than cancer and I suppose she's right.'

'Do you think you'll be able to cope with having my Dad at home?'

I didn't for a moment think she would.

'I've no option,' she said. 'But I think he'll pull himself together a bit when he gets home. I'll manage. I'll have to. He said to me, "Can I boss you when I get home?" And I said, "Of course you can." It'll be a great boost for him to know he'll be at home when you get back.

'I had a phone call from Tessa. She said she'd willingly come up

and help. She sounded very nice and concerned but I don't want her
to.'

'I don't blame you,' I said.

'Try not to worry,' my mother said. 'He's still alive, that's the
main thing.'

After the phone call we went out and I got drunk in a Japanese
restaurant. There was a sign on the wall of the restaurant that said
they'd be closing for a week because of family bereavement. It was
happening all over the place. There was nothing at all unusual about
sickness and death in the family. Next morning I had a hangover as
we set off for the Pinnacles.

The nearest town is called Cervantes, named after a whaling-ship
that was wrecked there in the 1840s. Early sailors who saw the
Pinnacles thought they were looking at a ruined city, a perfectly
understandable thing to think.

To get there we drove north up National Route One, the Brand
Highway. For a man in search of deserts it seems a totally inappropriate sort of road. Some of the early stretches of countryside that the
road passes through might almost be found in England. This could
be a country lane rolling through cultivated farmland, but even the
quietest English country lane has more traffic than did National Route
One. Before long, however, it stopped looking at all like England.
The spaces became too wide and open, and there were explosions
of tropical vegetation; palm trees and the illiberally named black boy,
a long, black, penis-shaped plant.

It took about four hours to get to the Pinnacles. Once there, signs
told us we were in a National Park. We had always known that this
was not going to be one of the world's wild places, but even so, I was
a bit miffed to find there was a three-and-a-half-kilometre one-way
designated loop of road that provided an easy scenic tour of the
desert. The loop was marked by rows of evenly spaced and sized
rocks, and it opened out in places to make lay-bys where visitors
could park, get out of their car and take a photo of Mom and the kids
standing beside some suitably gnarled pinnacle. Then they could go
home having done the Pinnacles. This was certainly what people all
around us were doing. In fact, when the specialised bus tour arrived
they all did precisely that as well.

The guy who rented us the Suzuki assured us we'd need four-
wheel drive on this trip. This was a lie. The loop wouldn't have
presented problems for a wobbly Reliant Robin. And there were
notices up everywhere telling you not to stray from the loop. It was

hard to believe that anyone was going to catch you if you strayed, but low-impact recreationists to the end, we didn't even think of straying, at least not in the car. On foot you could go where you liked.

The Pinnacles looked just the way they do in pictures. Every pinnacle had a flavour, a visual style of its own. Some looked like termite hills, some like cathedrals. Some were certainly phallic, others looked more like cottage loaves. They varied in size from taller than a man, to smaller than a little finger. Some were almost smooth while others showed complex innards, labyrinths and bur-rowings. Some showed the influence of Henry Moore, others were more Gaudí, while others still, looked like visions from one of those acid-inspired science-fiction illustrators.

The smallest of the pinnacles were rhizoliths, fossilised plant roots. They lay on the sand at ground level. However sensitive we were to the fragility of the ecology, it was impossible to walk without shattering a few hundred of these under foot. They broke with a dry, musical snap.

Fortunately, inevitably, we didn't have to stray far from the beaten track, or indeed from the designated loop, to find ourselves far from other people. In fact, heading west towards the sea and some white sand dunes, it was possible to indulge all sorts of desert fantasy, including that of getting lost. Being lost here would have been even more ignominious that getting lost in Kanowna. Fortunately we didn't do that sort of thing anymore.

We decided to walk to the white dunes. Flies clung to our backs. The sky was dark blue and there was a light breeze coming in from the sea. The sand we walked over kept changing colour, from many different shades of yellow, to cream, to off-white. The tiny pinnacles crunched under our feet. Bright-yellow flowers poked up through the sand. We passed slanted outcrops of layered limestone. Above us, even though it was only mid-afternoon, a sliver of moon appeared in the sky. After walking for an hour or so, the white dunes that had looked quite close now looked no closer at all.

We told ourselves we didn't need a destination. We spent the next hour or two just walking through the desert, just looking, taking a few photographs which we knew wouldn't look as good as the real thing. Despite the smallness and accessibility of the Pinnacles Desert, there was something truly, unassailably, strange and alien and beautiful about it.

Like all good day-trippers we began to think about getting home.

The sun was sinking, the shadows lengthening and making the desert look even more photogenic. But we had a four-hour drive back to Perth and we were leaving the country the next day, and part of us wanted to get back to the dreaded certainties of a hotel room with its mini-bar and in-house videos.

I am a great admirer of Spalding Grey, the writer of *Swimming to Cambodia*, but I have never been sure about his theory of the perfect moment. Spalding Grey needs a perfect moment before he can leave a place. It is the moment, event or feeling, which completely sums up and crystallises the experience he has had of a place.

There seem to me two problems with this. First, what do you do if the perfect moment fails to materialise? Do you refuse to leave and stay in a place for weeks or months, running up a vast bar bill and willing something perfect to happen? Secondly, what do you do if you have the perfect moment within half an hour of arriving in a place? Do you simply turn around and go home? Supposing I had had my perfect moment in the mall in Darwin on the first day: at the very least it would have made the rest of the trip seem a little superfluous. So I tend to think I can live without perfect moments, but that doesn't mean they don't happen.

We walked back to our lay-by and got in the Suzuki. The day trip was as good as over. We had seen our last bit of desert for a while. We decided to have one last tour of the loop. Halfway round we saw a big estate car full of teenagers, and beside it was a Land-Rover belonging to a Desert Ranger. I hadn't even realised they *had* Desert Rangers in these parts. The Ranger had got the driver out of the estate car and he was talking to him good-naturedly but very seriously. The Ranger was delivering a good telling-off, but we didn't know why. Then we saw why. The driver of the car hadn't obeyed the signs telling him to stick to the loop. He'd driven off it and left tyre tracks all over the sand. Then, with great authority and some sense of the ridiculous, the Ranger gave the driver a broom and made him sweep the desert, brushing away all his intrusive tyre tracks.

The guy was trying to look cheerful but obviously felt truly humiliated, which was exactly the Ranger's idea. I stopped the jeep and watched as the guy swept and swept the desert, trying to obliterate all signs of his and his car's presence. It was going to be a long job. I'd had my perfect moment. Now I was ready to go home and see my father.

3

Pink Fingernails and All
The Kingdoms of the World (Egypt)

In one sense I never really wanted to go to Egypt at all. I'm not entirely sure why. I think the main problem was all that civilisation. Not the current civilisation, obviously; *that* I could handle. But I couldn't handle all that ancient stuff; Cleopatra and King Tut, Osiris and Isis, the Valley of Kings and the Book of the Dead. I felt overwhelmed by all that.

I had a friend who had not done much to encourage my enthusiasm for Egypt, although he'd tried. He was called Alastair and he'd been one of our men in Cairo, and had some experience of the deserts of Egypt. I asked him how *he*'d do this trip.

'Pretty straightforward,' he said. 'Buy your Land-Rover in England, preferably the long wheelbase version, drive down through Europe to Brindisi, cross to Alexandria, and there you are, all set for the desert.'

I tried to hint that I didn't quite have the funds to start buying and transporting my own vehicle. Wasn't it possible to hire one when I got there?

'Yes,' he said, 'you can do that, but there *is* a problem. It changes from time to time, but at the moment if you hire a car in Egypt you have to hire a driver as well. It's a sort of job creation scheme. And frankly, I wouldn't trust an Egyptian driver further than I could kick him.

'The real problem,' he continued, 'is that ninety-eight per cent of Egypt is desert, and ninety-nine per cent of Egypt is a military zone. Therefore, any time you stray off the road and get into the desert proper you're almost guaranteed to be in army territory.'

Didn't that create unassailable difficulties?

'Not really,' said Alastair. 'You'll be driving along some dirt road and you'll come to a road block. There'll be a couple of Egyptian soldiers slouching at their posts, half-asleep, no laces in their boots, but with an AK-47 each. They'll point their guns at you and tell you the road is out of bounds and that you have to turn back. The way round this is to reach inside your cool-box, get out a couple of beers and wave them at the soldiers. They'll take the beers from you and wave you through. No bother.'

He assured me he'd done this countless times while driving through the Egyptian desert. But he had diplomatic immunity, I insisted. What exactly would be the position of an English tourist, driving around in a military zone, having bribed a couple of Egyptian soldiers?

'One of our chaps did get shot at,' said Alastair, 'but he *was* taking photographs of military installations. He rather thought that was what British diplomats were supposed to do in their spare time.'

At one point Alastair had thought my trip to Egypt sounded such a good idea he wanted to accompany me. It had its attractions. Yet I feared that he, as the man with the local knowledge, might impose his own version of the desert on me and not leave any room for mine. The hypothesis was never tested. Alastair's wife reminded him, gently but firmly, that his place was at home with her and the baby. A crestfallen Alastair confirmed that she was right.

So I decided I wouldn't go to Egypt. I thought I'd go to Israel instead, to the Negev, a desert that is very easily accessible, even from the holiday resort of Eilat. It was also possible to hire a car there and not be burdened with a driver. Moreover, I had read an article in *National Geographic* about the miracles the Israelis were performing in the Negev, transforming the desert sands into a green, fertile paradise. They were developing plants that grew happily in salt water, and breeding special, delicious-tasting camels that satisfied the local palate. I also read that there were sometimes international conferences on desert usage and how the delegate from Israel would get up and describe the miracles his country had performed, at which point all those pesky Arab delegates would get up and walk out, thereby shooting themselves in the foot and condemning their countries to poverty and infertility. Then I remembered I was reading the *National Geographic*.

Then Kuwait was invaded by Iraq, and suddenly the newspapers and TV were full of desert images, slightly *specialised* desert images, of tanks rolling over dunes, camouflaged soldiers crawling through the sand on their bellies, landmines exploding around them, but desert images nevertheless.

All this was happening in Saudi Arabia and Iraq Radio was broadcasting to the troops in English. One message said, 'Didn't you hear that the sand dunes in the Arabian desert move, and they have swallowed up many people and they will swallow you?' In retrospect it sounds as if Saddam Hussein had more faith in the Saudi sand dunes than he did in his own defences, but back then it sounded like a reasonably convincing threat.

I started clipping pieces out of newspapers, pieces with headlines like, 'Desert War Games Leave GIs Itching For A Fight.' Or 'France's Dogs Of War Beat Rats To The Desert.' Or 'Challenger Crews Get Fired Up For Duel In The Desert.' And when the fear of gas warfare was paramount there was a headline that read, 'Belsen In The Desert' but I thought that was trying too hard. I read about British troops sending little bags of desert sand home to their families. There was the story of a commander who was finding the desert too crowded. He complained he couldn't do any test firing for fear of hitting 'Bedouin Bob'.

The operation, of course, was initially called Desert Shield, a name that never made much sense to me. If the desert was being used as a shield, what exactly was being shielded? Kuwait? Well no, it was a little late for that. Saudi Arabia? The stability of the Middle East? American interests? Any of those things seemed to me to be worth shielding, but it surely wasn't the desert that was doing that, it was the fact that the allies had a massive military superiority over Iraq. Nevertheless, I agree that 'Military Superiority Shield' doesn't have much of a ring to it. The very use of the word 'desert' brings a certain class and romance to a war. Eventually the shield became a storm, and ultimately a sabre, but all that was some way ahead.

All this stuff was happening uncomfortably close to Israel, but for a time I thought I should make the trip anyway. There was a 'Doomsday scenario' in which Saddam, cornered, barking mad, with nothing to lose, would unleash his weapons on Israel, thereby 'turning it into a desert' and turning himself into a hero and martyr of the Arab world. However, I thought the chances of that happening while I was there were slim, and if it did I could always play at being a war correspondent. Then, the weekend before I was due to book my flight, they started handing out gas masks in Israel, to the Israelis that is, not to the Palestinians, and for all I knew, not to tourists. So I thought Israel could possibly wait for the next book.

In the meantime, my editor had offered the opinion that as far as audience expectation went, I really ought to write about the Pyramids. When people think about the desert, he said, they think about camels and pyramids and the sands of Egypt, and even if that wasn't the whole story on deserts it was a bit of the story that ought to be told. So, despite all the civilisation, I was going to Egypt.

The ancient Egyptians, as a matter of fact, didn't have camels. Camels weren't to be found in Egypt until the Persians invaded in 525BC. You might say that's long enough, but even in the First World War camels had to be imported from Libya and India to provide mounts for the Camel Corps because there weren't enough in Egypt.

Cairo is a desert city all right. It has an annual average rainfall of twenty-eight millimetres, which puts it well within our empirical definition of a desert. Gautier tells us that in the thirty-year period between 1890 and 1919 there were thirteen years when it received no rain at all, yet in 1919 it received forty-three millimetres of rain in one day.

But Cairo owes its fertility to the Nile rather than to rainfall. The Nile floods annually and as it recedes it leaves a rich silt which has washed down from the mountains of Ethiopia. Historically this has been good for Egypt and not so good for Ethiopia. However, the deforestation in Ethiopia is now taking place at such a rate that unprecedented amounts of silt are now going into the Nile, more than anyone wants or can deal with. There is so much silt that it's now actually gumming up irrigation systems. This is bad for Egypt, but it's even worse for Ethiopia, which now has the desert where it once had forests.

The Nile has always been a long strip of culture and civilisation, and these days it's a terrific source of bilharzia. For ancient Egypt it was also a border between the living and the dead. Life and the cities of the living were on the east bank; death, tombs, the Pyramids and necropolises were on the west bank.

I had always thought that the Egyptian section of this book would be the shortest. I looked at package tours. Maybe I could get a seven-day package holiday to Luxor or somewhere and from there go into the desert now and again. It didn't feel quite right. Then I saw a package that offered to take me to Cairo one day and bring me back the next. That felt much better. A week's package to the desert sounded pretty banal. A day's package sounded so banal it was good. It had just the right note of absurdity about it. It's also worth noting that the title of this book existed long before the book did. Two days in Cairo would offer a fairly authentic day trip, but the trip seemed appropriate because it fitted the title of the book; the title wasn't devised to fit the trip.

Also, mundane reality, Sue, who was coming with me, found it hard to take time off from her business in November. Christmas was not far away and that was when the retail side made all its money. Bucking goats in bathtubs, men being sheared by sheep, roaring lions who couldn't spell; these were what the public wanted at Christmas, and Sue had to be there to satisfy the demand. Paul Spooner, her star craftsman, had produced a Christmas limited edition of a skeleton flogging a dead horse.

I now knew Sue infinitely better than I had when I'd first invited her to come with me to the desert. We were good at travelling together, and she found the idea of spending one night in Cairo even more bizarrely appealing than I did, just so long as I was sure we were actually going to see some desert while we were there. I tried to be reassuring.

There was another pressing reason why I didn't feel much like making a long trip to Egypt, or anywhere else for that matter. My father had very recently died. My mother was grieving, as, in quite a different way, was I. I felt my mother wanted and needed to see me often, and a long trip would have prevented that.

The deal was that we flew to Cairo at seven a.m. on Sunday morning, saw a mosque and a bazaar, had a Nile cruise with buffet, and spent the night in the El Gezirah Sheraton. Bright and early Monday morning we got taken to the Egyptian Museum and the Pyramids and were then whisked off to a lunch featuring dancing horses (as entertainment, not as lunch). I reckoned we would be able to skip lunch, slip away from the group and wander the desert for a couple of hours before meeting up again in time for the return flight to England on Monday evening.

Naturally I wondered what kind of people went to Cairo for one night. The newspaper ad and the information sheet from the tour operator seemed to suggest there'd be about twenty of us. I imagined them well heeled, with a taste for 'the good things in life' but also with a taste for adventure. I thought they'd be craggy, lean, sun-tanned people who'd been around. They'd have done the rainforest and Bali and a couple of Himalayan walks and the volcanoes of Iceland, and they'd be regarding their night in Cairo in much the same way that my parents might have regarded a day out in Blackpool.

The group was not to assemble until we reached Cairo so we looked around the airport and then the plane asking ourselves, 'Does *he* look the kind of man who'd go to Cairo for one night? Does she? Do they?' We were about three hours into the flight when a representative from the tour company made an announcement allocating our room numbers for the hotel. That seemed a bit strange and it was then we realised that the whole planeload, a full 757's worth, over two hundred people, were *all* going to Cairo for one night.

Of course, it's all too easy to mock package tourists, but that doesn't mean it isn't fun. Yes, we were a checkered crew, mostly couples, and yes, mostly well heeled, far better heeled than I was. And although old and new money rubbed shoulders in the cramped airline seats, the fashion styles were remarkably consistent. The men had a taste for expensive sportswear: tennis shirts, tracksuits, trainers, and they liked to carry a lot of photographic equipment. The women (I didn't understand why) tended to have very long fingernails painted metallic pink. A lot of buck's fizz was drunk during the flight.

Sue and I had fun trying to spot the wife swappers and the wife beaters and came up with plenty of candidates for both. We also speculated on what kind of home-made pornography they liked to produce with their photographic equipment.

By now, people all over the plane were falling into conversation, and it appeared that one-night trips to Cairo were the kind of thing these people did. They 'took off' spontaneously, on the Orient Express to Venice, or cruised the Danube for a long weekend, or flew on Concorde to New York for the sheer, exuberant hell of it. They were 'into' travel, but they were also into comfort, and the men were the kind of thrusting, self-motivated, workaholic professionals who could get a couple of days off work but had trouble getting a couple of months. In that respect they were a little like Sue. I fitted in like a sore thumb.

There was, however, one guy who completely failed to fill the profile, who stuck out even more than I did. He was, for want of a better phrase, profoundly working class. He was a rough South Londoner, but not a successful, moneyed rough South Londoner. He wore a flat cap and a zip-up woolly under his tweed sportscoat. He appeared to have been in a serious road accident at some time and had lost most of one cheekbone, and where the skin grew over it, it was all dried up and looked a little diseased. His luggage consisted of one Marks & Spencer plastic carrier bag, and he wasn't much of a conversationalist, though that didn't stop him talking. Each time an announcement came over the loudspeakers he'd say, 'Wor, what's she saying, eh?' which meant that you couldn't hear what she actually was saying, and from time to time he'd yell out to nobody in particular, 'Wor, look at them clouds!' or 'Wor, it's a bit pricey this do, innit?'

He was harmless enough, but obviously not quite playing with a full deck, and totally out of place. He had a deeply unsettling effect on the sportswear and pink fingernail brigade, and I was extremely glad he wasn't sitting next to me. While he was in the loo and out of earshot, one of the women said very loudly, 'You don't expect to find that sort of person on a trip like this, do you?' If you put that in a novel it would look like crude characterisation but she really did say that.

I was tempted to think he might be a plant, a bit of comic relief, a common enemy to bring people together, at the very least a 'character' to provide material for any would-be travel writers on board. But the facial deformity and the skin disease seemed to be going too far.

I have often been amazed by the extent to which the desert can mimic other forms of landscape. Sometimes it can look like the sea or like snow, and on the flight to Cairo I looked down on to the clouds and they looked very much like long, smooth stretches of sand.

But the desert always takes you by surprise. I was sitting there reading my in-flight magazine and glancing casually out of the window and suddenly there it was: the desert. How long had it been visible? How much had I missed? It was, in fact, the Eastern Desert, that east of the Nile, and from this height it looked very flat. It was a dirty-yellow expanse streaked with paler-yellow weals. Some of these were dried-up river beds, known as wadis in these parts. They made patterns like the subdividing roots of a tree. Because we were in the air we saw the desert through gaps in the cloud and in places it was hard to tell where the clouds ended and the desert began, as they merged together in the haze.

Then there were long stretches of flawless, unscarred sand, followed suddenly by the thinnest burst of greenery before the land sank into the sea. We were above a bay, and across from the fertile coastal fringe, on the other side, was pure desert running straight into the water, and it had formed itself into short, tight curlicues like the tails of a paisley design.

As the plane banked we were over the desert again, flying lower now above a marked, ugly stretch, though I couldn't tell what the marks were. Scale was impossible to judge. There were tracks, but who could tell their size, and there were things that looked like giant worm casts. You could imagine this was a beach and that some God-sized giant had been dragging his toes through the sand, doodling with a stick, drawing designs that made no sense to anyone except himself.

Then there were two dark parallel lines through the desert. At first they looked like a railway track, but on closer viewing the lines were clearly not parallel at all. I thought it might be a pipeline, but then I saw it was actually a motorway, two jet-black lines of tarmac drawn through the sand, and huge trucks were visible moving along each carriageway.

Finally there were the outskirts of Cairo. Before the slums appeared there was a verdant agricultural area, long strips of field in dozens of different shades of green, and it was dotted with palm trees that looked from above like clusters of green asterisks.

At the airport three Kuwait Airlines 747s stood gathering dust on the runways, obviously going nowhere. Tourists were in short supply and we swept through the airport with an almost ominous lack of fuss, and got on to our six air-conditioned coaches, and suddenly we were out in the Cairo traffic. Cairo traffic deserves every bit of its legendary status. Thousands of vehicles mesh together, unhampered by rules, consideration or common sense. We had a one-man police motorcycle escort to get us through it. He had a smart uniform and a shiny BMW motorcycle with a very loud siren. He cleared lanes of traffic for us, beating on the windows of cars that didn't get out of the way fast enough. Sometimes he would ride ahead of us and stop whole cataracts of traffic so that the road we were coming to was clear. He only took two wrong turnings (the bus drivers didn't follow him) and he appeared to come close to killing himself three times getting us from airport to hotel via mosque and bazaar; but that seemed about par for a drive through Cairo.

El Gezirah, where our hotel was, is an island in the middle of the Nile. Cairo lies to the east, and Giza where the Pyramids are, lies to the west. The El Gezirah Sheraton is circular so that every room gets a view of the Nile. Some, I assume, must therefore get a view of the Pyramids and the desert too. We got a view of Cairo. A different sort of travel writer might have complained and changed rooms, though I think he'd have got short shrift from the hotel staff of the El Gezirah Sheraton. I looked down from our balcony on the nineteenth floor, down on to the tennis courts, the basketball court and the swimming-pool and felt I might lose the contents of my stomach. I tried not to look down.

The air was thick with haze; part pollution and part (I like fondly to think) sand and dust stirred up from the Sahara. The mini-bar in the room was empty. Our local tour guide had told us not to drink the water, not even to accept ice in our gin and tonics. The rest of the evening would be given over to the Nile cruise and buffet. The desert would have to wait until tomorrow.

There are eighty-odd Pyramids in Egypt, nine of them at Giza, but six of those are tatty little things, the Pyramids of the Queens, and they show how much status queens had in ancient Egypt. But when we speak in a vague sort of way about 'the Pyramids' we tend to mean the Great Pyramid of Cheops, which is indeed great, about four hundred and fifty feet tall, though its outermost layer has crumbled away like cheap pebbledashing; the Pyramid of Chephron, which is only slightly smaller; and the Pyramid of Menkoura, which is quite a lot smaller, though not nearly so small as the Pyramids of the Queens. These are the three that you see in the postcards and in the ads for Camel cigarettes. Three good big pyramids are good enough for most tourists, and were certainly enough for me.

The mythology surrounding the Pyramids is impressive enough: nobody knows how they were built, no corpse has ever been found in any of them, which is a little strange if they're meant to be tombs, and, of course, there are all sorts of theories about them marking the centre of the earth, or that they were built as landing markers for beings from outer space. Their desert location no doubt helps to foster the mythology.

I hadn't wanted to see the Pyramids any more than I'd wanted to see Ayers Rock, yet Ayers Rock had turned out to be a place of awe and uplifting spirituality (at least for me). The same could not exactly be said for the Pyramids. The Aboriginals have, with the white man's permission and with a good deal of compromise, insisted that Ayers Rock remain a holy site. Nobody is insisting on that for the Pyramids. They have been subjected to all manner of indignity, whether it was as a battleground for Napoleon or as a backdrop for a concert by the Grateful Dead. (The Dead tried to do the same thing at Ayers Rock and were told where to get off.) While I was there, school parties were using the lower steps of the Great Pyramid as a playground and picnic spot. The 'Tourist Police', mounted on their camels, could see nothing at all wrong in that.

The very top of the Pyramid of Chephron has been lost. Its point is blunted. In order that tourists can see exactly how high the pyramid originally was, a metal pole has been stuck in the flattened top, supposedly to the same height as the original peak. Of course, you could tell where the original peak would have been simply by imagining the point at which the lines of the Pyramid's sides would converge. However, this seemed to be some way from the top of the pole. It was the guide who offered this explanation for the pole, and she was not the most reliable of sources. For all I know, the pole may have been a lightning conductor.

Yet for all these indignities, the Pyramids manage to remain dignified. They look solid and immovable, though one knows they are not exactly either of these things. They protrude from the desert yet they are not *of* the desert. They do not exactly have an air of mystery about them, and yet they are definitely inscrutable. They have an irreducible quality. They cannot be explained away. They are elemental and not to be questioned. They are simply there.

There was a road that ran past the Pyramids to a sort of car park, a scenic spot, a place to which you can drive and then look back and see the Pyramids in all their ruined magnificence. You can also be hassled by the sellers of traditional crappy souvenirs. On the way to that spot we passed a number of cars, dusty old Fiats and Mercedeses, that had driven off the road and parked in the sand within sight of the Pyramids. The cars belonged to locals. They were having a day trip to the Sahara, maybe just an afternoon or a couple of hours. The doors of the cars were open and the owners sprawled inside, baking in the heat, looking in the opposite direction to the Pyramids.

You can imagine a time when the Pyramids stood isolated in the desert. Now the city has sidled right up to them. But that in itself produces an extraordinary effect. There is the city, then a line of pyramids, and then five thousand kilometres of nothing, if you call the desert nothing. It also means that the tour bus can drop you off at the Pyramid car park and you can walk straight into the desert while the rest of your party goes off for lunch and dancing horses. One optimistic member of the group thought these were 'dancing whores' and was later sadly disappointed.

The desert here goes by many names. Common sense would tell you that this has to be the Egyptian Desert, which in one sense it is, but to the English who fought there in the Second World War it was the Western Desert, and maps will often tell you this is the

Libyan Desert. However, these are all subdivisions of, other names for, the Sahara, a word that in itself means desert.

Before we could reach the wide open spaces of this desert we had to pass through a cordon of Arab boys and men who saw us as fair game, if not exactly easy pickings. Their line of patter was uncomplicated. They said many times, 'You English. Welcome. Tally ho. Shake hands. You ride camel. You ride horse. You make picture.' And they would then block our way with their horse or camel or themselves. The guys were persistent enough to be a pain, but after the naked, professional, aggressive hassling of Marrakesh they seemed like poor amateurs. We shook them off without too much difficulty.

Sue and I soon found ourselves alone in the sand, the Pyramids behind us, beckoning space and emptiness in front. We simply walked. I'd be tempted to say we walked in a straight line, but I know how hard it is to walk in a straight line in the desert. But at least we knew we weren't going to get lost here. The Pyramids, whatever their historical or mystical function, make a fairly unmissable landmark.

We knew the temperature was high, thirty degrees we'd been told, and yet, despite having come straight out of an English November, we didn't find it too fearsome or debilitating. It was moderately hard work to tramp through the sand but we felt perfectly happy and at ease. The prospect ahead, the 'view', was wonderful.

The horizon was high and more or less straight, the top of a ridge that fell away sharply to our left, sand giving way to the rock beneath. Although there were sand dunes around us, the landscape was essentially rocky, as if boulders were being pushed up out of the earth. It was a scene full of pale colours; buff browns fading and receding, becoming bluer with distance. Halfway to the horizon the silhouettes of two camels made swift, ungainly progress across our field of vision. It was the desert of cliché, but I was not going to knock it.

And then, inevitably, we gained a companion. He was, again inevitably, a little Arab boy, about ten years old. He had a sweet face and seemed bright, well fed, not abjectly poor. He was wearing a thick blue woollen sweater that looked far too hot for the climate. He was puzzled by us.

'English?' he asked.

'That's right,' I said.

'Tally ho!'

We carried on walking.

'I show you Pyramid,' he said, and pointed behind us.

'Wow,' I said, 'is *that* what those things are called? But naw, we don't want to see 'em.'

He thought we were dimwits and hadn't quite caught his drift so he took a coin from his pocket. He showed it to us and pointed out the resemblance between the image of the Pyramids on his coin and those big triangular things on the horizon.

'We know what a pyramid is,' I said, and we kept walking. 'Go away.'

'Why don't you leave us alone?' said Sue.

This was a silly thing to say but it was her first experience of small Arab boys. We walked on further, ignoring the kid, but he followed us at a distance of about fifteen feet. We stopped for a moment and he caught up. Sue and I took a drink of water. He indicated that he wanted some too. I wasn't sure I was doing myself any favours but I gave him a drink of water.

'Now get lost,' I said after he'd handed back the water bottle.

We continued to walk away from the Pyramids.

'Why you go *that* way?' the boy asked, a little frustrated now. 'Pyramids *this* way.'

And he stared out in front of him at the desert into which we were walking and he seemed very baffled indeed.

'What is that way?' he said, a little unsurely, perhaps thinking that we knew something he didn't.

'The desert,' I said.

Now he looked totally lost and confused.

'We're going that way into the desert,' I continued, 'and you're going your way back to the Pyramids. Maybe you'll meet some nice tourists there.'

We kept walking. He was still following us though with considerably less enthusiasm. It was gradually dawning on him that, incredible though it must seem, we really didn't want him to show us the Pyramids. As far as he was concerned that meant we were totally crazy but he still wasn't quite ready to give up. He plodded uncertainly behind us and every now and then we turned and shooed him away.

Sue said, 'Maybe if we give him some money he'll go away.'

I said, 'If we give him some money he'll *never* go away.'

I wasn't entirely sure about that but it sounded reasonable. By now we had picked up an interesting-looking rock with a fossil in it. Sue was carrying it in her hand, looking at it every once in a while. She turned again to see if the kid was still following us, and when she saw that he was, she made a gesture with her hand to wave him away. But she was holding the rock in that hand and it must have appeared to the kid that she was about to throw the rock at him. He cringed, stooped, raised his hands to protect his head. He looked as though he'd had quite a few rocks thrown at him in the past.

Eventually he left us. Once he'd gone I decided he hadn't been too bad. He had sort of amused me. I hadn't found him nearly as objectionable as I'd found the fossil seller in Merzouga. He hadn't threatened to 'spoil' my experience of the desert. I wasn't quite sure what that meant. Maybe I was becoming more cool and laid back, which might be another way of saying that my ideas about the beauty and solitude of the desert had become a little bit less tight-arsed. Nevertheless, as we walked on and found a suitably high place from which to survey the desert, there was the nagging fear that our boy might reappear.

Sue said, 'Are we safe out here?'

'Of course,' I said.

'Mightn't we get robbed, raped, that sort of thing?'

'No,' I said, 'that only happens in novels.'

We walked and stopped and walked some more, then sat for a while and walked again, drank more water, looked for interesting lumps of rock, took a few photographs; the usual stuff.

Photographs of the desert can always all too easily lie. By pointing the camera in the right direction, away from the road or the picnic tables or the beer cans, it is relatively easy to take photographs of what looks like vast tracts of virgin desert while standing in a place that is no such thing. Looking back towards the Pyramids from where we were now it was possible to take a photograph that made them appear utterly isolated in the desert, appearing to grow out of the sand; while another sort of photograph would have shown them adjacent to an urban sprawl, surrounded by tour buses and parties of day-trippers.

But I was having problems with tyre tracks. I could line up perfectly picturesque shots of sand and Pyramids, but in the foreground there would always be tyre tracks. These threatened to 'spoil' the composition. They were stopping me taking the kind of pictures I thought I wanted to take. The way round this was to convince myself that a tyre track in the foreground 'said something' about the relationship between desert, Pyramid and modern, mobile man.

*   *   *

In all, we were in the desert for about four hours. This does not mean that I established a bond of blood with the Sahara, and in fact we never strayed all that far from the Pyramids, but it wasn't bad for a day trip.

It was time to head back, but we thought we had time to scale one more rocky peak. We climbed up a jagged outcrop and expected to be able to look over it and see another stretch of open desert. However, what we actually saw were Cairo and Giza laid out below us in the distance. The desert ran down to a dusty road where it abruptly stopped, to be replaced on the other side of the road by farmland and then the city.

Climbing the outcrop we had heard nothing, only the sound of the wind and our own footsteps. Once we were at the top there was immediately the distant rising noise of a city, and much more insistently, the clashing sounds of many voices calling the faithful to prayer. The voices of the muezzin rose from the city, electrically amplified, loud, sharp, distorted, ghostly, chaotic.

We looked back at the desert. The thick bluish haze softened the contours of the horizon, hinting at an unknown world in that direction, just out of sight. The Pyramids stood above it all, equally softened, but solid, majestic and immutable. If one had the temerity to demand a perfect moment on such a short trip this would have done fine. And in this setting I began to think, as I often did, about my father and his death.

The moment I had got back from Australia, feeling tired, jet-lagged, suffering from some sort of stomach problem, I phoned my mother.

'Hello. It's me.'

'You're home?' my mother said.

'Yes. Is my Dad home from the hospital?'

'Yes.'

'How is he?'

'Not very good.'

'What does that mean?'

'I told him the flight was getting in at half past six and he said, "Make sure the door's open for our Geoff, make sure the front and the back door are open for him."'

My mother told me this as though it was the awful evidence of terminal mental decay and tragedy. I wanted to believe it was simple confusion.

'Do you want to speak to him?' she asked.

Obviously I did. It took a while for him to get to the phone and when he eventually came on he sounded very weak, very tired and obviously in some pain, but he still sounded very much like the father I had always spoken to. He was sounding perhaps a little softer and gentler than usual, but he was still himself. None of the lights had gone out yet.

'When are you coming home?' he asked almost immediately.

'I thought some time next week.'

'As long as that?' he said, his voice betraying disappointment and hurt.

'Well, it'll be a day or two before I get back to normal,' I said.

'You're not ill, are you?' he asked urgently.

'No, I'm just tired, a bit jet-lagged, you know.'

'Good, so long as you're not ill.'

'And you know,' I said, 'I've got some work I ought to do . . .'

I knew I was sounding hopelessly lame and inadequate. I think I was at least partly trying to avoid being overdramatic. Getting off the plane from Australia and immediately dashing to my father's bedside seemed too corny, too obvious, too much like soap opera.

'It's all right,' my father said gently. 'I mean, once you get here we'll have said all we have to say to each other in five minutes, won't we?'

I don't think this was intended to be some sort of terrible insult from father to son. I think he too was genuinely trying not to be overdramatic.

'I can't tell you how much we appreciated getting postcards from you while you were away,' he said, 'knowing you were thinking about us.'

This didn't sound very much like my father. It sounded too appreciative and sentimental by half.

'I was thinking about you all the time,' I said, which was very nearly true.

My father gave me some medical details about his condition and said he felt rotten but was surviving and asked how Sue was, and then he handed me back to my mother. I repeated that I was planning to travel home next week.

'Oh no, Geoff,' she said, 'don't leave it that long. Please don't leave it that long.'

I said I'd be there the next day, Saturday. A far more difficult journey than that to Australia, certainly than that to Cairo, lay ahead of me. I set off for Sheffield at six in the morning, drove up an uncrowded motorway and arrived at my parents' house before nine.

I went in via the unlocked back door and found my mother standing in the kitchen looking much saner and more composed than I had been expecting.

All she said was, 'You'd better go up and see him. Be ready for a shock.'

My father was in the back bedroom, what had once been my room when I lived at home. When I was near the top of the stairs I could hear his snoring, and he didn't wake up as I entered the bedroom. He was sleeping with his mouth and his eyes open and he was a great deal thinner than when I'd last seen him. His posture looked very uncomfortable. His head was thrown back at a strange angle and he was tangled up in the sheets. His face showed pain. His mouth was without saliva and his lips and teeth were coated with some brown sticky deposit from the medicine he was taking. I knew he was bedridden. I knew he was a dying man. And yet I had been braced for a much worse spectacle.

He woke up. He was pleased, though not very surprised to see me. We had a conversation of sorts. I asked how he was and he said 'Rubbish.' He asked how my trip had been and I said 'Great.' He asked how Sue and I had got on and I said we'd got on very well. I said I'd got some photographs to show him and was beginning to tell him one or two things about the trip but he fell asleep while I was talking to him.

That didn't seem very alarming. He was tired and he was ill. I looked forward to him waking up again and talking to him properly. I had bought him an Aboriginal carving of a desert animal and I thought he'd enjoy looking at that. He seemed better than I had dared to hope for. He was still my father. The personality, the man, was still there. I had no reason to believe that anything momentous or final had happened, but it had. My father and I never really talked again, at least not coherently. Something had happened, some switch had been thrown. His prediction of five minutes of conversation had been fairly accurate.

In retrospect it seems to me that he had been holding himself together until I finally arrived to see him. He'd seen me, we'd talked, however briefly, and now he was ready to call it a day, to let go. If I had stayed away longer perhaps he would have lived longer. If I had returned earlier his suffering might have ended that much sooner. It would be nice to report that his letting go was easy and peaceful but it was not. It was not easy for him, and it was not easy to watch, though the latter seems a trivial thing.

My mother showed me the array of medicines the doctors had prescribed. They were mostly morphine in one form or another and I now know that some of them were virtually pure heroin. My mother had been told the recommended doses to give to my father but it seemed that recommended doses didn't mean very much. However much my father needed he was to have. Opiate addiction was not going to be one of his problems. But it was perfectly apparent that the morphine wasn't wholly effective. My father was still in constant pain. One could only assume that he would have been infinitely worse without it.

'They didn't want him to come home from the hospital,' my mother said. 'But he wanted to so much that I had to let him.'

It appeared that a doctor and a district nurse called on alternate days, though, of course, there wasn't much they could do for him.

'Have you thought of asking for a Macmillan nurse?' I said.

I didn't know much about Macmillan nurses, but I knew they were attached to the local hospice, that they specialised in the care of terminal cancer patients and that they cared for the surviving spouses and families too.

'Oh yes, I was offered one,' my mother said. 'But I turned it down.'

'Why?'

'Because they'd tell him.'

'Tell him what?'

'Tell him he's got cancer and he's dying. I couldn't let them do that. Besides, I thought I could cope.'

Saturday afternoon was spent sitting by my father's bed, holding his hand, getting him to take his medicines, and trying to persuade him to drink some water. By now he had stopped eating. He was running on empty. There were still attempts at conversation but he was rapidly drifting away.

I said, 'Tessa sends her love.'

He said, 'Can I phone her?'

'Of course,' I said, at which point he tried to get out of bed and walk downstairs to make the phone call, a feat of which he was utterly incapable.

'But maybe not now,' I said.

He sank back on the bed.

'No, not now,' he said, 'but some time over the weekend.'

'Sure,' I said.

Then he fell back into sleep for a few minutes. His sleep was constantly broken. He would twitch, wake with a start and look around him, disorientated, and say, 'Oh, I thought I was falling.' Then he said, 'That bloke phoned about that car.'

'Which car's that?' I asked.

He had to think for a moment. He gave a long, wide-eyed stare around him. He no longer knew which car or which bloke. He no longer even knew exactly where he was. He was lost, bewildered, frightened, on the point of panic.

'It's okay,' I said, not knowing to what I was referring, and he seemed to be briefly reassured. But he kept trying to get out of bed. He was endlessly persistent and, to my amazement, still very strong.

'Where are you going?' I asked, putting a hand on his shoulder to restrain him.

'I'm going to work, where do you think? I'm going to knock those nails in. I'm going to see to that staircase. I'm going to put that wood in the loft.'

With difficulty I managed to persuade him that he didn't have to go to work today, that he should stay in bed, that he was ill; but from time to time he did need to get out of bed to go to the toilet. He would not use a bed pan or the commode sent by the hospital. So my mother and I tried as best we could to help him get to the toilet. It was very difficult to help him. He couldn't stand unsupported, but even our hands holding him to provide support hurt him intensely. Somehow or other we managed to get him to the toilet.

My father was always extremely, needlessly modest about his body and its functions. Once in the toilet he closed and locked the door. I could easily imagine him being trapped in there and being unable to open the door. We left him alone. We stood in the bedroom waiting for the sound of him leaving the toilet, a sound that would tell us he needed our help to get back to bed. But we didn't hear the sound, and he tried to make it back without help. We found him crawling on his hands and knees, in agony, his thin grey hair matted to his scalp, his pyjamas round his ankles. He had stopped in despair and rested his head on the floor. The effort had defeated him. He wasn't going to make it. He could go no further. This was a man who found the use of a bed pan intolerably humiliating. I thought at the time that seeing your father in this state, knowing how much he hated to be seen like that, was as bad as things could get, but I was quite wrong.

Very gradually, as Saturday wore on, my father lost the ability to speak, or at least the ability to make himself understood. The last intelligible words I exchanged with him were said as he stared ahead of him, his eyes unfocused, apparently staring at the bedroom's fitted wardrobes, wardrobes he'd built himself.

'If you lie here,' he said, 'you can see over that hill, and there are all these people dropping out of the air, dropping into the water, and the water's poisoning them. You're trying to do it on me. You're trying to poison me.'

I did my best to convince him that I wasn't trying to 'do it on him', that I wasn't trying to poison him, but I wasn't sure that he believed me.

Now he slept mostly, his mouth and eyes resolutely open, his breathing a catarrhal snore. And when he woke up and tried to speak, his voice still sounded like snoring. Occasionally I could make out words but mostly it was a thick nasal rasp that had the patterns and rhythms of speech but not the meaning. On the rare occasions when I thought I had worked out what words he was saying they were a nonsensical delirium.

His urge to get out of bed and go to work persisted, would persist until the very end. My mother and I spent hour after hour, initially trying to coax him and calm him down, eventually holding him down to stop him launching himself out of bed.

This went on throughout Saturday night and all day Sunday, a period of twenty hours or so, a period in which he deteriorated quickly and frighteningly, although for his own sake we wished he might deteriorate quicker still so that the end might come sooner and he might be mercifully released.

We knew that since there was nothing any doctor could possibly do for him, my mother and I had to stick it out, be tough and endure the sight of my father looking like a man who was being tortured. We were utterly impotent to stop his pain. By early Sunday evening he was having trouble breathing and we couldn't take it any longer. I had only been home a day and a half but it felt like an eternity. We called for the doctor who arrived and immediately sent for an ambulance. My father was strapped into a wheelchair and taken back to the cancer hospital. He appeared to be suddenly, excruciatingly lucid. He knew exactly what was happening to him and he was terrified. I travelled with him in the ambulance. On the way to the hospital we passed a depot where he had once worked. He said to the ambulance driver, sounding completely comprehensible, 'This is far enough. This is where I work. Drop me off here, please.'

At the hospital there was a private room and a bed with sides, which my father still tried relentlessly to climb out of. There were now tubes in his arms and up his nose, and an oxygen supply, and he seemed to be in more pain than ever.

He was like that for another twenty-four hours, his arms flailing, his legs trying to push his body up and out of the bed, a nurse or my mother or me trying to calm and settle him, to no avail.

By now he was naked under a single cotton sheet, a sheet which he threw off regularly as he struggled. It was the first time I'd ever seen my father naked.

Sometimes he would grab me, throw his arms round my shoulders and pull me to him. It felt as much like a boxing clinch as it did like a gesture of affection, but it seemed to give him just the slightest amount of comfort and by then that was as much as we could hope for.

I stayed by his hospital bed. It was hideous to see my father in that state, but I felt I had to stay there and watch for as long as I could possibly stand it. It hurt me to see him like that but I felt good that it hurt. By experiencing hurt I was sharing, in however slight and trivial a way, my father's pain. It seemed, in some terrible and futile way, to bring us together.

The last time I ever saw my father alive he was in that private room in that hospital bed. He was naked, terrified, delirious, in agony, fighting with me, with my mother, with the nurses, and fighting also with hosts of invisible, hallucinated enemies and demons. He looked like a concentration-camp victim, like a suffering Christ, like a corpse; and he was shitting himself.

I was not there at the hospital at the very end. It was ten o'clock Monday evening and I had taken as much as I could for that day. I was in my parents' house with my mother. The phone rang. My mother went into the hall to answer it. Not long after, she came into the living-room and said, 'He's dead.' We held each other and cried, and I remember saying 'Thank God' over and over again.

My mother said later that we should try to forget the final awful image of my father in the hospital bed, that we should try to remember the good times. I tried but it was hard to come up with any. I mostly remembered the misery of family holidays, of getting a telling-off or a clip round the ear from my father. I remembered all the arguments in adolescence about clothes and hair and girlfriends and staying out late. I realised I had always been afraid of my father.

After some time I came up with one happy image of him and me. After we'd had our tea, both while I lived at home and later when I came home to visit, we'd sometimes sit together with the television on, and he would start the crossword in the local paper. After a while he'd say, 'I'm stuck with this, see if you can get on with it,' and he'd hand over the paper and I'd do what I could until I was stuck too and then I'd hand it back, and so on. That was as far as I got in remembering the good times.

In my father's bedside cabinet I found a pictorial calendar for the previous year. I suppose he'd kept it for the photographs. It was published by the Jehovah's Witnesses. That didn't surprise me particularly. My father bought a copy of *Watch Tower* whenever the Jehovah's Witnesses came to the door, because he knew that everybody else in the street would tell them to get lost. No doubt he'd bought the calendar for the same reason. One of the photographs on the calendar showed a desert scene, of bare rolling mountains, with sun and clouds creating dappled patterns on the peaks. The photograph was captioned 'Wilderness of Judah (View to SW)' and in the centre of the picture one of the peaks was walled, and inside the wall were the ruins of a church. I read that this was the hilltop from which Satan showed Christ all the kingdoms of the world. It somehow seemed very important. I still have the calendar. And as I sat on a desert hilltop not far from the Pyramids, thinking about my father and his death, it seemed very important once again, though I couldn't say how.

At last Sue and I returned from the desert by much the same route that we'd come, through the cordon of those trying to sell us camel and horse rides, back to the Arabesque delights of the Mena hotel where we had a very late lunch and eventually met up again with the rest of the tour. A police escort saw us through Cairo traffic again, back to the airport, and only a few hours later we were standing in London in the November rain.

Despite my lack of enthusiasm for visiting Egypt, and quite apart from the chance to see the Pyramids and the desert, the trip had offered one opportunity I was particularly keen to seize, and that was to see some images of Anubis, the jackal deity, the Lord of the Mummy Wrappings, more or less *in situ*.

The Egyptian Museum in Cairo contains a carrying-chest in the form of Anubis sitting on a shrine. Here he is simply a jackal, not in the half-human form he often takes. He sits atop a golden chest that looks somewhat like a solid vaulting horse, his long tail hanging down one end of it, his paws out in front of him. His eyes, his collar, and the insides of his ears are picked out in gold. It is magnificent.

Paul Spooner, Sue's craftsman, as I've said, uses Anubis's image constantly. One of the simplest automata that Sue sold in her shop, and one of the most effective, was a little model of Anubis, about five inches tall. The head was painted black with whiskers and cold wicked eyes picked out in white. The body and limbs were bare wood, something called ramine, and they were hinged so that the figure could be moved and arranged in any number of more or less comical, threatening or mordant positions.

Long before my father started to be bothered by back pain it became obvious to me that he shouldn't be spending his days in unheated houses struggling to fit window frames and doors. It occurred to me that if he could set himself up in his garage with a jigsaw and a gas heater he could turn out these models of Anubis and have a nice easy retirement, with the possibility of making a fair bit of money if he turned them out at a reasonable rate.

He did get the jigsaw, bought some ramine, and made the first few trial attempts at cutting out the figures. When I went home to see him before my trip to Australia, when he'd first gone into hospital, there were some hesitantly cut arms and legs lying around on his workbench. But he never got as far as completing one. He was already in too much pain to concentrate on the work. Even setting up the saw and marking out the figures had been too much for him.

The figure of Anubis in the Egyptian Museum was far too ancient and substantial and mythic to be very relevant to the death of my father. The Egyptians say that by talking to the dead we bring them back to life, but I could never really talk to my father and I certainly can't now. At the same time I don't have many regrets about 'things left unsaid'.

At Christmas in her shop Sue sold little wooden figures of Anubis wearing golden wings. They were meant to be ironic variations on the Christmas fairy. Sue made them herself on her own jigsaw. She said how sad it made her. Earlier in the year she had imagined that come Christmas she would have been able to ring up my father and place an order with him for an extra few hundred.

Does any of this add up to anything? Do death and deserts, God and Anubis, package tours and Christmas gifts amount to some sort of nexus of meaning? I tend to think that such meanings are in the mind of the beholder and here the beholder was me, and yes, at times these disparate elements make a sort of sense, but not always.

Sometimes, for instance, I think the only connection between death and deserts is that while I visited deserts my father was dying, and that is purely accidental, it is not a meaning but an autobiographical detail. But then sometimes I also think that if these elements don't add up to anything, that's all right too. Why should they?

When I sat in a 'high place' in the desert by the Pyramids I thought about my father. I often thought and continue to think about him, but I specifically made myself think about him then, and perhaps it was only to establish a specious connection between me, him and the desert, a connection that would be good for my book. Sometimes one can be disgusted by oneself in the desert, but one can be equally disgusted anywhere.

4

Scenic Turn-Offs and
Industrial Tourism (USA)

Our trip to the American desert began and ended in Las Vegas. I had no urge to visit Las Vegas but flying there seemed a very efficient way of putting oneself in the middle of the desert, a way, in fact, of putting oneself in a Mafia-run gambling town surrounded by a cordon sanitaire of desert so that its wicked influence doesn't pollute the morality of the rest of the United States.

It was night as we flew in and I didn't have a window seat, but I was sitting next to a Minneapolis businessman who was taking his entire staff to Vegas as a thank-you bonus, and he *did* have a window seat and he insisted that Sue and I swap seats with him so we got a good view.

'This you have to see,' he said. 'I've seen it a dozen times and it still knocks me out.'

I looked out of the window and saw only impenetrable blackness.

'What would I see down there if it was daylight?' I asked disingenuously. 'Desert?'

'Desert,' he confirmed. 'The most barren, desolate, hostile piece of desert you ever saw in your life.'

I wished it was daylight. Then the plane banked and turned and out of nothing, Las Vegas appeared, or more specifically, the lights of Las Vegas; a band of orange and white illuminated dots, like a fairground that grew and revealed its true enormity as the plane got nearer. This was a fairground on the grand scale, a fairground as big as a city. Gradually we were able to make out individual buildings, hotels and casinos, neon sculptures, and such is the central location of the airport we seemed to be landing right in the middle of it all. After we'd landed we were close enough to see our hotel across the runway and the name Tropicana lit up in red letters.

The Tropicana was a fairly modest place by Vegas standards. It only had about two thousand rooms, six restaurants, two swimming-pools, four tennis courts and a golf course. Its real gimmick though was that it claimed to be an island. This wasn't strictly true, but there was a lot of water around, indeed they referred to the place as 'a five-acre water-park paradise' and it was possible to drink and gamble while sitting chest deep in water if you wanted to. But Las Vegas is a desert town all right and a lot of the hotels and casinos have names that use desert images. There are places called the Sands, the Dunes, the Mirage. There's a cheap, sleazy motel called the Oasis. There is even a hotel and casino called the Sahara, but I could never work out how many, if any, layers of irony there were in that choice of name.

To observe that Las Vegas is vulgar is about as astute as noticing that the desert is dry. Yes, of course it's vulgar. That's what it's *for*. All up and down the Strip casinos compete with each other to attract attention. The Excalibur, for instance, is shaped like a fairytale castle made out of Lego. Caesar's Palace has waterfalls and gold horses and sphinxes. The Mirage has fountains that erupt into flame every fifteen minutes throughout the night. Naturally, they all pulse and drip neon and they attempt to drag you inside with offers of cheap buffets and the chance to see circus acts or Tom Jones or the dolphins or the white tigers. If King Kong was captured today he'd be shown to the public in a Las Vegas casino. You couldn't get away with that in a real town, there'd be planning regulations and protest groups, but in the desert it's okay, it doesn't matter. What goes on in the American desert is nobody's business and most people want to keep it that way.

All the excess of Las Vegas is, at heart, a form of advertising. It is spectacle without responsibility. It says, 'Hey! Look at this! Step inside! Come and lose your money with us!' Because the truth is you have to lose your money *somewhere*, so it might as well be in a place that at least has some eye-catching window-dressing.

There are things to do in Las Vegas besides gamble. You can take in a show. You can visit the Liberace Museum. You can do a little shopping. But there really isn't any point going there unless you want to gamble. I didn't want to gamble and I felt like a freak.

Nevertheless, I went into the casinos. They are infinitely welcoming. They are very democratic. It doesn't matter who you are or what you look like, you're free to step inside and lose money. How many times can you walk into a joint that cost five hundred million dollars to build without being asked who the hell you are and what the hell you're doing there?

The people walking into Las Vegas casinos know that they're nobody special. There are a few grotesques and a few exotics, but mostly the town is full of just plain folks who are well aware that losing is their only option. They know they aren't going to walk out of there with pockets full of hundred-dollar bills or as the owner of a new, hot, red sportscar, and perhaps that in some way makes them content. Vegas confirms, what they always knew, that the world gives you precious little and even that little is likely to be taken away from you.

Of course there are stories about little old guys who put a dollar in a one-armed bandit, or a 'slot' as they're known locally, and then win three and a half million dollars. We talked to a waitress who assured us she'd seen that happen. Then there's the story of the guy who walks in from the desert carrying two suitcases. One of them's empty, the other contains half a million dollars. He goes to a roulette table and puts all the money on black. Black comes up. He wins. He opens the other suitcase, puts his winnings in it, and returns to the desert with two full suitcases, each now containing half a million dollars. But Las Vegas is inevitably a town of losers not winners. The multi-million-dollar hotels and casinos are built out of the money that gamblers have lost. If the gamblers won all the time there'd be no Las Vegas.

I stood in the casinos and all around me people were shovelling quarters and dollars into the slots. The urge to conform soon took over. If everyone else was doing it then surely I must want to do it too. Before long I was shovelling in money too. I even, briefly, got ahead, but that wasn't the point. To gamble in any circumstances is to submit oneself to the inhuman laws of chance and probability, but nothing is quite so submissive, quite so inhuman, as playing the slots. You become an adjunct to the machine. The machine demands your money and you give it more or less willingly. At times you feel you'll be glad when you've lost all your money because then, and only then, will you be free of the machine.

The change girls at the Tropicana wore badges that said, 'Ask me about Thursday.' I got a few dollars' worth of change from one cheerfully world-weary 'girl' aged about sixty.

'What happens on Thursdays?' I asked.

'Thursday is my day off,' she said.

My only previous experience of organised gambling was in Sheffield where my father had been a member of the city's two casinos. My father used to go quite regularly, usually alone since my mother didn't have any taste for casinos, but occasionally with me. I never liked it much. We played roulette. When I came out ahead, as I did once or twice, I got no great thrill out of it. When I lost, and I never lost more than a few pounds, I felt violently resentful. I would rather have spent the money on drink or on a book or record, or even put it into the hands of some bum on the street.

I've no idea how much my father lost, or was prepared to lose, but he lost it happily. He regarded it as the price of a night out. I said, sounding humourlessly Puritan I'm sure, that losing money didn't seem like much of a night out to me.

My father left me a little money when he died. I had a vague idea that I might take it all and place it on an evens bet, like the old-timer from the desert, and let chance decide whether I would double my father's money or lose it all. When it came to it I didn't have the nerve to do it for real but I went to watch the play at a roulette table and I mentally placed my bet, my father's money, on black. Even imagining it made me feel nervous. The wheel was spun and the ball careered around and came at last to rest in one of the two zeros. The casino had the rule whereby a zero meant I only lost half my bet, so I told myself I would keep it on black. The wheel went round again and this time black came up, so after two spins I was back where I'd started. I decided I would have left the money on black for the third time. The wheel was spun again and the ball fell into red. It would have taken me three spins to lose all my money. It could have been worse. I might easily have lost it all on the first spin. In some circles that would be called a good run for my money. But my father would never have done anything so rash as putting all his money on black. A run for his money was what he wanted from the casino, an evening's entertainment.

I had heard that Las Vegas was a good place to buy secondhand guitars. The theory was that people were so desperate to keep on gambling they'd even pawn their classic Fender Strat, and after they'd lost again guys like me could come along to the pawn shop and guy the guitar dirt cheap. The theory was wrong. I looked around the pawn shops and found they were full of wildly overpriced anonymous guitars that nobody in their senses would want to buy. As I came out of one of the shops I was approached by a great-looking but frazzled black woman. She was very skinny, young, wore a tight tee-shirt, and messed-up hair.

'I wonder if you'd like to bless me with a seventy-five cent stake?' she said.

At first I wasn't sure if she was saying 'stake' or 'steak'. Even in Las Vegas, a place of very cheap deals on food, I doubted that you could get a steak for seventy-five cents, but I wasn't sure. I looked at her blankly.

'If I could just get a stake then I could get ahead.'

'Yeah?' I said.

'Yeah. I could take that seventy-five cents and maybe I'll get lucky and turn it into a million dollars in one of them casinos.'

'You think so?' I said. 'I think you'd probably lose.'

'You know what? So do I.'

She shrugged and laughed. The thought of losing didn't depress her. I should have given her seventy-five cents, but I didn't. And neither did I give money to the Vietnam veterans begging on the Strip. I thought I'd leave the blessing to the guys who'd had big wins in the casinos. As I walked away from the girl I could hear her shouting after me. I suppose in most places in the world she'd have been shouting abuse, but I turned round and heard her repeat, 'I said, by the way, I really like your shirt.'

There were a few black people gambling in Las Vegas but the casinos were mostly full of the white middle and lower middle classes. There were plenty of black dealers and maids and parking valets and change girls, and I think Vegas believes that's the way things should be. Some Americans feel the need to apologise for Las Vegas. They say, perfectly truthfully, that not all of America is like that, but apologies seem unnecessary. Not all of England is like Blackpool but I don't feel I have to apologise for Blackpool. I think the Americans who apologise for Vegas do so because they fear that this is the real America. They fear that America is not really about civil rights and freedom and canyons and wide open spaces and culture and good books. They fear it is about cheap gimmicks, gawdy come-ons and greed. I think they're right to have that fear. Las Vegas is America's picture of Dorian Gray, kept not in the attic but in the desert.

We saw Las Vegas as a particular manifestation of desert life, but we were not planning to stay there long. Nobody plans to stay there long. Our plan, and it was not very well formulated, was to visit the deserts of California and Arizona, with perhaps an excursion into New Mexico.

Sue and I did many things together but we felt by now that travelling was probably the best of them. In fact there were times when it felt as though travelling was the *only* thing we did very well together. In the deserts of Australia and even in Egypt, our relationship had been concentrated but very simple. We drove, we walked, we looked at the desert. We shared a sense of wonder.

In England there were many distractions, lots of domestic issues; our friends and families, our jobs and our neuroses. Sue's business, like any business, demanded vast amounts of time and energy from her. I wanted to be helpful but had no desire to get bogged down in a world of leases, mortgages, escalating business rates and interest charges. I know some people thrive on that sort of thing but I'm not one of them. Unfortunately, Sue wasn't one of them either, and the person who came home from Cabaret Mechanical Theatre was as stressed, worried and depressed as I would have been in her position. Any kind of change from that exhausting pressure was welcome, and the desert was a huge change indeed.

It's a truism to say that women tend to change their lives to fit in with their men far more than vice versa. Sue often said how different her travels, if not her life, might have been, if she'd met someone other than me. Even if she'd fallen in love with some other writer, it might have been one who was commissioned to write a book about trains or opera. Sue might have found herself travelling the world looking at old steam engines or productions of *La Traviata* rather than deserts.

There are four large deserts in the United States the Great Basin and the Chihuahan, which we weren't planning to visit, and the Sonoran and the Mojave, which we were. The Sonoran, which is sometimes called the Colorado, is the desert of Arizona and New Mexico, while the Mojave is essentially the Californian desert, although a portion of it, including Las Vegas, is in Nevada.

The United States are not, by English standards, densely populated, and the desert areas are thinly populated indeed. Nevertheless, they are all very well travelled. People cross and recross the country, enjoying recreation, making their own explorations, getting to out-of-the-way places; with the result that nowhere is truly out of the way. Compared with Western Australia, for instance, the American desert is swarming with people.

America is a well-classified country. All the dramatically beautiful areas of desert are designated as National Monuments, that's places like Death Valley or Monument Valley. Beyond these are desert conservation areas, desert state parks, designated recreation and scenic areas. Even the word 'wilderness' has an official definition within this scheme of things. This makes it hard to convince yourself that visiting the American desert is going to be much of an adventure, and we were doing other things that were less than adventurous. We would be travelling by rented saloon car rather than by rugged four-wheel drive, and we would be staying in motels rather than camping out. We did want to see some of the great desert sights, especially Death Valley, but we had a well-founded suspicion that a tour round the National Monuments wouldn't in itself be all that fascinating. The real story, we thought, would happen between destinations.

We had three projects that we thought we might complete on this trip. The first dated from the first night Sue and I had spent together; that was to get married in a chapel in Las Vegas. The second was to get a tattoo. The third, the only one that I was very serious about, was to spread my father's ashes in some suitable desert place.

My mother and I had disagreed about most of the arrangements for my father's cremation. For example, she wanted to hold the wake at the Co-op. I thought it should be held at home. My mother thought Tessa shouldn't be invited to the funeral. I thought she should because I thought my father would have wanted her there. I lost most of these arguments. But most crucially we disagreed about what should happen to my father's ashes.

My mother wanted them to be buried in the grave belonging to her mother and father, my grandparents. I didn't want that. I thought the point of having a cremation was that you did away with the grave, you avoided having one place to which you then made dutiful and solemn pilgrimages. Ashes were meant to be dispersed, returned to the earth in a more generalised way, not returned to one six-foot-deep plot. Indeed, the crematorium had a garden in which they scattered the ashes if asked. I would have settled for that. My mother insisted on the grave.

Strangely enough, as part of his work with the council, my father had been involved with maintenance and repairs at the crematorium. I had always thought that when you collected the deceased's ashes it was unlikely that you got the ones belonging to your particular deceased. I had imagined it was a slapdash business and that they gave you any old ashes they had to hand. My father had thought this too, but while working at the crematorium he'd discovered they went to great lengths to ensure you got the right ashes. That was some-what consoling.

It was my job, after the cremation, to go along and collect my father's ashes from the crematorium. I went the day after the funeral and was given a heavy parcel wrapped in brown paper, with a label identifying my father. I had to carry this parcel through the car park, past people arriving for other cremations.

I sat in my car and opened the paper wrapping. Inside was an opaque jar made of gold-coloured plastic. It was shaped like an old-fashioned sweet jar. I unscrewed the lid and looked inside at the ashes. They were coarser than I'd expected, and far less homogen-ous. They were primarily soft, pale grey but there were flecks of black soot and small fibres that were completely white. It did not conform to the ordinary idea of what ash was like.

I had made up my mind about what I was going to do with these ashes, at least with a small portion of them. I had been to a super-market on the way to the crematorium and had bought a small plastic container with a screw-top lid, and a plastic spoon, and I scooped the equivalent of a couple of handfuls of ash into the container. I did it as carefully as possible but little grey clouds of ash escaped and ingrained themselves in my car's carpet and upholstery.

The amount I took was a small proportion of the whole, and I thought there was little chance of my mother knowing that I'd taken any. I had already decided I would take this token amount and scatter it somewhere in the American desert. I didn't know whether or not my father would have approved of this, but at the very least I thought he wouldn't have objected. I was well aware that I would be doing this for me, not for him.

Thus the fiction that I'd talked about so glibly to the people on the truck in Morocco was becoming a reality. I was making it a reality. It would give my trip to America a greater sense of purpose.

In the event, I wasn't able to take the ashes without telling my mother. I felt too guilty. I asked, very gingerly, if it was all right with her if I took them. I was expecting an argument, but she said that was fine by her. I was relieved and very surprised.

I had been told that the only way to get through US customs with any rapidity was to dress like a 'straight'. My daily dress is hardly freakish, but I arrived in the United States wearing a formal jacket, a blue and white striped shirt and a sober tie. My passport still said I was a bookseller though I hadn't done that job for some years. It was true that I still wanted to sell books – the ones I'd written – and there are some countries in the world where it isn't prudent to announce via your passport that you're a writer. Nevertheless, my passport did to that extent contain false information and I saw it was possible for an immigration official to bounce me out of the country for that reason if he chose.

Far more worrying was the jar containing my father's ashes. I had no idea whether or not it was illegal to transport human remains across international borders. I thought it was probably the kind of thing you ought, at least, to ask permission for. I hadn't asked. Once you start asking permission for something you give somebody the power to say no, and since saying no must be one of the few pleasures such people have, I thought it best not to give them the opportunity.

I had imagined a scene where the US customs official went through my luggage and came across my father's ashes. Wordlessly he would open the jar, look, sniff, remove some of the ashes, taste them, offer them to his colleague . . . 'And what exactly *is* this substance you're carrying, Mr Nicholson?'

But it didn't happen. Bored officials waved me through customs and immigration formalities. Nobody questioned my luggage or my profession, thanks, no doubt, to my smart, formal appearance.

I had no specific idea where I would spread the ashes. I thought it would be obvious when the time came. The right location would make itself known. It would certainly not be in or around Las Vegas.

I'm a sucker for most of the pleasures that come from driving a car. I'm not silly enough to believe that driving has anything to do with freedom, but a car gives you mobility and independence in a way that no ecologically sound public transport system is ever going to do. Neither is any public transport system ever going to take you to some wild and lonely spot in the middle of the Mojave desert. There is some pleasure and some romance to be had from driving too fast along open, empty desert roads. This may have been turned into a cliché by too many road movies, but most clichés contain a lot of truth.

In England, any enjoyment you experience from the automobile has to be tinged with a certain guilt. It's obvious to anyone that there are too many cars in England. There aren't enough roads, and attempts to create more of them will mess up the environment still further. You sit in a traffic jam on the M25, you see the poison cloud spreading over the countryside and you feel guilty. In America you can shed this guilt.

Outside of a few urban centres it's impossible to function in America without a car. Everything about the culture encourages you to be mobile, to drive long distances, to use many gallons of cheap gas. If the status quo changed, if, say, gas became too expensive, if people had to give up their cars, the whole system would fail, the whole house of cards, consisting of malls and motels and suburbs and drive-in banks and restaurants, would collapse. You know all this anyway, but it hits you with absolute force the moment you take your rented car out on the American road. You can see with complete clarity why America would be prepared to go to war in order to preserve that status quo.

The America we arrived in was still bubbling with post-Gulf War euphoria. There were American flags in stores and in bars, and there were posters up all over the place saying how much everyone supported Desert Storm. You could buy all sorts of regalia; buttons and tee-shirts and even door mats, welcoming the boys home again. There were signs around announcing forthcoming victory parades, and as a special way of doing the welcoming, yellow ribbons were tied around old oak trees, or indeed any and every other kind of tree.

We spoke to a woman who worked in a cowboy-boot store who told us her son was 'over there' with Desert Storm. As we talked a little more it became clear that she had a rather nebulous notion of 'over there'. Her son, it turned out, was stationed in Oxford.

Every time I pumped gas into our car, gas costing about a third of what it cost in England, I was reminded of the war aims in a way I never had been at home. In America cheap gas was something worth fighting for. But hell, in England we'd never had cheap gas in the first place, so what had *we* been fighting for exactly? Principles? Above all else the Gulf War had been great for American morale. It enabled people to feel good about themselves and about their country. America *had* learned the lesson of Vietnam; that war is a terrible thing if you lose.

Vast areas of the American desert are given over to military bases and test ranges. American soldiers and pilots were familiar with desert terrain long before they went to Saudi Arabia. The American desert had stood them in good stead for fighting against Iraq. These areas are obviously not open to the public. You can't expect to be allowed to go cruising through military zones and I didn't want to, and obviously any country that has a military is going to have areas set aside for their training; but as I drove past endless forbidden military zones, I kept asking myself whether they really needed so much room. We had been told during Desert Storm that intelligent missiles could fly vast distances and pick out a target no bigger than a barn, so how come missile ranges at home had to cover several thousand square miles?

I knew that to really do the desert in style we should have been driving something low and red and heavy on gas; a Corvette for choice. However, we'd booked a Geo Metro, an 'economy car'. But there was some computer problem at the Alamo rental office and the man behind the counter, who was called Chance Meng, told us we were getting a Buick Century Custom for the same price. This was called a 'standard car' and it did seem like just about every other car on the road; big, characterless, power everything, and with the cornering capacity of a bowl of soup. Later we were grateful for the power steering and the air-conditioning and the cruise control, but the Buick was not a car we ever learned to love.

On Saturday morning we set off from Las Vegas heading for Death Valley. If I had one piece of advice to give anyone who wants to see the American desert it would be this: don't go on a weekend. I realise this sounds absurd. However, such is the American taste for the great outdoors that any spot in America which has any sort of reputation for being worth seeing will be packed solid from Friday night to Sunday afternoon. If you visit the same place on Monday morning there will still be one or two stragglers but nothing compared with the weekend. Another option, of course, is to choose places that don't have any sort of reputation for being worth seeing; but we weren't ready for that yet.

Death Valley really is one of the world's truly elemental places. The shapes and textures of the earth are naked and visible. There are mountains, faults, alluvial fans, dunes, and a vast, scarred salt pan. The place is harsh, raw, utterly unsympathetic to mankind, and anyone who has any illusions about the gentle bosom of Mother Nature should start here. To look across the vast empty salt pan and see the jagged snow-peaked mountains beyond, to experience that emptiness and desolation and that heat, is to believe that one is seeing a scene that's a throwback to some time before man, or perhaps a glimpse of what the world will be like when man's gone. Either way one is awed by Death Valley's sheer indifference to humanity, by man's irrelevance in this place.

On the other hand, Death Valley contains several spots where you can get a not-bad dry martini, and on paper at least, that might make it my idea of the perfect desert place.

Death Valley isn't really a valley at all. No river ever ran through here. More correctly it should be called a graben since it was created by the twisting and stretching of the earth's crust. This is 'basin and range' country, though it's hard to think of Death Valley in terms of anything so domestic as a basin.

There are some statistics about Death Valley that can't fail to impress. It contains, at a place near Badwater, the lowest point in the western hemisphere, at 282 feet below sea level. The temperature has been known to reach 134 degrees, not quite a world record, Libya has had it hotter, once. Temperatures of 120 degrees are common in Death Valley. The average annual rainfall is 1.9 inches, but there are plenty of years that get no rain at all. And even if it got a hundred and fifty inches of rain a year, the potential evaporation rate is so high it would still be a desert.

But unlike many desert places, Death Valley is, which is to say it has been made, highly accessible. There are good roads, lots of campgrounds, plenty of accommodation, none of it cheap. There are plenty of signposts, the visitors' centre is excellent. You can pick up all kinds of maps and guides that enable you to drive round Death Valley and know what you're looking at. This isn't all bad.

We arrived mid-afternoon. We knew we'd arrived because we saw the National Monument sign, and the moment we passed it we saw a man walking in the road, in the middle of our lane, his back to us, walking into the vast emptiness of the valley ahead. There was nothing on that road for miles. He was as much in the middle of nowhere as anyone could wish to be and he was without shelter or water. I slowed the car down and gave him a good looking-over as we got closer. He wasn't trying to hitch a ride, in fact he seemed to be barely aware of our presence. He was dressed in denim, a cap pulled down over his eyes, his mouth slightly open. He looked glazed, stunned, a little crazy. We could have stopped and asked him what was up, but, you know, Death Valley is Charles Manson territory. Only a dangerous lunatic would be walking alone out there and who's going to stop for a dangerous lunatic?

People who know Death Valley well reckon that if Manson had remained cool and kept his head down, he could have stayed in Death Valley for the rest of his life and nobody would ever have found him. The big mistake he made was to set fire to an extremely expensive Clark Michigan skip-loader belonging to the Desert Rangers. That was the last straw. Never mind the drugs, the thefts, the kidnapping, the murders, once he'd done that and offended the rangers there was no way he was ever going to escape justice.

There are two places to stay in Death Valley if you aren't camping. One is Furnace Creek, of which more later. The other is Stove Pipe Wells. This was not high season, nevertheless, the only place to stay in Stove Pipe Wells was a 'De Luxe 49-er Cabin'. De Luxe means expensive and 49-er cabin means a hut with two big beds and a colour TV. It was a rip-off but this was our first night in the desert proper and we weren't going to carp.

The name Stove Pipe Wells came about because the well there, the only source of water for many miles, was constantly being covered up by drifting sand dunes, so a tall stove pipe was stuck in the ground to mark it.

Yes, Death Valley has sand dunes; good sand dunes, if not great sand dunes. They only cover an area of about thirty square miles and the tallest is only about eighty feet high. Nevertheless, they are spectacular. We managed to get there as the sun was going down, creating sharp ridges in the dunes and casting one side of them in velvety shadow. We viewed them from a spot known as the Devil's Cornfield. In front of the dunes there were clumps of a bush called arrowweed that did indeed look like corn stooks, and behind them were the mountains of the Amargosa Range. I think it was the most picturesque, if not the most dramatic, desert view I have ever seen. Lots of other people obviously felt the same way and as the sun sank the roadside was lined with people filming and photographing the view.

But we waited a little longer, for that period when the sun had slipped out of sight behind the mountains but while there was still plenty of light, and we took off driving along one of the main roads through the valley and it felt as though we had the place entirely to ourselves. The owners of the motorhomes and campers were safe in their campgrounds and we drove through an empty desert landscape where the rocks glowed with pinks, purples and shadowy blues. And at that moment I could think of nowhere I would rather have been. Yes, we'd be spending the night in this dodgy cabin with pool and restaurant not far away, and yet for a while we were able to revel in the, and I use this word carefully, glory of Death Valley. There was something there that we tourists and all our works couldn't taint.

*   *   *

A lot of work has been done to try to reduce Death Valley to a number of 'sights'. There are for example Zabriskie Point, the Devil's Golf Course and Dante's View. These places are all dramatically beautiful and we wanted to see them. You would have to be a rock not to be impressed and moved by them, but they could all be reached via a good paved road, and they might even all, after a fashion, be seen without leaving your car. This inevitably changes their status.

Timing is everything. It was a weekday evening when we eventually visited Zabriskie Point. It was about seven o'clock. We were the only people there. The sun was low and the shadows were deep and there was a wind blowing that whipped and shook our bodies and wouldn't let you stand upright.

Zabriskie Point is actually just a viewing area from where you can see a range of bare, streaked multicoloured rocks. The colours run from tawny brown to dark grey, with splashes of cream and lime green. The rocks are sharp and crinkled and resemble the twisted backbone of ancient creatures pushing up through the earth. In that light, in that wind, you could feel you were seeing something truly strange and primitive. But had we been there on a sunny Saturday afternoon along with thirty other people, it would have been very difficult to feel that.

There's a rotten film by Antonioni called *Zabriskie Point*. It was made in the late sixties and is about teenage rebellion, police brutality, freedom. It had music by Pink Floyd. It was that kind of late-sixties film. At one point the hero, who has stolen a plane to assert his credentials as a free spirit, makes love to some girl at Zabriskie Point and suddenly all the rocks are alive with dozens of other naked couples all doing the same thing; a whole generation loving each other was the idea, I guess. Anyone attempting to make love in the vicinity of Zabriskie Point on a weekend would certainly get a good talking-to from a Desert Ranger. They would probably also get an audience.

Mr Zabriskie, after whom the point was named, was not much of a free spirit. He had been a banker and an undertaker before he found success with the Pacific Coast Borax Company who were digging borax out of Death Valley. Long before Death Valley was a tourist attraction it was *the* place to mine borax. The aftermath of borax mining is still visible just across the road from Zabriskie Point, and is still very ugly.

The Devil's Golf Course is a large, flat plain of salt and gravel that the action of wind and rain has cut into vast, spiked crystals. These crystals are far too big and sharp to walk over, not that there is anywhere to walk to across them, except deeper into the plain, a plain that's so flat and so wide that as you look across it you can see the curvature of the earth. We stood and were duly awed, and that's about as much as you can do with the Devil's Golf Course. There wasn't as far as we could see a way of 'participating' in it.

We weren't alone as we looked at the Devil's Golf Course. We drove along the dirt road to the parking-area from where you get the best view and found someone already there. There was a small red van covered in stickers showing how well travelled the owner was. The owner was sitting in the driver's seat struggling with a camera and tripod that he'd managed to set up a couple of feet from the car without actually getting out. The guy was grizzled, bearded, grey, and then he did get out of his car. It was a great struggle, and as he emerged we saw that his body was twisted and crippled and that he moved with enormous difficulty. He thrust two metal crutches out of the car ahead of him and supported himself on them just long enough to press the camera shutter. Then he fell back into his seat and started wearily to haul in his photographic equipment.

It would be patronising to make too much of this episode but you had to admire someone who refused to let his body's failings make him immobile. From the outside it was easy to believe that this man saw some kind of resemblance between the gnarled desolation of the landscape, and the similar gnarlings of his own body. Here was someone who perhaps *could* participate in what he saw at the Devil's Golf Course.

Of course I realise the absurdity of going to tourist spots and then complaining about the presence of tourists, and it wouldn't matter what time you went to Dante's View, you would always find company. The curving mountain road rose about a mile from the bottom of the valley. As we ascended the car radio picked up radio stations with increased clarity, and after a long, low-geared climb we found our-selves on top of the mountains in a wide parking-area with litter bins and a variety of information boards headlined, 'Growing Up Dry', 'An Army Of Caterpillars', 'A Manual For Man'. But beyond the parking-area the land dropped away frighteningly and we were look-ing down on the salt pan that is the floor of Death Valley. In places the pan was a gleaming, flawless white, elsewhere it had blue and pink markings and tints, crinkled lines and edges that resembled rivers and waves. On the other side of the valley there were mountains rising two miles from its floor. They had snow caps and their sides were stained by the flows of water and silt that had washed down them over millennia.

The Dante in question here is not some employee from the borax mine, but the Dante of *The Divine Comedy*. However, I'm not sure about the implication that this view is a glimpse of Hell. But there is something ungodly about the bleached vacancy of Death Valley seen from this angle, from this high place. Certainly if the Devil brought you here and said you could have all that you surveyed, I'm not sure that you'd want it.

The particular company we found at Dante's View was a seventy-eight-year-old woman called Nancy. It wasn't all that obvious she was seventy-eight, nor, at first, that she was a woman. That was because she was dressed in motorcycle gear; well-worn black leather jacket and pants, mirror shades and a helmet. The helmet and shades remained in place all the time we talked to her. And her voice didn't even sound very female, being a dry, cracked, metallic rasp.

She began by telling us her age. Then she told us she'd been all over the States on her huge Honda Gold Wing, and that her next trip was going to be to Helsinki where she was going to meet up with a Finnish motorcycle club and ride to Russia to meet Gorbachev, if he hadn't lost power by then.

I wasn't sure, even given the extent of the changes going on in Russia, that Gorbachev would want to hang out with Finnish motorcycle clubs, even if they did include a seventy-eight-year-old American lady. I began by not believing her. I thought she was one of any number of odd old people who engage tourists in conversation and don't feel any need to tell them the truth. She did seem a little strange. Her skin was taut and washed out, and she had some sort of metal plate in her jaw, and she did have this strange voice. However, I could believe she was really seventy-eight, and she was certainly riding a Honda Gold Wing.

She said she hadn't been a biker all her life. She'd learned to ride when she was seventy. Before that she'd been into airplanes. Oh no, I thought, here we go into the realms of complete fantasy, but the more she talked the more it all made sense and the more I was convinced that it wasn't fantasy at all.

She'd been a flyer for Standard Oil before the Second World War, as had been her husband, and when the war started he'd become a fighter pilot and she'd become a pilot of cargo planes, and eventually that was to explain everything. She was flying in convoy across the Atlantic, delivering cargo to Lincolnshire, when a lone, stray Messerschmitt spotted them and attacked. The attack was brief and not fatal but Nancy's plane was damaged and the landing-gear couldn't be lowered. At the airfield in Lincolnshire, aware of her plight, a ground crew spread straw over a wide area to cushion her belly-flop landing. She almost made it, but as she came down she tipped a wing, the plane crashed and caught fire. They got her out alive but not quite quickly enough. Her arms, legs and pelvis were broken, and her face and lungs were burned by the flames. That explained the voice, the skin, the metal plate, and perhaps it explained why she kept herself hidden under leather, helmet and mirror shades.

Now she lived in California, had an apartment in San Francisco and a place in the country that she rented out, keeping just one room in it for herself. But she didn't like California too much these days. 'California used to grow fruit,' she said. 'Now it grows houses.' It sounded like a much-rehearsed line but I enjoyed it. She said if I was interested in deserts I should go to the Joshua Tree National Monument, and she gave me an interesting piece of advice. 'Don't be afraid to talk to the ugly Americans,' she said. 'They're terrible snobs, but once you talk to them they're not so bad.'

Which brings us neatly enough to the Furnace Creek Inn. Of course, most Americans would claim not to know what you're talking about if you suggest that their country is riddled with snobbery and class distinction. The Furnace Creek Inn might have been designed to educate such people.

Furnace Creek is the other place to stay in Death Valley apart from Stove Pipe Wells. A couple of nights in the De Luxe 49-er Cabin were enough. A change would be as good as a rest. So, knowing nothing at all about the place, we went to Furnace Creek. Tourists there can choose between the Furnace Creek Ranch, which is a sort of dude cabin affair and the Furnace Creek Inn, which is a three-hundred-dollars-a-night luxury hotel stuck out there by the borax works. We went for the Ranch. It wasn't a big decision. But the Ranch was full, and the receptionist there said we should try the Inn.

'But doesn't that cost three hundred dollars a night?' I asked.

'Usually yes,' she said. 'But they have a special rate at the moment and we can offer you a double room for a hundred and sixty.'

'I still think that's more than we wanted to pay.'

'Okay, how about a hundred and twenty?'

'I don't know, that's still quite a lot . . .'

'Okay, ninety-five dollars but that's as low as I can go, and that's what it would have cost you if you'd stayed here at the Ranch.'

'Okay, ' I said. 'You talked me into it.'

'You have to go to the desk at the Inn, tell them that Ann sent you, and tell them I said ninety-five dollars.'

The Furnace Creek Inn was built in the 1930s, and Hollywood movie stars would race out there from Los Angeles and spend wild weekends in the desert. Reyner Banham, author of *Scenes in America Deserta*, and a man whose opinions on the desert I generally respect, writes, 'The whole Furnace Creek operation is an oasis of luxury and expensive fantasy that I can get along with – if economic necessity makes my stays as rare as they are short.'

Here he has the advantage over me. I could not get along with the Furnace Creek Inn at all. Or, let's be specific, at least I couldn't get along with the smooth greaseballs who worked behind the reception desk. There were several of these, and although they had different techniques for doing it, they all managed to piss me off royally with their finely honed snobbery and condescension.

The first greaseball we encountered was tanned, fleshy, in a blazer, wearing a lot of gold jewellery and affecting a fake English accent. We turned up looking dirty, sweaty, like we'd been in the desert maybe, without any jewellery, but at least our accents were authentic. I said that Ann had sent us.

'Oh *did* she? I suppose she quoted a hundred and sixty dollars.'

'Ninety-five,' I said.

'Ninety-*five!*' he exclaimed, and he looked as though someone had waved a bundle of used toilet paper under his nose, which oddly enough was pretty much what I felt like doing to him.

Having told us we couldn't park our car in front of the hotel and that he couldn't possibly find anyone to help us with our bags, and that our room was right next to the lift shaft, he wished us a pleasant stay.

The Furnace Creek Inn stands on the bleakest part of the floor of Death Valley, all hacienda-style arches and tiled roofs, landscaped gardens with palm trees and green baize lawns. It looks out over the salt pan the way a riviera hotel would look out over the sea. It does look like an oasis, or possibly like a mirage. It has something of a movie set about it. Seen from a distance it looks like a cardboard cut-out, all façade and no depth.

In the evening we sat for a while in the lobby looking out at the valley, and a viciously strong wind started to blow, bending the palm trees, stirring up the swimming-pool. It was as if nature was

reminding hotel guests that however comfortable the beds and however good the dry martinis, this was still one of the world's wild
places.

Our room was fine, and the barman who made our martinis wasn't
a slimeball at all, but the hotel was awash with stupid pretensions.
However, it was the hotel 'library' that enabled me to sneer back at
the Furnace Creek Inn with a clear conscience. The library consisted
of a small room in which there were four small tables, around each
of which there were four winged armchairs, as though reading was
some kind of boardgame for which you needed a foursome. The
books, there weren't very many of them, were enclosed in a glass-
fronted bookcase. They were rather bruised and tatty, but from
neglect rather than constant use. The pride of the collection was
something called *The Lifetime Reading Plan* which outlined a programme of reading through the world's great classics. None of these
was to be found in the library of the Furnace Creek Inn. Sidney
Sheldon was about as good as it got. There was, however, a run of
the magazine *Arizona Highways* from the early seventies that would
have graced any barber's shop. I thought of stealing something to
show my contempt, but concluded that the coolest thing would have
been to *add* something. I wasn't that cool.

On check-out it took an ageing, bronzed, sporty male receptionist
a very long time to notice my presence. He was deeply engrossed
in a smiling conversation about winter gold packages with two suck-
ers who were presumably paying three hundred dollars a night. I
wanted to come up with some superbly efficient and devastating
putdown. In the event I said, 'Don't worry, I'll carry my own bags.'
I think it was wasted on him.

In the battle between Death Valley and organised tourism I think the
Valley just about wins on points. The signs and the self-guiding tours
and the car parks and the snotty hotel make the place popular and
accessible, and certainly do a lot to make it safe, but that doesn't
mean that people don't die there. Death Valley is too big, too monumental, too dangerous, ever to be entirely tamed. The sights to be
seen at Death Valley are genuinely magnificent and are genuinely on
the grand scale, but if anything they're too big, too operatic, to leave
much room for a personal response. You can't think of Death Valley
as 'yours'. You cannot appropriate it and you cannot love it, and that
is precisely why it is able to survive.

*   *   *

At various times in my enjoyment of deserts I have been a bit sniffy about sand dunes. They represent the scenic, 'easy' version of the desert. They are emblems rather than the things itself. Unarguably they make up only a tiny fraction of the world's deserts. They are not what most deserts are *like*. Nevertheless, the desert south-west of America has quite a few patches of sand dunes and we found ourselves going to several of these.

Death Valley has, as I've said, dunes of its own, but we wanted to visit some that were less well known, less accessible. We wanted to find, I know it sounds crass, some dunes we could have a personal relationship with.

A little way outside the boundary of Death Valley National Monument, to the west, are the Panamint Dunes. They do not cover a very great area. From the road they look like a very small patch of white sand on the lower slopes of the Panamint Mountain Range. But the patch only looks small because it's ten miles from the road. In fact, the dunes soar up to two hundred and fifty feet. I liked to think of them as dunes for the connoisseur. The difficulty in getting to them only added to the pleasure.

As we drove out of Death Valley the main road climbed up and up into the Panamint Range then suddenly swooped down on to a wide, dry lake bed, Owens Lake, before rising up again and disappearing into the next set of peaks.

The lake bed was dry and cracked. In places it was pure white, while in others it looked like old, beige, flaking skin, or like pieces of a completed jigsaw puzzle with each piece curling at the edges. In one spot we found a small circle of wet mud containing dozens of tiny worm-like creatures, twitching and dying as the pool dried out.

There was a sign forbidding all vehicles from driving on the lake bed, which was fair enough, but in true, irritating, California style the sign explained that this was 'to preserve cultural values'.

We drove along the rough dirt road that headed along the edge of the lake bed towards the dunes. The soft suspension of the Buick probably made it seem a much worse road than it really was; nevertheless, it was a rugged ride. After about five miles the dirt road veered away from the dunes towards an old mine. From here we were on foot.

This was not a place you could easily get lost in. We could see the dunes ahead of us, looking considerably bigger now, and we simply walked in the direction of the highest dune. It took a long time, about two and a half hours, but it was still early morning, it wasn't too hot, and we were feeling intrepid.

The first part of the walk was easy enough, over the dry lake, then on to firm, gravelly ground dotted with creosote bushes. There was plenty to see; butterflies, lizards, some coyote tracks, and after about ninety minutes we reached the start of the dunes. The sand didn't appear nearly as white as it had from far away, nor so bare and enticing, but this was only the edge. The tallest dune, the one we'd been heading for, still looked miles away. We tramped on, stopping from time to time to rest and drink water.

The basic advice on water in the desert is that you should drink a gallon a day and that you should always drink before you get thirsty. The first problem here was that a gallon of water is extremely heavy, and I was being a bit of a hero and carrying enough water for both Sue and me. The second problem was that as I took my unfit, short-breathed body up the dunes, I was thirsty all the time.

Even halfway up the dunes we could turn around and be impressed by the sight and sensation of colossal space at our backs. There were mountains on all sides but they seemed very very far away, and at the foot of the mountains, long stretches of desert ran eventually into the lake bed. I was only intermittently able to savour this, how-ever, since dragging myself up the two-hundred-and-fifty-foot sand dune was taking up rather a lot of my attention.

I kept telling myself that the difficulty, the sheer hard work and physical exertion required was crucial to the experience. If one had been fit and healthy and could climb sand dunes with a single bound, reaching the summit wouldn't have been nearly such an achievement.

Sue abandoned her climb about two thirds of the way up the dune, not because she lacked breath or stamina, she said, but because every now and then she looked down and saw that she was already a hundred and fifty feet high and was terrified. I tried to tell her that even if she fell she wouldn't hurt herself. Hell, some people rolled down two-hundred-and-fifty feet dunes for the fun of it. But she stayed where she was and I didn't blame her. I don't usually have much of a head for heights either, but dunes seem not to affect me. Besides, I had other things to worry about. My heart was knocking against my ribs, my temples were pounding, I was in pain from the effort, and I thought I might well have a heart attack. I realised that a heart attack out here would be pretty final. My chances of getting to hospital quickly were not good.

But you know as well as I do that I didn't die on the Panamint

Dunes. After a lot of slightly masochistic effort I got to the top of the dune and sat there looking around me, and I realised I wasn't going to die. I felt great but I also felt empty; not because the desert had in any metaphysical way drained me, but because sheer exhaustion had done the same.

The Panamint Dunes were hardly a 'find'. I'm sure that plenty of people make their way up and down them every year, and I'm sure they do it with more style than I did. But certainly from where I was perched there was not another soul in sight (except Sue), and the rest of humanity felt very far away.

When you sit in a high place, in or above the desert, you tend to feel, in several senses, 'above it all'. You feel, even though you ought to know better, superior. You feel high and mighty. The plebs, the low-lifes, don't get up here where you are. You feel an enormous sense of deflation when you have to go back down to their level. If you're smart you're a little ashamed of these elitist feelings, but if you're honest you may as well admit to them.

While I was sitting on my dune there was suddenly a deep rumbling, a sound that seemed to be throbbing and rising from inside the earth. My first thought was, oh my God, you avoid the heart attack only to die in a massive California earthquake. It really did sound as though the earth might be about to split open, but then I saw the source of the noise. It was nothing inside the earth, and in fact the source of the noise was not in the same place as the noise itself. It was a jet fighter flying faster than the speed of sound.

You might well think that a supersonic jet fighter smashing across the desert sky and making an unholy noise as it went, might spoil the moment, yet it didn't. The speed and power and thrilling loudness of the plane seemed, perhaps curiously, to fit with the experience. Besides, who but a churl or a commie would deny the boys the right to fly and train here? If it hadn't been for training flights like this maybe Desert Storm would never have happened.

One of the best things about climbing sand dunes is that the return journey is infinitely quicker and easier than the ascent. Another attraction is that finding your way back is nice and simple; you just retrace your footprints in the sand. Unless there's a sandstorm.

Being stuck in a sandstorm two hundred and fifty feet up the Panamint Dunes would certainly have made a traveller's tale, but I'm afraid we were down and back at the car before it started. It came out of nowhere, out of a clear blue day, and in seconds the air was so thick with sand that visibility was down to a few yards. We made it to the café and gas station in Panamint Springs, sheltered and ate hamburgers as the sand and wind lashed at the windows and whipped at the café's awning and twisted and bent its trees.

Towards the end of the trip we visited the Kelso Dunes in the Devil's Playground, which have a reputation for 'singing'. You are supposed to climb to the top of a dune, push some sand down the leeward side, and as the sand falls it should make a singing noise. I'd been told that conditions had to be just right before this happened so I hadn't got my hopes up too high.

I got to the top of a dune, a highish one, again Sue had given up along the way, and I threw some sand down what I took to be the leeward side. There was no singing. So I jammed my foot into the face of the dune to cause a small avalanche; and to my utter amazement a deep, eerie noise stirred inside the dune. I'm not sure you could call it singing exactly. It was something of a moan, something like a fart, something like an elephant's trumpeting. It was strange and yet it was comical.

When it was time to come down the dune I ran down this long, steep, leeward face. My feet plunged a foot or so into the sand and each step created this loud, laughably mournful sound. It was as if the sand was talking, groaning at me, responding badly to each step I took. It was truly mysterious but it was fun, and perhaps by then I had learned not to be so sniffy about sand dunes.

It was an easy drive from Panamint Springs to Manzanar, the site of one of the notorious 'relocation centres' used for Japanese Americans, or Nisei as they were known, in the Second World War. Sometimes these relocation centres are called concentration camps.

The story of how America treated its Japanese and Japanese-descended inhabitants after Pearl Harbor (many of whom were US citizens) becomes increasingly well known as it recedes into history. They were rounded up and packed off to camps, usually in the desert. The camps tended to be 'sand and cactus sites' and the literature frequently refers to them as 'godforsaken spots'. The idea is that God is not present in the desert. And just as the desert protects godly citizens from the evils of Las Vegas, so it was to protect them from the evils of the Japanese.

Although the internees were mostly from California they were dispersed to camps in Arizona, Utah, New Mexico and Nevada, as well as to a few non-desert states. These states weren't always keen on being used as a dumping ground for what they took to be California's problem. However, it was soon discovered that wherever a camp was built, government dollars soon gave rise to small, localised economic booms. The camps cost five million dollars to build and five million dollars annually to run. This represented big economic activity in a sand and cactus site.

Today Manzanar is on the main tourist drag between Mojave and Bishop. This is serious recreational territory. Traffic screamed up and down that road hauling trailers full of motorbikes and speedboats, jet skis and just plain ordinary skis. This is a place to have a good time. Independence and Lone Pine, which are Manzanar's neighbouring towns, are green, fertile places. Manzanar, however, is pale, dry, dusty desert. That's because in 1919 the city of Los Angeles bought Manzanar. They didn't want it for itself, but for its water. It had plenty back then, enough to support a decent agricultural community, but Los Angeles wanted the water for its own needs and took it all away by aquaduct. Manzanar turned into desert, and that's how it was when the Japanese arrived, and how it still is today.

However, it was hard to think of Manzanar as an entirely godforsaken place, tucked in as it is between two beautiful sets of mountains; the Panamints and the Sierra Nevada. Ansel Adams, who was a friend of the camp's second director, found it scenic enough to want to photograph it in 1943. He wrote:

> I believe that the arid splendour of the desert, ringed with towering mountains, has strengthened the spirit of the people of Manzanar. I do not say all are conscious of this influence, but I am sure most have responded in one way or another to the resonance of their environment.

This sounds like bullshit to me. I suppose, all else being equal, you might as well be locked up in a place that's pretty rather than in a place that's ugly. I like to think I'm someone who responds positively to the 'resonances' of the desert, but I also think that the resonances of being a captive behind barbed wire might dull my appreciation of Manzanar's arid splendour.

There isn't a lot to see at Manzanar these days, although that which remains has been artfully preserved. Guilt might have been assuaged by getting rid of the camp completely, clearing away the barbed wire and the stones that were foundations for the camp's huts. However, it has all been left as a grim reminder, and I think you have to find that admirable.

The building that used to be the camp auditorium is now the Inyo County Equipment Shop. It is fenced off, and inside the fence there are cars and trucks and machinery belonging to the county, and there is an inscrutable sign on the wall of the building that says, 'Please Park Outside' as though in the past a lot of people tried to park *inside* the building.

One photograph by Ansel Adams shows an elaborate garden built at Manzanar. In the photograph there is a log bridge, a pergola and a pond. We saw no bridge, pergola or pond, but there was a flowerbed. It was contained by a circular stone wall, perhaps twelve feet in diameter and two feet high. Desert scrub grew equally happily inside and outside the bed, but someone had used their finger to write in the mortar of the wall while it was still wet. The inscription said, 'Made by Wada and crew June 19, 1942 AD.'

There were two sentry boxes still standing. They were built in quasi-Japanese style, and it seemed odd that anyone would have concerned themselves with such architectural detailing at the time the camp was built, but the boxes appear in an Adams photograph looking much as they do today.

If nothing else, the experience of imprisoning 110,000 nisei has created a wonderful opportunity for retrospective self-flagellation. A metal sign on one of the sentry boxes said, 'May the injustice and humiliation suffered here as a result of hysteria, racism and economic exploitation never emerge again.' The sign was erected by the local department of parks and recreation. If there had been 110,000 Iraqis living in California at the time of Desert Storm the effectiveness of the wishes expressed on the sign could have been properly tested.

We spent the evening in Lone Pine and sat in Jake's Bar drinking draft Bud and watching a badly tuned TV set. We saw on the news that earlier that day in Los Angeles scores of American children had painted a 'peace scroll' to send to 'the children of Iraq'. It would have been pointless to ask *which* children of Iraq, or to wonder how Iraqi children of any sort would react to a painting three feet high and several hundred feet long, that depicted American aircraft and exploding bombs interspersed with wobbly peace symbols.

But we needn't have worried. The voice-over explained that the real purpose of the painting was to act as therapy, to help relieve the stress those poor Los Angeles children had suffered as a result of the Gulf War.

The Interstate 40 heading east from Kingman to Flagstaff in Arizona could be used to demonstrate how rain-shadow deserts are created. Kingman is certainly dry and desert-like but the land rises to the east and the scenery gets greener and greener, and by the time you're in Flagstaff you're up among lush pastures and pine trees and we even saw patches of snow. But once you're past Flagstaff, you're over the mountains, the road starts to descend and you're in the rain shadow and therefore in the desert. All the rain has fallen on the western side of the mountain and you're in a landscape of wide, flat, dry, plains dotted with pale-blue buttes, mesas and triangular peaks.

It was around here that we began to pick up Navajo radio stations. Some were broadcasting entirely in the Navajo language. Others played Country and Western songs and in between them the announcements and commercials came in both Navajo and English. At least that's what I assume was going on. A male voice would be speaking Navajo, lots of 'h' and 'k' sounds, but every now and again you could pick out words like Chevrolet or Furniture Warehouse.

There were also in English, radio ads for the Adobe Grill in Flag-staff and for their 'stress-management happy hour'. I think this just might have been a joke. There were also ads for a series of education tapes called 'Hooked on Phonics' which promised to give you a 'dyna-mite vocabulary'. These people definitely weren't joking at all. And as I was listening to the ad we were overtaken by a pick-up truck. It was towing a trailer on which there was a fifteen-foot-tall plaster head of a shark; jaws wide open, teeth exposed, fresh air wafting through the mouth. And I thought, yes, that's exactly the sort of thing you see in the desert.

The joy of it, of course, is that once you've seen it, it's gone. The best guide book in the world couldn't tell you how to have that experience. Whereas, with Monument Valley, for instance, to which we were now heading, though not very quickly or directly, just about any guide book can tell you what you're likely to see and experience there. And that was pretty much what we were going to see and experience too.

Monument Valley is cowboy-movie country. John Ford used it as a location for nine of his movies. When the cavalry comes to the rescue in *Stagecoach* they charge right between two of the most picturesque buttes. They wouldn't get away with it these days.

There's a theory that John Wayne developed cancer because he spent too much time filming in the desert and was exposed to deadly amounts of radiation, the fall-out left over from desert testing of nuclear weapons. I enjoy a conspiracy theory as much as the next man, but it seems to me unnecessary in John Wayne's case. As my father had proved, you didn't need hidden radiation sources in order to get cancer. You can get cancer by smoking sixty cigarettes a day like John Wayne did. You can still get cancer even if you don't.

We spent a night at Winslow, a place that sometimes describes itself as 'thirty miles from nowhere and two miles from Hell', but that makes it sound a lot more interesting than it really was. A lot of the motels there had signs up saying they were 'American owned' by which they meant that they weren't owned by native Indians.

Monument Valley is on Navajo land, and to get there from Winslow we needed to pass through both Navajo and Hopi Indian reservations; the Hopi reservation being a large square within the much larger rectangle of the Navajo reservation. Border disputes are common and cost the American government a wad of money to sort out.

The Navajos and the Hopis live very differently in the desert. The Navajos live on the low plains, plains just green enough to sustain a few skinny cattle and horses. The Hopis live on top of three high mesas, separated from the plains by sheer six-hundred-foot cliffs, whose chief function historically was to protect the Hopis from the warring Navajos. The Navajos were once semi-nomadic and even now they like to live well apart from their neighbours. Dwellings are scattered thinly but evenly through the reservation, far enough away from each other that you wouldn't have to worry about your next-door neighbour throwing a noisy party. The Hopis, however, cluster together in tight little villages where it would appear that your neighbour is aware of your every move, and you of his.

We visited the Hopi Cultural Centre and had lunch in the restaurant there that was the sort of place you might find in any mall in America; except that ninety per cent of the customers were Hopis. I admit I was surprised by this. I hadn't expected to find Hopis in the Hopi Cultural Centre any more than you'd expect to find British people in the British Museum. But there they were, and some of them were eating traditional Hopi food, which specialises in beans and fried bread, although more were eating from the all-American salad bar. And although the Hopis have unmistakable physical and facial characteristics, they were dressed, they talked and behaved like mall visitors everywhere.

After we'd eaten we drove a few miles beyond the Cultural Centre and pulled off the road. We were on a rim, the edge of one of the Hopi mesas, the one known, unromantically, as Second Mesa. Much of the Indian land had been fenced, but not here. We were able to get out of the car, walk to the mesa edge and look over the land. It was like being in the upper circle of a theatre, in the 'Gods'. Cracked rocks fell abruptly, treacherously down to the Navajo lands below. Away to our left a car had come off the mountain road and lay on its back some way down the cliff face. We sat there for a long time just looking. You couldn't claim this was a great beauty spot. It certainly wouldn't have been worth erecting one of those signs saying 'Viewpoint'. And yet we enjoyed the spaciousness, the peace and tranquillity of the place in a way that I had a shrewd idea we weren't going to enjoy Monument Valley.

I felt a considerable sense of intrusion at being on the Indian reservation at all. There was no denying that we were there to gawp, although I was gawping at the desert rather than at the Indians living on it. But intruder or not, I was determined to drive up and down a few dirt roads in search of something to write about. We headed for a place called Dinnebito. We had no particular reason for going there. I just had a hunch it might be interesting. Sometimes these hunches pay off, but not in Dinnebito. The place had some shacks, some trailers, some old cars, some new pick-up trucks, an Indian 'boarding school'. Two glaring young Indians crossed the road very slowly in front of the car, playing a game of slow-motion chicken. Would I stop to let them cross? Would I swerve round them at speed? Would I, always a possibility, simply run them down? They looked as though it was all the same to them.

We left Dinnebito without stopping and drove on via Tuba City to Kayenta, a place that is known as the Gateway to Monument Valley. All the way there the scenery offered suggestions, slight impersonations, of Monument Valley, tall blue and red buttes rising out of the flat beige desert.

I phoned my mother from the motel in Kayenta. This too was a form of impersonation, it had echoes of the phone calls I'd made from Australia. This time we didn't have so much to talk about. There were no urgent reports on my father's condition, no latest bulletins from the hospital.

When I was twenty-one I spent four months travelling round the United States and never phoned home at all, just sent my parents a few terse postcards. Now, pushing forty, I phoned my mother every other day when I was at home, and even in the American desert I felt a duty to call home at least once a week. When I was young I imagined that as I got older I would become increasingly free of my parents. That hadn't happened. Now that my mother was a widow I felt an enormous, and not unwilling, duty to her. And death certainly didn't have anything to do with freedom. When my father was alive I phoned home regularly enough, but between calls I didn't think of him much. There was no reason to. I knew what he'd be doing; going to work, growing runner beans, tinkering with his car. Now that he was dead I thought about him all the time.

So I asked my mother about the weather and about the garden and if she'd done anything interesting. She said she hadn't been able to do any gardening because it had been raining. Of course, she had never done any gardening at all while my father was alive. Now it was an 'interest' for her. Before leaving for the States I'd been home to plant some perennials and to sow some seeds; California and Arizona poppies. I suppose I was hoping to bring a bit of desert to the suburbs of Sheffield. My mother assured me that she never did anything interesting these days, but I wasn't sure that she ever had.

Monument Valley is, in one sense, very easy to see. You can see it very clearly from many miles away and it looks pretty much the way you expect it to; giant columns, hands, fingers of craggy rock pointing up at the sky. But most of us want to see it at close range. There was a two-dollar entry charge to get inside the area designated as National Monument. There was a visitors' centre from which you could take archetypal photographs of the valley. There was a souvenir shop and a cold drinks machine and some stalls selling Indian souvenirs. There was a seventeen-mile loop drive around the various buttes and pinnacles, and you could stop your car here and there and take slightly less archetypal photographs. Some Navajos would take you on bus trips around the loop and get you to places that were forbidden to ordinary self-driving tourists. We didn't want to take the bus tour. We weren't even sure that we wanted to drive round the loop. We'd have been happy to just go for a walk, but you couldn't even go walking unless you had a Navajo guide.

So we thought, since we were there we'd do a quick circuit of the loop and then get out of Monument Valley and look for a more interesting dirt road. There was everything to suggest that the loop, although unpaved, was an easy enough excursion even in a Buick Century. This was not the case. The road was rough, potholed, difficult, in some places downright dangerous. The amount of concentration needed to get round without plunging into craters or getting stuck in sand, or piercing the underside of the car on some sharp boulder didn't leave much scope for appreciating the view. The loop was also supposed to be one-way, but nobody seemed to have told the drivers of the Navajo buses that.

The absolute nightmare high point of all this was negotiating the car up a steep incline into a blind corner with a thirty-foot drop and no fencing. You had to make sure you had enough speed to prevent getting stuck in the soft sand, while at the same time trying to stop the wheels skidding and taking you over the edge. Personally I was wrestling too hard with the car to realise how petrified I was. Sue, as helpless passenger, had to be petrified for both of us. When she tells the story now she says she was 'wet with fear'. She says she felt absolutely certain we were going to be hit by a bus coming round the blind corner and that we'd plunge over the edge and die in a ball of flame. It's one thing to do this in some uncharted bit of desert. In the scenic loop round a National Monument we thought it was a bit much. At various points of the loop there were little dead-end roads you could drive down. These were signposted as scenic turn-offs, a change, I suppose, from scenic turn-ons.

The Navajos grazed their sheep through Monument Valley. When we came across an Indian shepherdess and her flock it almost appeared that she and they had been deliberately placed to give the scene an extra picturesque detail, like swains in an Augustan landscape. However, there was an Indian camp at the base of one of the buttes that was wretched and slummy and was anything but picturesque. They sold jewellery and crafts and they had signs up saying 'No Photography', though why anyone would want to take photographs of a wretched, slummy Indian camp I don't know. Several photography enthusiasts I spoke to agreed it was a scenic turn-off.

Tell an Englishman you're writing a book about deserts and he'll say it sounds like hard work because surely there's nothing there in the desert to write about. Tell an American and he'll say be sure to see the Kelso Dunes and Death Valley and Monument Valley. The American imagines the desert as a series of visual events, whereas the Englishman imagines it as an emptiness. Of course, the Englishman is likely to be less familiar with deserts than the American, but I suspect it is my Englishness that makes me enjoy precisely that emptiness. Monument Valley was positively crammed with visual events, far too many. It didn't feel like the real desert at all.

There was also, of course, no shortage of people at Monument Valley, but by now that didn't really surprise me. Edward Abbey, the author of *Desert Solitaire*, has a lot to say about what he calls 'industrial tourism'. He is against it, which is perhaps to say that he is broadly against people; an attitude that is not uncommon among desert enthusiasts. I would agree that there are far too many people in the desert, but of course I'm one of them. Abbey would probably have disapproved of me and my activities, but Abbey too was a person cluttering up the desert. There is a perfectly logical position that says if you really love the desert you shouldn't go there. But most of us aren't that logical.

Abbey was writing in the late sixties. I'm sure things have got worse since his day, but the principles of tourism in America continue much as he knew them. The current thinking is that above all else the great American beauty spots should be accessible. There should be a paved road, helpful rangers, maps, a short self-guided scenic drive, all the things that enable visitors to 'see' the place with the minimum of fuss and exertion and in the least possible time.

Abbey is not a great believer in accessibility. He suggests there should be a kind of self-selection based on the inaccessibility of great desert places. If in order to see Monument Valley, you had to drive along thirty-five miles of dirt road, then hike for a couple of hours, the number of visitors would drop dramatically. This would save wear and tear on the place and, much more importantly, it would change the relationship between the people and the places they visit. This seems to me undeniable. Undoubtedly I enjoyed the Panamint dunes far more than I enjoyed the dunes of Death Valley, and that had a lot to do with the fact that it was a real effort to get to them. And the simple fact is, people are more appreciative of things when they've expended a little effort over them.

Abbey was a Desert Ranger and no doubt he saw the worst of desert tourism, just as barmen see the worst of drinkers and as booksellers for that matter see the worst of book buyers. But I met a few rangers who were not exactly depositories of sensitivity and earthly wisdom either. A typical exchange between ranger and tourist would have the ranger saying, 'How long have you got? A couple of hours? Then you should do the two hours' scenic drive.' Perhaps this is inevitable, but not once did I hear a ranger tell anybody that they should go to a bleak lonely place and contemplate the higher mysteries.

It comes down, I think, to the question of what it is we are meant to *do* with landscape, with places of great natural beauty. In one sense there is nothing to do. Beauty is useless. Most of us simply want to look. We might want to walk through an interesting-looking valley, we might want to take photographs, but that isn't really doing anything. It's much harder to interact with a desert than it is with Disneyland. At Disneyland there's lots to do, and for a whole class of tourists Disneyland and Monument Valley are equivalent attractions.

I tend to agree with Abbey that you can't see a place simply by driving there, parking, taking a ten-minute look and then going home. I think this is a fairly Philistine response to landscape, but then I'm the kind of elitist who would think that, aren't I?

No, you can't see Death Valley or Monument Valley in ten minutes, but you can't see them in a couple of days either. It takes years, maybe a lifetime to 'see' these places fully. It might be Fascist to suggest that some people are never going to be capable of seeing these places properly, but at the moment even the ones who might be capable are having their chances spoiled. Good roads, clean rest rooms, visitors' centres, scenic loops, seem to obstruct the view every bit as much as a solid brick wall would.

At the end of *Stagecoach* John Wayne gets the girl and together they ride off into the desert, and one of the bystanders who's watching them go says, 'Well, that's saved them from the blessings of civilisation.' For the rest of us, I think, it's already too late to be saved.

Of course, there was no question of scattering my father's ashes at Monument Valley. It was far too 'public' a place. If anyone had seen me depositing them here, they would probably have reported me for littering or polluting the precious desert environment.

My enjoyment of the desert, it will be obvious by now, doesn't have much to do with a love of nature. In fact, it was the absence of flora and fauna that first attracted me. But this absence is, of course, illusory. If you know where and how to look, the desert is absolutely full of life. You can find all kinds of publications with titles like *Our Living Desert* that confirm this, and the desert is a wildlife-documentary maker's idea of heaven. What I especially like is the fact that in the desert, nature takes on outlandish forms. Camels and kangaroos, road runners and horned lizards have a compelling quality to them that English wildlife just doesn't have. The horned lizard is one of my American favourites. It defends itself by squirting blood out of its eyes into the eyes of predators. Inventive huh? However, if there's one thing that symbolises the American desert more than anything else, it has to be the cactus.

I have read, and I find this hard to believe, that each of America's mainland states has a native cactus. I find it hard to envisage what kind of cactus is native to New Jersey, but it was in a book so it might well be true. Certainly cacti hybridise like crazy, so the number of different varieties is colossal. However, when I think of a cactus I think of one of those with a tall central trunk with two arms sticking out of the sides and curling upwards; the kind of cactus you see in cartoons and on menus in Mexican restaurants. It is called the saguaro.

One of the great things about cacti is that their names often describe them quite accurately. The barrel cactus looks like a barrel, the pin-cushion cactus looks like a pin cushion. There's the fish-hook cactus, the organ-pipe cactus, the hedgehog cactus, the prickly pear. I got reasonably good at identifying these, but none of them is as appealing as the saguaro.

The saguaro lives in Arizona and northern Mexico, and in small numbers in California. Its flower is Arizona's state flower. I think, however, it owes its symbolic status to its sheer size and character. It can be very big indeed, up to fifty feet tall, it can live to be two hundred years old, and most important of all, it can appear intensely human.

We were driving south from Sedona to Phoenix when we saw a sign for a place called Bumble Bee, and suddenly the hills were full of saguaros. They looked like human beings, standing on the slopes peering over each other's shoulder to get a better look at what was going on down in the valleys.

We had thought we might stay in Phoenix and do some city things, but when we saw the size and complexity of the place we just couldn't be doing with it. We decided to head east out of town to the desert along a road labelled, slightly mysteriously, the 60/89. Its mysteries remained intact as far as we were concerned. My memories of Phoenix are of driving for several hours through urban congestion, getting tangled up in airport approach roads, finding several places that sold nothing but used hubcaps, and in some despair taking a road called University Avenue, which seemed to be going more or less where we wanted to go. University Avenue ran for about thirty miles. When it began it was strictly, densely urban. There were tall apartment blocks which eventually gave way to suburban houses, which in turn gave way to trailer parks. It also became increasingly desert-like or at least the emblems of the desert became more insistent. The cacti in the gardens got bigger and bigger. There were seven-foot-high prickly pears, then ten-foot-tall chollas, then fifteen-foot saguaros.

We drove, for no good reason, to a place called Superior. Superior to what I don't know. Along the way all the hills and mountains were crowded with saguaros, but Superior was almost above the saguaro line. It was a town that had seen better days. In the main street were closed-down motels and laundries and auto-part stores, and someone had gone berserk with a spray can on all the boarded-up buildings. On one he'd sprayed a magic mushroom and the face of a hippy smoking a joint, and he'd been up on the roof of the Hamburger King and where the sign showed a cute cartoon chef carrying a burger, he'd sprayed out his eyes and had written 'All U Can Eat'.

Our motel in Superior was very popular with the local copper miners. They obviously liked soft, shapeless beds, crumbling stucco walls and badly tuned TV sets. There was a call box outside our door and there was a miner shouting down the phone, 'I need a good lawyer, and I need him now!'

Superior's main attraction for us was its proximity to the Boyce Thompson Southwestern Arboretum, a thirty-five acre patch of cultivated desert that makes an ideal primer on desert flora. A lot of this kind of priming goes on. In Tucson there's the Sonora Desert Museum, and in Phoenix there's the Desert Botanical Gardens, scene of the annual Phoenix DesertFest. There was nothing at all wrong with the Boyce Thompson Southwestern Arboretum. There were more cacti and succulents than you could ever wish to see in one lifetime, all clearly labelled and well displayed. It was educational. We learned things. It was good background for my book. But, I don't know, I found it fairly depressing. It wasn't the arboretum's fault. I think it was the combination, the accumulation of ersatz desert experiences, partly at Death Valley, profoundly at Monument Valley, that was so debilitating. The real thing seemed to be elsewhere, somewhere that I hadn't been to yet. And I didn't know where it was. I came out of the arboretum ready to scream. Surely we could find a bit of desert that was more like a desert. We found it, rather surprisingly, and entirely by chance, at the Tom Mix Monument.

Now this was not a *national* monument, you understand. It was not a monument like Death Valley or Monument Valley. To be absolutely specific, the Tom Mix Monument is a stumpy stone obelisk with a droopy, riderless, cast-iron horse on top. It is situated in a rest area on the Pinal Pioneer Parkway, not far south of the prison town of Florence. It was a remarkably liberal rest area. There were canopied picnic tables and ready-built barbecues, and nobody would object if you slept in your car there overnight, although camping as such was forbidden.

A plaque on the obelisk confirmed that this was the spot where Tom Mix's 'spirit left his body'. Mix was a cowboy actor who made a lot of movies in Arizona. He had no trouble with cancer. He died in 1940 when he crashed and rolled his coffin-nosed Cord. The guy was in his sixties, and probably ought to have known better. Perhaps, on the other hand, he wanted to die a young man's death.

What makes his memorial rest area such a wonderful place is that it's in the middle of a cactus plain. We had been driving through the plain for some time, looking for a road or track that went deeper into it than the highway along which we were driving, but we hadn't found one by the time we got to the rest area. We parked, drank some water and saw there was a gate that led from the rest area into the cactus plain. There was no sign telling us to keep out. We walked through the gateway and found ourselves in a kind of desert wonderland. There were tall saguaros, dotted with large holes in which woodpeckers and owls had made their homes. There were prickly pears, hedgehog and barrel cacti bursting into rich orange and purple flowers. There were desert marigolds, and lizards snickering through the sand.

This was not a great, dramatic piece of territory. It was really just a strip of desert between the Pinal Pioneer Parkway and the more modern Interstate 10, a strip no more than forty miles long and fifteen miles wide, yet it was great to be there. It looked right. Despite its proximity to road and rest area, there was a feeling of isolation there. It was not one of the world's desolate spots, but it was certainly a good deal more deserted than a lot of the desert we'd seen in America so far. It was a great way to make acquaintance with saguaros. It gave us just enough optimism to risk going to the Saguaro National Monument in Tucson.

Tucson is a desert town, make no mistake. If you don't believe me, just take a look in Yellow Pages. You might live there in the Desert Willows Mobile Home Estate, buy your car at Desert Toyota, get your spectacles at Desert Optical, eat at the Desert Rose Café, have your metal recycled at Desert Metal Recycling. You could even learn scuba diving at the Desert Divers Scuba Centre.

But Tucson is a *big* desert town and it's growing rapidly. The Saguaro National Monument is barely outside the city limits, and as Tucson eats up the surrounding desert it's quite conceivable that a time will come when the Saguaro National Monument will be a tiny one- or two-acre park surrounded on all sides by the suburbs of Tucson.

In fact, there are two Saguaro National Monuments, one east of Tucson, one west. We picked the eastern one. The place does, in one sense, show the desert in pristine condition. The place was free from beer cans and spent cartridges and dumped automobiles, in a way that much of the American desert isn't. It was well managed. The picnic areas and the Cactus Forest Drive were well managed too. It was possible to park in one of the lay-bys and walk along one of the hiking trails and you could be fairly certain of not running into other people or their debris, which we did, and it was fine, but frankly I'd rather have been in the Tom Mix rest area.

We drove past a lay-by which was occupied by an interesting-looking couple. They were photographing a hillside full of saguaros. He had a shaved head, wraparound shades, and a heavy walrus mustache. She was very slender and dark and was wearing a flimsy, short skirt. As we passed, the wind gusted and the woman's skirt blew up. She was wearing nothing underneath, and although she must have been aware that we were passing in the car and could see 'everything', she made no attempt to hold the skirt down. It made my day, and I thought it probably didn't entirely spoil hers. I'm not sure that this was a desert experience *per se*, but it's something that's never happened to me in the city or the suburbs.

That night we stayed in the No-Tell Motel in Tucson; a cheap, badly air-conditioned place with mirrors, a waterbed and a twenty-four-hour dirty-movie channel. Maybe the desert was getting to me. I would be far too embarrassed to seek out a motel or hotel in England that had a dirty-movie channel, even if such a thing exists. But we were in a desert town so it was okay.

For this really to have worked I guess one or more of the dirty movies should have been filmed in the desert. Alas, most of them had been made with limited means in motel rooms much like the one we were staying in. I half imagined that we too were being filmed, by some hidden camera, behind the mirror say, and that this movie would then be shown to other people in other, similar motel rooms, who would themselves be filmed by other hidden cameras, and so on. Eventually the whole world would have seen the whole of the rest of the world making love to each other. It would be a very safe version of sexuality.

I had thought that the desert outside Tucson might have been a good place to scatter my father's ashes. My reasons for thinking that seemed a little eccentric even to me, but they were as follows.

In 1954, in 'the desert outside Tucson', Wilhelm Reich did some experiments with a piece of equipment called a cloudbuster, a device which he believed would make the desert fertile. Reich, of course, is the 'inventor' of orgone energy, a positive bioenergy, in fact life energy itself. By Reich's accounts it is connected with sexuality, found in living organisms, but also present in the atmosphere in a free state.

Reich believed there was some connection between orgone energy and nuclear radiation. At the time of the Korean War he did experiments exploring the possibility of orgone being used as an antidote to radioactive fallout. He posited the existence of Deadly Orgone Radiation (DOR) as the equal and opposite or ofgone. Among other things, he suggested, DOR caused cancer, therefore orgone energy might be part of a cure for cancer. He also thought that accumulations of DOR in the atmosphere might be responsible for droughts and for the formation of deserts. The cloudbuster would disperse accumulations of DOR in the desert outside Tucson, induce rainfall, and thus the desert would no longer be a desert at all.

It seems to me that you don't really need the existence or presence of Deadly Orgone Radiation to explain the existence of deserts. The simple, geographical explanations have always been good enough for me. Nevertheless, in the patch of desert where Reich conducted his experiments rainfall *was* unusually high, though that doesn't prove anything, naturally. However, while Reich was pointing his cloudbuster at the Arizona sky he became, according to his own accounts, involved in a battle with hostile craft from outer space. Fortunately he saw them off with the cloudbuster.

It seems to me that even if you *were* involved in a space battle with hostile aliens, you would, if you had the slightest smattering of common sense, keep it to yourself. Reich didn't keep it to himself. He wrote the book *Contact With Space* and destroyed what little credibility he had left at that point.

The accepted wisdom is that Reich started out sane and ended up mad. The difficulty is knowing when he crossed the line. From a layman's leading of Reich, and of his critics and supporters, I'm prepared to believe that there is an energy in the world that we might as well call orgone. It does seem possible that this energy is connected in some inverse way to the negative energies of radiation, and it seems not inconceivable that orgone might fit in with a cure for cancer. Whether this has anything to do with deserts I'm not sure, but Reich's desire to make the desert fertile seems reasonable, not even very unusual, and certainly not mad.

The problem I have with all this is that curing cancer seems to me neither here nor there. I was horrified by my father's death from cancer, but it was not the cancer that was horrifying, it was the pain he had to go through that was horrifying. I suppose we would all like to die of some disease that took us gently and without pain, but that doesn't always seem to be an option. We talk of cures for cancer or AIDS or heart disease as though by curing them we would somehow have cured ourselves of death. We talk as though if only our doctors were clever enough or ingenious enough, and if they were given enough money and time, then we could stamp death out altogether.

The only 'remedy' for death that I can see is to live fully and well, not entirely without pain or misery (I suspect that's not possible) but with determination and tenacity. And I realise, of course, that 'living well' is a luxury that is only permitted in societies that have arrived at a certain level of affluence and stability. To travel through the desert and to then be able to write about travelling through the desert, are two of the things that make me think I am 'living well'. They make me feel very alive. That's why I find it hard to accept Reich's thesis that deserts are caused by the accumulation of something 'deadly'. My own experience tells me this isn't exactly the case.

Anyway, I had thought, perhaps hoped, that this coming together of ideas about life and death, cancer and its cure, barrenness and fertility, might make 'the desert outside Tucson' the right place to scatter my father's ashes. In the event I knew it wasn't. I felt that any bit of desert I chose immediately outside Tucson might very easily be the site of a brand new housing and shopping complex within the next few years. The ashes remained in the container in my luggage.

It was a Sunday and another bad day for seeing the desert. We had spent the night in Deming, New Mexico and were on our way to the White Sands. The White Sands were another National Monument, but they were so curious and disquieting (at least they were in photographs) that we thought we ought to see them.

We had lunch in Las Cruces, in a place that appeared at first to be called Jack Ruby's Restaurant, but in fact was called Jack *and* Ruby's. The waitress thought Sue had the most wonderful English accent. She clearly thought mine was nondescript and not wonderful at all. From Las Cruces we drove through a town called Organ, and suddenly the highway crested a hill and then plunged into enormous desert space. Plains and mountains opened out before us, pale creamy yellows in the foreground, dun-coloured isolated peaks and pale aquamarine mountains in the distance. As the road made its descent the car was shaken by strong winds, and we came across what must surely be the world's most unusual rest area.

In fact, I suspect this is quite a famous rest area. A photograph of it appears as an album cover ('Strange Meeting' by Power Tools if you're interested). It's a big rest area and has no tables or barbecues or obelisks, but it does have men's and women's toilets, trash cans, commanding views of the desert, and, what really sets it apart, a twenty-foot-tall US Army missile. The missile just stands there at one end of the rest area looking very strange.

Experts could no doubt tell you what kind of missile it was. I can tell you it was long and thin, white with a black point, and with black tips to its fins, and that someone had sprayed the words 'Acid Trips' on it. As with saguaro cacti, it was a vertical line in an otherwise predominantly horizontal scene.

The presence of the missile seemed at first completely bizarre, but once you realise that most of the desert you're looking at from the rest area is the White Sands Missile Range, its presence is a lot more understandable. They have serious problems at the range about what to do with old or unused missiles. There's a kind of missile garden at the range, but that isn't open to the public, and in Alamogordo, the nearest big town, the Chamber of Commerce has a collection of missiles decorating its car park, and the Space Hall of Fame, also in Alamogordo, has a whole heap of them littering its back yard.

The road we were travelling on ran right through the range, and, we were told, it got closed from time to time as and when they launched missiles. It would have been bad public relations if a stray warhead blew up a Winnebago full of happy vacationers.

Most of the side roads had military road blocks, and there were jeeps parked in the median, and heavy-looking military types posed around, peered through binoculars as though they were doing something really important. Maybe they were but their body language looked a little fake to me.

The White Sands we were going to didn't have much in common with the missile range except its name. The range was bare rugged desert. The National Monument is the world's largest gypsum dune-field, at about three hundred square miles. To be strict about it, gypsum is quite a different substance from sand, but it would be a hard man and a geologist who drew the distinction. The place is, and I'm quoting here, 'an alabaster "sea" of ceaseless geological action . . . an unearthly pure-white landscape that shimmers and drifts in continual motion.' This is true.

In photographs and even sometimes to the naked eye, the White Sands look like fields of snow. They ripple. They give you snow blindness. You could imagine the solidity of rolling green hills just below the white surface. Between the dunes, however, there were flat areas sprouting yucca plants that had only recently ceased flowering, and there were coyote prints and snake tracks in the gypsum, and, of course, the temperature was pushing ninety degrees. You couldn't seriously think you were in the Alps.

We had to pass through a roadblock and show our passports before we were allowed into White Sands, but I think that had more to do with fear of illegal immigration than with worries about our infiltrating the missile range. We paid our entrance fee and drove in among the dunes. The road was made out of compressed gypsum and the edges of dunes spilled on to the surface. The dunes were not especially high but their sheer whiteness was magnificent.

Needless to say, we were not alone. The form on a Sunday at White Sands seems to be that you pull off the road at the earliest opportunity, park, get out of your car, find the nearest dune, climb it and then roll down it. There were literally busloads of people doing this.

Amid the dunes there was a wide, flat picnic area, again built on compressed gypsum. There were barbecues and shelters made of corrugated iron, painted red, blue or yellow, and shaped like billowing sails. A couple of families had brought volleyball nets with them, which they'd set up in the picnic area. No doubt the dunes made a nice setting for volleyball but you felt they were missing the point.

We went into the dunes. We didn't go far. The wind that we'd first encountered on the road was now blowing hard through the dunes. In the distance a sandstorm looked like thin, tattered curtains drawn across the landscape. It was flapping and angry and spectral. The sky was cloudy, only patchily blue, and the wind threw sharp grains of gypsum into our faces. It was obvious that despite the Sunday crowds we only had to walk a couple of hundred yards into the dunes in order to be completely alone, but that missed the point too. It wasn't that we simply objected to *seeing* the volleyball-playing, dune-rolling crowd. We objected to their very existence. We could have got all irritated and holier than thou about it, but we were learning to cope with industrial tourism. We simply decided to come back on Monday morning.

We spent the night at the Desert Aire Motel, Alamogordo and were back at the White Sands for eight o'clock the next morning. The crowds had gone and so had the sandstorms and the wind and the clouds. The sun was shining and the sky was a bright blue and the dunes looked even whiter than they had the previous day.

We parked beside a likely-looking set of dunes and started to walk. There are American feminists of the south-west who ask whether man's penetration of the virgin desert was and is an act of conscious defloration and defilement. I find the idea of deflowering the desert an odd one, but I would admit there's pleasure to be had in leaving your footprints in an otherwise untouched stretch of sand. However, I think the pleasure has more to do with exploration than with defilement. You can allow yourself the fantasy that you're the first person ever to have set foot here. I'm not sure that to lose one's virginity is, in any case, to be defiled, but in the present case virginity was quickly and easily restored. Come the next strong wind and my footprints would be smoothed over as though I'd never been there.

Visitors don't explore the White Sands as extensively as they explore other places, and that was a source of pleasure too. At White Sands there are few roads, few designated sights or beauty spots. The dunes are much of a muchness and so people feel no need to press on into their centre. This means that those of us who do press on find ourselves thrillingly alone.

Sue and I walked in as straight a line as we could for about an hour and a half. The sun was still low, the air was fresh, and the white sand was cold to the touch. This was not a landscape of high drama or epic beauty but its power came about because the dunes appeared to run to infinity in all directions. There was a strange and wonderful silence that morning. There were no birds singing and no sound of wind. It was a completely peaceful and comforting silence. There was, and I know this is a problematic word, a feeling of elemental cleanliness about the place.

It was here that I deposited my father's ashes. I had made the decision the previous evening. I had somehow known that this would be the right place and the right time, although the White Sands looked a very different place now than they had the previous day.

As I came through customs into the United States it had felt as though I was carrying a substantial quantity of ashes. Now, in the face of this white emptiness it seemed I had not brought nearly enough. This was only ever going to be a symbolic gesture yet it now seemed I had barely enough ashes to make the symbolism work.

I think I had always imagined there would be a good strong wind blowing when I opened the box of ashes and released them, and that they would be instantly carried away and dispersed. In the event, the air was perfectly still, and from a seated position I poured out the ashes so that they formed a tiny grey dune amid the vast, flawless white gypsum expanse.

I took a photograph, not of the ashes themselves, but from the spot where I was seated when I did the pouring. Looking at it today, the photograph is pleasingly undramatic. It was not a scene of high drama, but one of a simple, and perhaps slightly bathetic act. I realise there must be those who would think that a tourist attraction adjacent to a missile range might not be the most satisfactory place to deposit your father's remains, and I probably wouldn't argue with them. But I thought it was better than burying them in a cemetery in Sheffield. It was the best place I could find.

The pile of ashes remained quiet still, waiting for the next wind that would blow them away, making them part of the desert, the same wind that would smooth over my footprints as though I'd never been there.

Sue had been with me when I poured out my father's ashes, but she had said nothing. She'd drawn away and given me enough room and time to do whatever I needed to do. It was only as we got in the car and started driving away that she said, 'I think he'll be happy there.'

A part of me wanted to sob, to let go, to let the tears run down my cheeks, and let grief take hold of me and have a damn good cry. But I didn't do that. I put my foot down and kept on driving, back through the missile range, into the desert.

In her novel *Play It As It Lays* Joan Didion always refers to her characters as being *on* the desert rather than *in* the desert. If I'm not careful I find myself talking and writing about being out in the desert; a sloppy but not meaningless construction.

Maria Wyeth, the central, you might say only, character in *Play*

It As It Lays comes from a town called Silver Wells, a desert place
that no longer exists and has become part of a missile range. The
novel talks constantly about the desert yet the desert is never
described. Reyner Banham calls this 'a cheap but brilliantly effective
literary device'. He writes, 'The thin web of words is a cunning
incitement to the reader to fill in the diagram with private visions,
deserts of the mind, images – biblical or otherwise – of unbearable
moral vacuity and mislaid purposes.'

I think he is right. I think Joan Didion does use the desert as a
literary symbol, as an emotional correlative for her heroine's crippling
inertia, and it is more powerful for being undescribed. However, Joan
Didion is a writer adept at finding unbearable moral vacuity and mislaid purposes just about anywhere she looks, in Las Vegas certainly,
and also in Bogota, Saigon, Miami.

I'm not sure that I have found moral vacuity and mislaid purposes
in the desert, but I know what Reyner Banham means, and I think his
phrase is one of breathtaking elegance. I carried it with me through
America like a mantra, or maybe like a catchy line from a Top Forty
hit, like 'Tie a yellow ribbon round the old oak tree.'

And then we went to Ajo, pronounced Ah-ho. Ajo is the town you
would probably plan to stay if you were going to visit the Organ Pipe
Cactus National Monument, which is what we were doing. As we
approached it from the south there were a couple of billboards advertising motels, apparently in town. These billboards, however, were
situated just a few yards outside the town boundary, and the motels
themselves were situated outside the boundary too, on the north
side. But this wasn't at all obvious from the billboards and we spent
a lot of time driving round the town centre before we worked it out.

Ajo came into existence because of copper. There was still a vast
hole in the ground, an open pit where the copper was extracted. The
edges of the pit had been built up into a big rim, and you could see
them from just about anywhere in town. The hole was one of Ajo's
tourist attractions. I'm not sure what the other tourist attractions
were. We saw a couple of signs in the centre of town that said
they were pointing towards 'tourist information' but we never found
anywhere that offered any.

No motels and no tourist information might suggest that Ajo
doesn't welcome visitors and yet there was much about the place
that was very welcoming. Right in the centre of town was a green
park with irrigated lawns and tall palm trees. The park was a perfect
square and around it was the Spanish-style Plaza with a supermarket,

a bank, a real-estate office, and a closed-down movie theatre, all tucked away behind long, white arcades.

A lot of people on the street were Mexicans. That wasn't very surprising. Ajo is only about forty-five miles from the border, and the ones who were Caucasian all looked very, very old. I saw that many of the old white men had limps or terribly hunched backs, and I wondered if these were the results of mining injuries.

I later discovered that the injuries were unlikely to have been sustained in the copper pit. Ajo was being much touted as a retirement centre. They got their injuries elsewhere, in their previous jobs. One town slogan was 'retirement living at 1950s prices' and Ajo was also plugging the idea that it was the 'place where summer spends the winter'. But summer, of course, had to stay in a motel out of town.

Our motel was called the Marine. I don't know why. Our room had a French window that looked out on to a cactus garden with a picnic table. Beyond that was an empty patch of desert with saguaros, behind which the built-up rim of the copper pit was clearly visible.

Close to the motel was what had once been an orchard. There were no trees in it now, but the irrigation system was still in place, pieces of black pipe with sprinklers stuck up out of the ground, one where each tree had been. There was a barbed-wire fence around the orchard but it had been broken down in several places. There was a building inside the fence, some kind of warehouse or packing plant, and despite the signs warning off trespassers, it had been thoroughly broken into and smashed up.

Not far up the road was a laundromat. It sat amid a pile of derelict washing-machines, fridges and beds, and the skulls of longhorn sheep were mounted on the white wall of the laundromat that faced the main road. It was weird, but maybe bleached bones make a good advertisement for a laundromat.

The patch of desert with the saguaros looked inviting. Sue and I got a can of beer each and walked out. The invitation was one we probably shouldn't have accepted. On closer inspection we saw that far from being empty, it had been used as a dumping-ground for domestic and industrial waste. There were tin cans, piles of car tyres and heaps of anonymous, useless machinery, all kinds of mechanical junk. There were people living nearby, no distance away from the mess, each with a small square of desert on which they'd placed a trailer or built a small house. Some had gone as far as to build white picket fences around their plot, but most looked unfinished and uncared for. Some weren't much more than shacks. There were some barns, some one-car garages, and a familiar clutter of trucks and old cars, most of which weren't in service. And each little home had its own big dog keeping guard.

We'd been walking for half an hour or so when it started to get dark. We didn't want to encounter any rattlesnakes so we set off on what we thought was the direct way home. However, after walking for a while we found ourselves not back at the motel but amid the trailers and shacks, not sure of the way, and as we got close to any of the dwellings, the savage barking of some unseen animal would start. We couldn't tell whether these dogs were tied up or not, whether they were issuing warnings to keep out, or whether they were baying for blood; and we weren't keen to find out. As we moved from one plot, the dog belonging to the next would start howling. Before long, dogs were barking madly all around us.

We took a dirt road that led away from the dogs and the habitations, and we lost our bearings on the motel. We stood in the gathering darkness, in a filthy patch of desert, fearing rattlesnakes, not sure where we were but aware that most directions would bring us into closer proximity to some vicious, crazed-sounding dog, and perhaps its vicious crazed owner. We stopped. We didn't know what to do next. Nothing we might do seemed very sensible, although doing nothing seemed the least sensible of all. We had ground to a halt. We stood still for a long time, saying nothing and not moving. This was quite a different way of being lost in the desert. At which point I did experience a frightening, if not strictly unbearable, sense of moral vacuity and mislaid purposes.

I suppose, above all else, I have combated moral vacuity and mislaid purposes in the desert by simply having to search for material. It is easier to find your purpose when you have a deadline for your book and you've already spent the advance. But if I were a Joan Didion character that probably wouldn't make much difference.

From Ajo we had the purpose of seeing some organ-pipe cacti. These are a form of saguaro, but instead of being upright and humanoid with arms, they have clusters of long, straight, armless stems, and look at least somewhat like a set of organ pipes.

The Organ Pipe National Monument is tucked in the south-western corner of Arizona, satisfyingly far from any centres of population. Consequently it is comparatively deserted, certainly for a National Monument. We drove along a dirt road to a place called Alamo

Canyon, which is in the foothills of the low but rugged Ajo mountain range.

We parked and we walked. We didn't go so very far before we found a big black rock and sat on it. At first we looked closely at the mix of cacti and paloverdes and the occasional lizard. But before long I wasn't looking at anything at all and I certainly wasn't thinking. I was just sitting on a rock in the desert, not observing or having lofty thoughts and certainly not in any sense gathering material. I was just existing, just being there.

I felt gradually 'emptied out'. My personality slowly diffused out of me. I am tempted to say that I had a feeling of great peacefulness, and yet it might be truer to say that all the mental equipment with which I felt *anything* had been briefly disconnected.

I'm deeply suspicious of anyone who would claim to be 'at one' with the desert and yet it seems to me that the kind of vacancy, the lack of movement or desire that I experienced in Alamo Canyon was undoubtedly because of the landscape I was in. It would not have happened to me had I stayed in London or Tucson or Las Vegas. That is what the desert can do, and I was perfectly willing to let the desert do it to me. There was nothing mystical or mysterious about the experience. It was simply a time when it felt good not to feel anything. It did not last long, maybe an hour, but that time of doing and being nothing amid the organ-pipe cacti was as important and as enjoyable as any period I have ever spent in the American desert.

As we neared the end of the trip we began to think about getting a tattoo. It had its appeal. We weren't sure what kind of design we wanted but I thought a cactus was the most likely choice, a saguaro to be positioned on the left biceps. We were only moderately committed to the idea. We would have to find the right tattooist whose designs were stylish enough to make us want to mutilate ourselves for life, and we would have to find him on a day when we both felt brave enough to have our skins pierced.

I used to know a barman in Colchester whose forearms were entirely covered with large blue smudges. These were tattoos he'd had done in Egypt. He'd been in the army, had arrived in Cairo, got drunk, and found a local man on the banks of the Nile who had a tattooing needle connected to a car battery. This wasn't a man you could ask to give you just a small bluebird or butterfly. You had to give him your skin, put your trust in him, and he would doodle all over your arms as the spirit took him. As my friend the barman had discovered, it didn't really matter much whether or not you liked the finished design since within a few years it would spread and turn itself into a blue smudge. Egypt, despite its desert connections, was not the place to get a tattoo, I had thought. America would surely be better; better inks, better designs, better hygiene.

My grandfather had been tattooed, with ships mostly, but I recalled that he had a ring tattooed round the base of one finger. I thought it must have been very painful to have done. My father, despite his time in the Navy, of course had no tattoos. That would have been far too flamboyant for him, and he would have been horrified at the idea of his son getting one. It seems to me that a lot of nonsense is talked about the father's death liberating the son, yet I knew I wouldn't have been contemplating getting a tattoo if my father had still been alive.

I had already read an article in a magazine called *body art* (it's the lack of capitals that make you, rightly, suspicious) about a world-class tattooist who lived in a place called Twentynine Palms in the Mojave desert. I didn't think we'd be going anywhere near there on this trip so I hadn't even bothered to note down the guy's name or reread the article. However, if by some chance we found ourselves in Twentynine Palms, I thought it would be a small enough town that a world-class tattooist wouldn't be so hard to track down.

Inevitably we found ourselves in Twentynine Palms. I remembered two things from the article. The tattooist said that when you start out tattooing you feel the needle going into somebody's flesh and you ask yourself, 'Am I creating art or am I just making hamburger out of the person I'm working on?' The answer, he said, is that you're probably making hamburger. He also said that he'd be prepared to tattoo a swastika on somebody's buttock if they had a sexual fetish for swastikas, but not if it was just a signal of anti-Semitism. He sounded like a man I could do business with, if I could find him.

Twentynine Palms was much bigger than I'd imagined. It has a population of seven and a half thousand, and just north of the town there's the Twentynine Palms marine base which covers a few hundred square miles of desert and contains a lot of marines. The town was eager, not to say hysterical, to welcome its servicemen back from Desert Storm. The motels offered cheap rates to servicemen, the used-car lots offered them special low-deposit deals, insurance companies offered them easy-start policies. We had seen plenty of yellow ribbons on our travels but never in such profusion as in Twentynine Palms. Yellow ribbons were tied round anything and everything vertical: street lamps, the signs for fast-food restaurants, telegraph poles, mail boxes, road signs, and of course palm trees, though there seemed to be more than twenty-nine of them. In fact, yellow ribbons were tied round telegraph poles and trees all along the highway from Twentynine Palms to the next town of Joshua Tree. It was hard to see this as a spontaneous gesture of welcome. Fifteen miles of yellow ribbon takes some organising. You might even need the marines to take on a big job like that.

No doubt some of the marines would be heavily tattooed. There were two tattoo parlours in Twentynine Palms and they were both full of customers on the days we were there. I didn't see how I could go into one of the parlours and say, 'Are *you* the world-class tattooist I've read about, or is it the guy who runs the other place?' Presumably each would say he was the world-class tattooist and the other guy was the schmuck. I suppose I could have asked him his views on buttocks and swastikas and anti-Semitism, but I didn't have the nerve. In fact, even if I did find the right guy I didn't particularly like the idea of baring my flabby white biceps in front of a roomful of battle-hardened marines. Sue and I decided, without much heart-break, to drive out of Twentynine Palms and abandon the idea of the tattoo. It had only been a whim anyway, we told ourselves.

As we got to the edge of town we drove past a used-book store. I didn't get a very good look at it. It was a small, slightly rickety, one-storey building, but I did notice a sign saying the business was for sale. Sue and I were still occasionally exercising some low-level fantasy of making a living in the desert.

'What books do you think they read out here?' I asked.

'Cowboy books,' said Sue. 'Zane Grey, Louis L'Amour,'

'No,' I said. 'I bet you're wrong. I bet they all read Jane Austen and Dickens.'

Sue said, 'I'm sure you *could* run a business out here if you were selling something people really wanted. What do people here really want?'

We thought of beer and pick-up trucks, and we thought of gambling and sex, and weren't sure we wanted to be in any of those businesses. Then, I still don't know why, I decided to turn the car around and have a look in the bookshop.

Outside the shop there were cheap paperbacks in cardboard boxes, and the inside of the shop looked dark and unwelcoming. There were two guys sitting inside the doorway, deep in conversation, and I hovered on the threshold, not sure that I wanted to go in.

Then the younger of the two guys, who was sitting at a desk in a manner that implied he owned the place, said, 'Come on in, folks. Come on in and see what we got. We got *books*. We got a *lot* of books. If you can't find anything here worth reading there must be something wrong with you.'

I thought this wasn't a bad bookselling ploy. If a potential customer wanted to show there was nothing wrong with him, he had, by this logic, to buy a book. We browsed in the shop. It opened out into several cramped rooms. The shelves were full of mostly rough old paperbacks, though neither Jane Austen nor Zane Grey seemed much in evidence. I looked, slightly desperately, for a book that would prove there was nothing wrong with me. The two men were having a long aimless conversation. They were talking about a restaurant in New York. The older man was saying that everybody knew this restaurant, even though he couldn't remember the name. And even though he hadn't been there for fifteen years, he was certain it was still in business. The owner of the shop was saying he hadn't been to New York in years either, and when he had been there he'd never had enough money to eat out in restaurants. You would think this ought to have been a short conversation but they were able to drag it out for a very long time.

I found something to buy, a copy of *National Geographic* containing an article with the title, 'The California Desert: a worldly wilderness.' As I was paying my dollar for the magazine I got my first good look at the owner of the shop. He was about fifty, lean, strong, with straight black hair brushed forward to disguise a receding hairline. He was lacking one or two teeth and he had a lot of tattoos. He was wearing a loose, long-sleeved shirt that was neither showing nor exactly hiding the tattoos, and you could see a woman's legs tattooed on one arm, what looked like stylised flames on one hand, and there was the edge of some big design on his chest that burst out of the shirt's open neck, though there was no telling exactly what the design was.

It didn't take much to get him into conversation. He was interested that we came from England and he had a story about being in England the day we joined the Common Market, and another about why he never celebrated New Year. Finally it was Sue who asked, 'Do you know any good tattooists in these parts?'

He thought for a while, not because it was an effort to think of a good tattooist but rather as if he was wondering whether we were the kind of people with whom he wanted to share what he undoubtedly knew.

'You serious?' he asked.

'Well, yes,' I said. 'If we find the right tattooist.'

He thought for a while longer before he said, 'It's a pity you weren't here a year ago. A year ago I was in business as a tattooist myself.'

It was then that I realised that this was, of course, our man, the one I'd read about, the world-class tattooist of Twentynine Palms. His name was Cliff Raven and the shop was called Raven Books.

'What kind of tattoo did you have in mind?' he asked.

'Oh, you know,' I said, 'something to do with the desert.'

He looked interested.

'Like a cactus,' I said.

He looked considerably less interested.

He said, 'Well, you know, there are a couple of tattooists in Twentynine Palms.'

'We saw them. Are they any good?'

'Let's say I won't recommend anyone in Twentynine Palms. Where are you going next?'

'Barstow.'

'No, I won't recommend anyone in Barstow. Where after that?'

'Las Vegas and then back home to London.'

'Oh well, I know a great tattooist in London,' he said and he proceeded to give us details of a London tattooist, Mr Sebastian. 'I'm sure he could do you a cactus as good as anyone else.'

Of course we were a little downhearted. We didn't want a London tattooist to give us a cactus tattoo. We wanted a desert tattooist to give us a cactus tattoo. In retrospect I see we played it wrong. We should have said, 'You're Cliff Raven and we've come five thousand miles to see you. Please come out of retirement and do your stuff.' We should have said, 'Here's our skin. Tattoo us as the spirit takes you.' But even so I think he still might have thought it was beneath his dignity to break out his tools just for the sake of a couple of white English arms.

So we didn't get tattooed in the desert and we didn't get married there either. Partly it was because getting married in a kitsch little chapel on the Strip in Las Vegas had seemed like an interestingly tacky idea when we were in London, but once we'd seen how it really was in Vegas, it seemed simply tacky. Too many other people were doing it. We had seen them arriving in hired limos driven by washed-up-looking chauffeurs. I think, more importantly, Sue and I were too happy not being married to each other to want to risk changing and potentially spoiling it. At times our relationship seemed infinitely robust but the moment anyone starts presuming that their arrangement is strong, stable and enduring is the very moment the fates are likely to guarantee its collapse.

The day we met Cliff Raven was the same day we landed in Room 206 of the Desert Villa Inn in Barstow, when we drank tequila and Orange Maid and I felt happier than I could ever remember; the scene that opened this book. It is said, usually by rather unreliable sources such as agony columns, that love is not so much about finding the right person as about becoming the right person, and certainly I felt more 'right' in the desert with Sue than I had in a similar situation with my ex-wife three years earlier. I suppose that would have to be regarded as an achievement.

Unmarried and untattooed we would soon be returning to England and we had completed only one of the three tasks I'd set myself for the desert. But we'd done the important one, scattering my father's ashes.

On the way to Barstow we passed five white crosses planted in the dirt of the road's soft shoulder. They were carefully made and placed. Each had a small metal plate with a name and the dates of birth and death. There were also bunches of fabric flowers and a solar-powered lantern so that the crosses would be illuminated and visible at night.

These were by no means the only roadside crosses we saw in the American desert. They were always poignant yet always enigmatic. They never told the whole story. I tended to assume they marked the sites of car crashes, but it was possible, for all I knew, that they commemorated those who had been lost in the desert.

But I don't know why anyone would erect crosses like these. I don't know what effect the person who erected them would want them to have on me. As a way of marking some private grief the crosses are both too public and too briefly glimpsed to have much effect at all. They turn all too easily into rather banal warnings to drive more carefully or to treat the desert with more respect. Perhaps they are intended as a form of *memento mori*, in which case they work just fine, but then everything in the desert is a *memento mori*: the dust, the heat, the bleached bones, the dead cacti, the wrecked cars. And what is a more effective *memento mori* than the expensive tawdry of Las Vegas? Here is a town built on human desire, greed, money, glamour; and these too shall pass away.

We had a day and a half to kill in Las Vegas before our flight home. I kept asking myself whether my father would have enjoyed Las Vegas, and I concluded that he would. Perhaps he'd have liked it more than the White Sands. It was easy enough in Vegas to find a roulette wheel or a blackjack table with low enough stakes that you could take your money and make it last a good while. Even the one-armed bandits were set up to give you a reasonable run for your money.

I'm not a great believer in gambling metaphors but I think that's all my father was looking for from life; not great wealth, not great excitement or joy, but a fair run for his money. It seems to me that his stake ran out some time before he was ready to leave the table. I wouldn't say he was cheated, but I think he never realised just how badly the odds were stacked against him. I'm fully aware that very many people face far worse odds.

My last view of the desert was from the plane out of Las Vegas. I had made sure I had a window seat. From above the desert looked pale and flattened, like a diagram. The paved roads looked like long, flowing scribbles. The dirt roads and the dry river beds looked like scars, the marks left on the fragile body of the desert after some particularly tricky bit of surgery.

We would soon be back in London and I knew it would seem small, mean, dirty and cramped after the desert. But that was where I lived, had my friends and did my writing. I belonged there and operated far more effectively there than I did in any desert.

It seems to me absurd to attempt to draw 'conclusions' from one's day trips, but I think we all need souvenirs. I take photographs, buy postcards, pick up rocks, but my main souvenir is also my main reason for having travelled in the first place; this book that is not the one I thought I would write; this book that is not quite memoir, not quite autobiography, not quite travelogue.

As I write now, the desert, my father, and certainly my dead marriage, seem very far away. It's easy enough to get back to the desert. You can go there on a day trip. My father is always with me in some sense, but he remains largely inaccessible. I could never have written about him while he was alive, wouldn't have known how, and perhaps to write about him now is an attempt at a sort of literary resurrection, but I know that I've written about his death rather than his life. I didn't know him as well as I would have liked, but I think that's not unusual for fathers and sons. I miss him more than I ever thought I would, not that I ever gave much thought to what life would be like without him.

My marriage seems, at this distance, to have been an irrelevance and its end inevitable. I no longer feel I'm the person I was when I was married. I certainly don't feel like the person who wanted to stay married. I can't remember exactly when it stopped hurting me to think about it, but now I hardly think about it at all. I'm not sure this has anything to do with deserts.

The death of my father didn't so much remind me of my own mortality (I think I was well aware of that long before he died) so much as confirm what I always more or less knew, that the things we see around us that appear fixed, reliable and permanent, may be none of those things. I can see how you might say that the desert is more fixed, reliable and permanent than many things, but that was never my conscious reason for going there.

The end of a marriage, the death of a parent, are things that hurt, and there's no denying that, for me at least, things hurt less in the desert. The desert makes you feel small and it makes your pain feel smaller, but no doubt the same might be said for mountains or oceans or rainforests.

I am back from the desert, and let's face it, I was never there very long. I'm still living in a small room in London and I'm still writing. I often wish I was in the desert and I'm sure I'll go back there before long, but I'm a day-tripper and I know it. I don't want to spend the rest of my life in some forbidding spot in the Mojave or the Sahara or Western Australia, but occasional forays into a landscape that is arid, desolate and unwelcoming may be what's required to make the rest of life more tolerable. There are still plenty more deserts in the world. There is still an appetite for the desert in me.